ISBN 978-1-331-91516-4
PIBN 10253412

1 MONTH OF
FREE
READING

at

www.ForgottenBooks.com

By purchasing this book you are eligible for one month membership to ForgottenBooks.com, giving you unlimited access to our entire collection of over 1,000,000 titles via our web site and mobile apps.

To claim your free month visit:

www.forgottenbooks.com/free253412

PRINCIPLES OF INSURANCE

VOLUME I: LIFE

THE MACMILLAN COMPANY
NEW YORK · BOSTON · CHICAGO · DALLAS
ATLANTA · SAN FRANCISCO

MACMILLAN & CO., Limited
LONDON · BOMBAY · CALCUTTA
MELBOURNE

THE MACMILLAN CO. OF CANADA, Ltd.
TORONTO

PRINCIPLES OF INSURANCE

VOLUME I: LIFE

BY

W. F. GEPHART

**PROFESSOR OF ECONOMICS IN WASHINGTON
UNIVERSITY**

New York
THE MACMILLAN COMPANY
1917

Norwood Press
J. S. Cushing Co. — Berwick & Smith Co.
Norwood, Mass., U.S.A.

PREFACE

THE literature on insurance is considerable in amount, but that which is accessible for use in schools and colleges is meager. Government documents, official reports of insurance companies and of organizations of insurance officials and employees, pamphlets and published addresses on the subject are the chief sources of the best information on insurance.

It is therefore because of the conviction of the importance of insurance, the character of the literature, and the increasing importance of the subject in the curriculum of educational institutions that this discussion is offered.

The two volumes on life and fire insurance are offered, not as a complete discussion of these two important forms of insurance, but rather as a statement of what is conceived to be the more important considerations which should receive study in a general course in life and fire insurance. The material has been selected on the basis of the author's experience in teaching the subject, his experience in the business, and his association with insurance organizations. As textbooks, they will need to be supplemented by the instructor, by reference reading as well as by the use of policy forms, company reports, government reports, and other available material.

The author is aware that his discussion of certain questions relating to the regulation of insurance is opposed in some cases to the prevailing public sentiment and practice. But it has been the purpose, not only to state as briefly as possible the important facts and principles of life and fire insurance, but also to provoke thought and discussion on certain mooted questions in insurance.

An effort has been made to select such readings on each topic as would be most helpful. Much of the best literature is either in pamphlet form or in the insurance journals. An exception is made in the case of insurance statistics. Such annuals as the Insurance Year Book of the Spectator Company leave little to be desired in the way of statistical literature. An exception is also to be made in the case of the German and French literature, much of which is of a very high character and in general much more extensive than the literature in English. Few references to this literature have been made; first, because most of it is not accessible to the reader of this book, and second, because this is an elementary discussion of the principles and practices of insurance.

W. F. GEPHART.

WASHINGTON UNIVERSITY.

CONTENTS

CHAPTER I

CHAPTER II

CHAPTER III

Policy. The Group Policy. An analysis of the policy contract.- Early forms of the policy. The judicial interpretation
of the contract. The effect of competition and legislation
on the liberalization of the contract. Difference in state
laws. The payment of the premium. Title to the policy.
Assignment. Insurable Interest and Beneficiary Right
distinguished. The Disability Clause. Loans on Policies,
their extent and evil. Difference in judicial interpretation
and insurance theory as to the nature of the contract. The
forfeiture clause. Cash Surrender Value Clause, its development and significance. Incontestability Clause. Annuities,
their early character, and later development. The Calculation
of an Annuity Value. The number and amount of different
kinds of policies in force.

CHAPTER VII

The Premium defined. Kinds of Premiums. The Level
and Natural Premium distinguished. The Net Premium. Calculation of the Net Single Premium. Calculating an Annuity.
The significance of interest accumulations. Calculating the
Net Premium on a Whole Life, a Limited Payment, and an
Endowment Policy. The Gross Premium. The Loading, its
basis and methods. Percentage and Flat Loading. Premiums in Assessment and Fraternal Companies.

CHAPTER VIII

The origin of the Reserve. The Reserve as a mortality
fund, and as a reinsurance fund. Methods of increasing the
Reserve. Calculation of the Reserve. The Terminal Reserve. The Individual Reserve. Proof of the adequacy of
the Reserve. The necessity of the Reserve. The Reserve
of an insurance company compared to the reserve and surplus of a bank. Valuation defined. Methods of Valuation.
Preliminary Term, Select and Ultimate Methods compared.
The relation of the Reserve to the Cash Surrender and Loan
Values. The Determination of Paid-up Insurance Value.

PRINCIPLES OF INSURANCE

CHAPTER I

LIFE INSURANCE AND ITS HISTORICAL DEVELOPMENT

Insurance Defined. — Insurance is an agreement among individuals of a group or between these individuals and another group called an insurance company under the terms of which each contributes to a fund out of which contingent losses in part or in whole are paid to those suffering the loss. Under normal conditions the payments to the insured individuals or their beneficiaries are paid from the individual contributions and their accumulations. In some cases, however, such as extraordinarily large losses by a fire insurance company, the stockholders of the company may be compelled to pay the losses in part or in whole. But this is unusual and when it does occur, the stockholders expect past and future contributions from the insured to compensate them for these unusual payments.

Character of Insurance. — Insurance is therefore in all its forms a method of coöperation among members of a group subjected to a risk whose frequency can be calculated with a large degree of certainty. The group as such assumes and distributes the risk, thereby reduc-

B   I

ing the risk for each member. The agreement for the insurance takes the form of a contract in which the duties and rights of each party, the insured and the insurer, are specified. The contract specifies a money payment or its equivalent in the event that a contingent loss is suffered by the insured on the condition that he makes specified payments to the insurer. Insurance provides against some of the consequences of accidents and uncertainties. Insurance does but little to prevent such accidents nor does the payment usually compensate in full for the loss suffered. It seeks only to mitigate pecuniary loss which happens to the few during any short period. In the case of life insurance the payment is not assumed to represent the monetary value of the life insured, for life lends itself only to very rough calculations of its value to the family of the deceased individual. In fire insurance the payment does not ordinarily represent the total value of the property and certainly does not compensate in full the owner of the property. The disorganization of his business as well as many items of it, material or otherwise, either are not included in the insurance policy contract or have no market value equal to their value as an integral part of his property.

The payments made by the insured, which are called premiums, represent the anticipated shares in the loss of the insured. These payments or premiums are usually paid in advance, for in a certain sense that which is purchased by the insured is protection against the chance of loss. No insured individual has any cause for complaint because he has made payment without securing an actual monetary return from the insurer. The life still lived, the property not burned, the body not injured by accident, the surety bond not paid, each should be valued more highly than any sum paid by the insurer to the beneficiary or the insured.

Insurance is not, therefore, a creator of wealth. It is not directly productive. Its primary economic function is to distribute the loss of destroyed wealth or life. It doubtless has an indirect effect in producing wealth in that it not only often encourages thrift in the case of life insurance, but it also makes possible the more efficient use of wealth by accumulating the results of many individual acts of saving in a large single fund, available for productive purposes. This result is especially important under the modern system of capitalistic production when the opportunity for the wise investments of small amounts of productive capital are not easily known or available to those who can or do save only small amounts. Insurance has, therefore, become a large and complex expression of the simple system of coöperation, under which each contributes a small sum to a fund to indemnify in part or in whole against a loss by any other individual of the group similarly situated.

Life Insurance Defined. — Life insurance in its strict sense is an agreement between one individual and the other members of a group or with a company by which the group or the company agrees to pay to the beneficiary of the insured a certain sum upon his death. In its present development the sum paid becomes due either at death or at the close of a stated period. It may be paid to the insured or to some other individual or organization. The agreement takes the form of a contract between the insurer and the insured in which the insurer agrees to pay the sum to the named beneficiary on condition that the insured pays certain sums at stated intervals or in one sum and agrees further to comply with other named conditions. The sum to be paid bears no necessary relation to the value of the life of the insured. Nor do the sums paid by the insurer bear any direct ratio to the particular sum which has been paid in by the insured. There is necessarily some relation between the total amount of insurance which an individual may purchase and his earning power, but this has very little practical significance, since but very few individuals carry the maximum amount of insurance which their earning and saving powers would enable them to possess.

Life insurance is primarily intended as a protection for those in some manner either from necessity or circumstances or from choice of the insured affected by his death.

Social Aspect of Insurance. — Insurance has therefore often been characterized as a social institution and especially as a family institution. A principle underlying every proper insurance contract is that the insured should not in any manner directly benefit from his insurance policy. That is to state, the contract, especially in life insurance, brings no gain to the insured, but on the contrary has been made with the prime purpose of protecting those who are in some manner benefited by the continued life of the insured. It may therefore be readily recognized how closely it is connected with the present family organization. It is a method of distributing the effects of losses. It is a mutual agreement among many to assume the burdens suddenly falling upon a few. It is also a method of capitalizing future time and energy against premature death. This feature of life insurance may be illustrated by the following example. Suppose an individual at thirty years of age is earning $5000 a year. He may purchase $100,000 of insurance with one half of this year's salary which, in the event of his death during the year, will at 5 per cent return to his family the $5000 a year income which if living he would have earned for them. Insurance is therefore based on the fact that a single life has either potential or actual value.

Insurance **and the** Family. — From this description of insurance it is evident that there could be no considerable development of insurance until society had progressed to the stage in which (a) the family was definitely established with social obligations and rights, and (b) the individual, as an individual, was valued as a member of society. Until the definite sex relations of the monogamous family were established, there could be fixed no definite obligations upon the different members of the family organization. However, in the monogamous family organization women and children assumed a position at once more definite and important than in the previous family organization. Affection and a sense of responsibility both operated to place definitely upon the husband the duty of caring for his wife and children. To a less degree only did he feel the obligation of caring for his parents and those of his wife. Thus the possible widow and orphan and infirm parent became a source of solicitude for the husband, who was urged by the definite family bond to make provision from his labor for their care and maintenance. ·

Insurance and the Individual. — In the second place, society had to develop to the point of valuing a life as an individual life before insurance could arise. In the earlier history of civilization it was only the exceptional individual, the king, the warrior, or the priest, whose life had any considerable value. Division of labor had not proceeded far, and the work of the masses was so simple, that the loss of any one person was not greatly missed, since almost any other person could do his simple task. With the progress of society and the corresponding minute divisions of labor, the life of each came to have a definite value to the other members of the group, so that it has come to be of great importance to society that each perform his allotted task and make provision for meeting his obligations.

Each individual comes into the world in possession of that rich heritage from the past which makes most members of society debtors throughout life. If in addition a man does his share in perpetuating the race by assuming the family relation, society has a right to expect that he will make proper provision to prepare his children to become efficient members of society by providing a fund out of his surplus earnings to equip them properly for life and for the maintenance of his widow in the event of his premature death. Otherwise his family may become a charge upon society. They are a form of debts which must be paid, and it is a kind of dishonesty when no provision for their care is made, no less culpable than that in which a man refuses to pay his monetary debts. Life insurance thus not only provides for dependents, but it also prevents an increase of the dependent class. The normal development of the family of the deceased husband is permitted, since provision has been made for the education of the children and the maintenance of the wife, which provision the husband would have made, had he lived. Thus since society is an organism made up of individual units and is benefited by whatever benefits the units, life insurance promotes the well-being of society by properly caring for the social unit, the family.

In addition to these purely material values which life insurance secures for the family, it undoubtedly does much to promote the best family life by strengthening mutual affection, by recognizing and meeting family obligations. It doubtless also adds to the efficiency of the family because it relieves the members of it from an anxiety about the future. Life insurance, then, promotes a sense of responsibility, it strengthens family ties, it creates unselfishness and thus produces a high type of a social individual by inculcating the idea of sharing burdens and of practicing widespread collective coöperation. The direct economic values of insurance are no less evident. We have seen that it makes possible the proper training of the children of the insured by providing a fund for their education, thus relieving society both of the burden of support and that of training. It also relieves the insured from anxiety about the future and contributes powerfully to his efficiency in his daily work.

Insurance and Thrift. — Life insurance enforces thrift, for the ordinary contract calls for the payment on the part of the insured of definite sums at stated intervals. Through lack of foresight or will power few men will save unless under pressure. There is a constant temptation to overvalue the present as compared to the future, not because the latter is uncertain in the minds of most men in their productive years, but because of the intense pleasure of present consumption and lack of imagination in visualizing the pleasures of future consumption. Even a large number of those who voluntarily save do so intermittently. The savings bank depositor is constantly tempted both to make his deposit less than he is able to make it and to spend it for conveniences or luxuries. But the possessor of a life insurance policy comes to look upon his premium in much the same light as the giver of a note or mortgage looks upon the interest. It must be paid. Out of the surplus earnings of his productive years, a sum is annually set aside for obligations either already created by his family connections or for his own maintenance after his productive years have passed. If it is a form of a policy which matures in the latter part of a man's normal lifetime, it may often be invested more wisely as well as more profitably because it is a considerable sum and the individual has had years of experience in business. Meanwhile, during the interval the small yearly contributions of each policyholder are combined with those of millions of others and constitute an enormous fund of accumulated capital with which to conduct, when it is loaned, the large-scale industrial enterprises of modern times. While the rate of interest secured to the individual policyholder on his annual premium may not be large in the abstract, yet through a long series of years it nets him in many cases a greater sum than he would be able to secure if he were compelled to attempt to keep his small payments continuously invested without loss. Desirable and safe investments are found for these collected funds, which could not be secured by the individual contributors to the fund. Then, too, the final payment to the beneficiary of the sum secured by his small annual payments is certain, even though the assured pays only one year's premium. This may seem inequitable to those who pay into the fund for many years, but we shall see later that the computations are so made that the average result is fair to all.

The life insurance company by its small collections from many sources brings together large borrowers and many small lenders. Life insurance indirectly creates wealth by enforcing thrift and saving and by inculcating habits of regularity in living. It directly affects the distribution of wealth in that it is a fund collected from the contributions of many and distributed without any necessary relation between the amount paid in and the amount paid out, so far as any one individual is concerned. That is to say, the principal sum may be paid after only one year's premium has been paid, the members of the insured group having, by the very fact of their becoming members of the society, mutually agreed to bear each other's burdens. We cannot understand insurance unless we thoroughly understand this principle, viz., that insurance is based on the idea of mutuality.

Economic Aspect of Insurance. — Life insurance combines the principles of protecting against loss by premature death with that of the accumulation and investment of funds. It converts income into capital in that the small annual payment or payments become a capital fund which is paid in whole or as an annual income to the beneficiary. The capital fund is not necessarily related to the annual payments which were made by the insured. It may be many times this small sum. In case the income of this large sum is paid annually to the beneficiary it is not necessarily equal to the small sum which the insured paid as a premium. Concretely expressed, this means that one annual payment of $50.00 by the insured may bring to the beneficiary an annual income of $200, thus emphasizing the fact that life insurance is not individualistic in its character. It is essentially mutual, that is, coöperative. No question of individual fairness or equity can arise. Life insurance is collectively always fair and equitable, though from the viewpoint of the ordinary market transaction it may be individnally quite unfair.

Conditions Precedent for Insurance. — The conditions precedent for insurance are: (*a*) There must be a risk of a general loss which neither the insured nor the insurer can prevent or hasten; (*b*) a large number of persons must be exposed to the risk; (*c*) the casualty contemplated must be likely to fall upon a comparatively small number during any short interval; (d) the probability of its occurrence must be capable of being calculated with some approximation of certainty; (e) the loss, when it does occur, must be considerable enough to be worth providing against; (f) the cost of the provision must not be prohibitive to large numbers of persons.

Origin of Insurance. — Insurance as a science is based upon the theory of probabilities, and most of the above conditions are concerned either directly or indirectly with this theory. Condition (e) and (f), for example, secures the large numbers necessary for the proper working of the law of average; condition (c) protects the operation of this law; likewise conditions (b) and (a) assure the results of this law.

Interesting attempts, illustrating considerable ingenuity, have been made to trace modern life insurance back to the remote centuries. These attempts, however, do greater credit to the resourcefulness of the authors than to their appreciation of facts. While no present-day social or economic institution has arisen absolutely intact without earlier ideas and often similar institutions, yet the historical method of explaining present institutions often becomes exaggerated when it seeks to find the germ of every present business and social organization in the remote past. This is especially true in the attempt to trace the history of life insurance into the far distant past. The confusion results in mistaking the fundamental idea underlying insurance with the present expression of that idea in modern life insurance companies. It has been stated that life insurance is based fundamentally on the idea of coöperation, or helping one another to bear burdens and unexpected losses. It has also been stated that life insurance is closely related to the family organization. It is certainly true that man had not far progressed before he perceived the advantage of coöperation, but it does not follow that anything corresponding very closely to the modern complex form of coöperation, called insurance, was developed. The basis of modern life insurance is not primarily the fact of death, but the uncertainty of it. Death was doubtless a great mystery to early man, but to be able to predict death was beyond his speculation. It is this uncertainty of death and the appreciation of its significance which is responsible for modern insurance development. That is, because man has been able to realize the importance of this uncertainty he has been constrained to provide against the misfortune incident to his untimely end. If each could know his length of life, many would provide by saving against the results of death without the intervention of insurance. What man cannot know individually is in a sense made known to him by the institution of insurance, or at least his ignorance of this fact is completely discounted by his association with others in an insurance organization which protects those dependent upon him against this unknowable fact — the time of death.

Before there could be a system of modern insurance it was necessary to have not only the idea of coöperation and family affection thoroughly imbued in man, but also a scientific knowledge of the frequency of death, together with an opportunity for the investment of funds. Commercial or business considerations, quite as much as family considerations, have been responsible for the development of present life insurance, for the modern insurance organization is quite as much an association of capital as of individuals to protect themselves by this capital accumulation from certain predictable losses.

Precursors of Insurance. — It is more accurate therefore to consider present life insurance as an institution which has developed during the past three centuries and to consider the earlier organizations, somewhat resembling insurance, as simply expressions of the idea of coöperation. The historical development of insurance thus considered divides itself into two periods: (*a*) early forms of coöperation somewhat resembling insurance and (*b*) the modern period of scientific insurance. But it must not be understood that all organizations denominated insurance during the past three centuries were of true insurance character. There are at present organizations claiming to use the insurance principle which are as unscientific as those of an earlier date. This may be due to the fact that they are essentially of a gambling or wagering character or because they are sincerely attempting to apply insurance principles to impossible conditions. Insuring for a consideration against unpredictable events or collecting inadequate funds for a pension scheme are but some of the many examples of the impossible attempt to apply insurance principles.

The Roman Collegia. — Among other earlier precursors of modern insurance the following may be noted : (a) agreements with money lenders to provide money for purposes of ransom in case of capture where an individual went on commercial ventures to foreign lands or religious wars or pilgrimages; or an agreement whereby the money lender paid double or treble a certain sum if the voyager returned, or paid certain sums to his family in case he did not return.　(b) the Roman Collegia.　These were organized for a variety of purposes, but usually in the early period had a religious aspect. They were associations of priests, or of artisans or of neighbors.　They often provided suitable burial for their members by contributions from each member of the college.　These organizations flourished both under the Republic and the Empire.　They did much to cultivate the feeling of fraternity and indirectly doubtless aided the members in many ways other than providing burial.

Guilds and Insurance. — (c) The Guilds.　This term is used to include a great variety of organizations which existed during the Middle Ages, and not simply to the best known forms, the merchant and craft guilds.　The occasion and need for their existence is to be found in the absence of any strong central government to protect the individual; in matters of administering justice and poor relief, as well as in the change which was occurring in the family organization as a protector of its members with the development of the system of land-proprietorship and the feudal system.　The guild organization became an expression of the strong family feeling which existed among the Germanic peoples and which under the developing order was being restricted in its expression.

These guilds assumed a great variety of forms with a great variety of purposes, yet they were bound together by the fraternal feeling of a desire to aid and protect each other. In many cases a strong religious purpose existed along with the duty to assist the members in time of distress and death. Traces of such organizations are found as early as the eighth century, and by the eleventh century the Merchant Guild was well developed. It is impossible, however, to establish fixed dates for the origin of any particular form of the guild. For our purpose it is only important to consider all these forms of the guild as an expression of that fraternal spirit which has assumed various forms of organization and which lie at the base of the modern system of insurance. There is no close connection between modern insurance and these early associations except in so far as they had the same psychological and social basis for their formation.

Financial Basis of Insurance. — Insurance as a system could not exist previous to the money and credit system, even if the earlier peoples had known the laws of mortality. It was necessary to have money to store up wealth. It was also necessary to have widely diffused private property and the relationship of debtor and creditor before modern property insurance could exist. Then, too, the use of loaned capital for productive purposes did not develop on any large scale until modern times, and modern insurance is very dependent upon the opportunity to loan capital for long periods at certain rates of interest. The prohibition of interest taking and the restrictions upon loaning what little capital there was during the ancient and middle ages would have precluded the existence of insurance if all other conditions had been favorable.

During the period of Mercantilism suggestions were not infrequently made for a system of life and property insurance under the direction of the state with the prime purpose of furthering the development of the state, since the protection of the individual from the results of misfortune meant a larger and stronger population and the property insurance meant larger capacity for paying taxes to the state. Like all other aspects of mercantilism the immediate object was the development of the State and only incidentally the benefit of the individual. Under the succeeding system of laissez-faire there was an abandonment of the suggestions of state direction of insurance, and in its place arose the beginning of private insurance projects. In modern times there is found in the system of insurance a combination of insurance as an enterprise of the private undertaker, as an expression of the age-old fraternal feeling of a desire for mutual aid, and finally insurance as a state enterprise. Examples of the first are to be found in private stock insurance organizations, although these also express the fraternal spirit. The purely mutual associations illustrate the second characteristic, and the developing systems of state insurance illustrate the third. It is, however, important to understand that all plans of state insurance have for their prime purpose the good of the individual, and only in a very secondary sense is there found, as in the times of mercantilism, the object of furthering an impersonal State. In other words the modern democratic State, as distinguished from the mercantile State, is considered as finding expression only in the individual; that is, the State finds its well-being in the well-being of its citizens, the people thus losing their identity to form a collected body, called the State.

Annuities. — (d) Another precursor of modern insurance was the purchase of annuities, that is, an arrangement by which a certain payment was made to an individual at stated intervals either for life or for a definite number of years. To do this it was necessary to have mortality records, and we find that the Roman jurist Ulpian compiled in A.D. 364 a mortality table for estimating the value of life annuities. This table, considering the imperfect records, was remarkably accurate. It was not an uncommon practice among the Romans to bequeath to faithful retainers an annuity. Annuities were also oftentimes given to members of the family other than the eldest son.

By the sixteenth century the purchase of annuities had become common in the commercial cities of Europe, although they were not based on very scientific plans, especially after the fall of Rome, when the data and tables collected by the Romans were lost. It was also a practice in this early period to insure the lives of individuals who held life interests in estates. Any one entitled to receive during his life a rent or a pension could sell insurance on his life for the provision of his family. All these precursors of insurance were unscientific for the reason that scientific insurance must be based on accurate statistics of lives, especially death rates for all ages, in order to know when payments must be made and in what amounts they will be demanded. The state of society precluded such an institution as modern insurance. Life was too uncertain. War was a game at which kings played. Princes of smaller territories often waged war against their neighbors. Quarrels with fatal results were common. Violence was the rule of the time, and single lives had little value. Plagues, pestilence, and famine were dangers ever present in almost every region. Unsanitary conditions of living were a characteristic of even the most civilized people if measured by present-day standards. Medical science was in its infancy. The duration of life was a lottery, subject to so many accidents that the probability of its duration could be measured in no way. It is, therefore, evident that life insurance, except as a wager or hazard, could not exist.

Early Vital Statistics. — One of the first efforts to collect vital statistics was made in 1592, when the first London Bills of Mortality were published. Since 1603, their publication has been continuous. The original purpose of their publication was to allay the fears of the people of London who had been periodically subject to the plague. Deaths were reported to the parish clerk, who compiled and published the number of deaths and their causes. The attention of scholars was later directed to this data, and deductions as to death rates were made.

In 1644 John Graunt published a work in which he

attempted to place a value on the duration of life, as shown by these Bills of Mortality. However, his data were far from complete for the purpose of insurance, since they often did not give the ages at which the individuals died, nor was there any information in regard to births. It was not until Dr. Halley, the Astronomer Royal, published in 1693 a mortality table based on the vital statistics kept by the town, Breslau, together with mathematical formulas for calculating annuities, that the real basis of insurance was established.

In 1742 Simpson, a mathematician, extended the work by making a practical application of the theory of probability to the valuation of life annuities. These last enumerated facts made possible a transference of life insurance from an experiment to a science, although experimental insurance and gambling under the guise of insurance have not yet disappeared.

Early Life Insurance Organizations. — In 1698 a public office for life insurance was opened in London under the name of the Mercers Company, and in 1699 the Society for the Assurance of Widows and Orphans was established on the plan that each one of the 2000 members should pay an equal sum and each family should receive an equal sum upon the death of the insured member.

The Amicable Society, of London, the first purely mutual company, was founded in 1706. Several other companies were formed during this period, but most of them failed to use whatever little accurate scientific knowledge there was on the subject. All of them charged the same premium rate regardless of age. Most of them were stock or proprietary companies, all of which had failed or failed at the culmination of speculation, the bursting of the South Sea Bubble in 1720. The Amicable Society alone survived in 1720, but in 1721 the Royal Exchange and the London Assurance Companies were formed, both of which are yet in existence. It was not, however, until the organization of the Equitable Society of London in 1762 that life insurance was successfully placed on a scientific basis. The company employed the mathematician, Dr. Richard Price, who would now be called an actuary, to determine the premiums which they should charge. He drew up the Northampton Table of Mortality and from this event insurance as a science may be said to date.

Life Insurance in the United States. — In America the history of the development of insurance has necessarily been different. Many of the settlers were doubtless familiar with the history and operation of the English and continental companies. It was not, however, until 150 years after the first settlement of the country that a life insurance company was organized. Population was very sparse, accidents and dangers of death were numerous, mutual helpfulness generally prevalent, few were even well-to-do, and data as to birth and death rates were very incomplete. In 1759 there was organized what is now called the Presbyterian Ministers' Fund, under the title of " A Corporation for the relief of Poor and Distressed Presbyterian Ministers and of the Poor and Distressed Widows and Children of Presbyterian Ministers." This society gradually developed into a modern insurance company and still exists as an excellent insurance organization. It accepts as risks only ministers. The ministers of the Episcopalian Church organized a similar society in 1769.

Early Life Insurance Companies. — The Insurance Company of North America, of Philadelphia, was organized in 1794 and although other companies were organized from time to time, life insurance as such did not develop much until after 1835. In that year the New England Mutual Life Insurance Company was chartered by Massachusetts. This company was established on the plan of the old Equitable of London, which, during the preceding twenty-five years, had been very successful. The Equitable of London was a purely mutual company, but the legislature of Massachusetts required the incorporators of the New England Mutual to guarantee a capital of $100,000. Owing to the difficulty of persuading capitalists to supply the money, the company was not able to begin writing policies until 1843. In the meantime a stock company, the General Life and Trust Company of Philadelphia, chartered in 1836, had been doing considerable business. It had provided for a division of profits with its policyholders, thus furnishing an example of what is called a mixed plan, that is, a stock company sharing profits with policyholders. Some of such companies permit a partial management of the company by the policyholders. Owing, however, to the great New York Fire in 1835, which caused a failure of many of the stock fire insurance companies and the subsequent organization of the mutual fire insurance companies which seemed to be successful; and owing further to the success of the mutual marine and mutual life companies in England, the mutual plan as applied to life insurance came into great favor in the United States. The Mutual Life of New York was organized in 1842, the New England Mutual of Massachusetts began writing business in 1843, the Mutual Benefit of New Jersey was organized in 1845, and the New York Life in the same year. From 1843 to 1859 fifteen other companies were organized, and the aggregate amount of insurance in force at the latter date was $150,000,000, an amount less than any one of several companies is now able to write in a single year.

The period from 1860 to 1870 was a golden age in the life insurance business. Notwithstanding the opening of the Civil War and the fear of insurance officials that the insurance business would decrease, it showed a remarkable increase. During the decade seventy-seven new companies were chartered, making a total in 1869 of one hundred and ten companies with almost a billion and a half of dollars of insurance on their books. This period of expansion was followed by one of depression, extending from 1870 to 1880. The cause of the remarkable growth of insurance during the preceding period and the consequent period of depression may be grouped under the following heads : —

Characteristics of the Early Development. — First. Insurance was a new idea, which in its application promised to satisfy the very strong characteristic of the Anglo Saxon to make provision for his family.

Second. Actuarial science had not developed to

any great extent in America. These numerous companies, most of which had been organized on the mutual
plan, were patterned after the old Equitable of London,
which now had a successful history of over a century.
However, they did not follow very closely the plan of
the Equitable. Interest rates were much higher in
America, and this led practically all of them to charge a
premium only from 30 to 60 per cent as large as the
Equitable charged for the same policy. In the early
history of the companies, when the death rate was low,
even the collections of these lower premiums were more
than sufficient to meet the claims against the companies.
The companies found themselves with much unused
money on hand. This led most of them to promise,
and many of them to pay, enormous dividends. Later,
when some of the companies perceived these mistakes,
the competition with other ignorantly or dishonestly
managed companies led them to continue the policy by
issuing scrip certificates for these larger dividends.
These were redeemable at a future time, frequently at
death. When the death rates increased, as the company became older, these promises of large dividends
could not be kept, and many policyholders were disappointed.

Third. Many of the mutual companies in their
desire to make the buying of insurance easy and because they had more than sufficient funds to meet the
few early death claims accepted notes for the premiums
due. The policyholder was led to believe that his
dividend accumulations would amount to as high as
50 per cent of the premiums due, but future events

so sadly disproved this, that many were unable to make payments due for unpaid premiums and were forced to give up their insurance. The people who knew little about the principles upon which scientific insurance should be conducted came to believe that insurance was a " swindle " and refused to purchase it.

Fourth. The seeming prosperity of insurance companies caused many new companies to be organized for the purpose of a speculation or for pure swindle.

For these reasons the failure of companies became numerous after 1870, and the panic of 1873 greatly accelerated the movement, so that by 1880 the amount of insurance in force, as compared with 1870, had decreased about 50 per cent.

The period from 1880 to 1905 may be considered as the one in which the companies were placed on a thoroughly scientific basis. It is further characterized by a systematic business organization of the companies, a liberalization of the contracts, and a very great increase in the expense of securing business, due in part to the great rivalry of companies, in part to the general adoption of the deferred dividend system, and in part to the invasion by some companies of foreign countries to secure business. The amount of insurance in force during the period increased 500 per cent, reaching in 1905 twelve billions of dollars. This refers, of course, as does all our preceding statements, to level premium or ordinary life insurance. The development of other kinds of insurance is described later.

Characteristics of Modern Life Insurance. — The year 1905 is chosen as the close of a period because that year marks the beginning of change in the relation of the state to the conduct of the insurance business. Previous to this date the states had laid down in general laws the terms upon which companies could be organized; many of them had well-organized insurance departments, but the character of the relation of the state to the business preceding 1905 may be described as that of a general supervising nature. In the preceding period of fierce competition and loose supervision many well-defined evils arose. In a contest between two parties for control of the management of a prominent New York Company facts were disclosed which led to an investigation by the State of New York and subsequently by other states of the management of several insurance companies. The result in the end was the subjecting of the business of insurance to much more detailed regulation than in any other period in the past, either in the United States or in foreign countries.

Laws were passed regulating the amount of commission to be paid to agents, the total amount to be spent in securing new business, the surplus, the plans of apportioning dividends; the amount of new business to be written, the requirement of certain provisions in all policies, and particularly greater publicity. As a result the insurance business is at present more minutely regulated in the United States than in any other country, and in fact little further is left to be regulated. There is already some evidence of a reaction along certain lines against such strict regulation, for it is becoming apparent that some of the regulation was unnecessarily burdensome to the companies and subserves no real interest of the policyholder. However, some unwise legislation was to be expected after the disclosure of the evils of the period of lax regulation. Then, too, such gross misrepresentations were made at the time of the investigation as to exaggerate the evils and bias the minds of the legislators who in general knew little about the business. Great injury has often been done to the insurance business through a failure on the part of the legislator to understand the character of insurance. It is a business of such complexity and the ignorance of the general public regarding it is so great, that sometimes their representatives in the legislatures are used by men acting from personal motives of oppositiou to the business or by those seeking popular favor by the common practice too prevalent in these latter times of attacking anything that is big. Probably most of the injury has resulted, however, not from evil intent, but from lack of understanding, and it is encouraging to note that more and more the legislatures are depending upon their insurance departments to recommend the passage or defeat of measures which affect insurance.

Insurance Legislation and Education. — Although there is yet considerable opportunity for making the state departments of insurance more efficient, the improvement in department work during the last years has been very marked. It must be admitted, however, that preceding the legislative uprisings following the disclosures of 1905, the companies themselves had done little to inform either policyholders or the public as to the character of the business, and hence were not in position .to expect many sympathizers or supporters. Happily, efforts since then have been made which, if continued, will do much to make impossible both the existence of many of the internal evils complained of in the past as well as the enactment of unwise laws designed to regulate, but which in their operation restrict the business. The campaign of educating the people to understand the principles of insurance and to appreciate the benefits must be vigorously conducted and long continued. There is scarcely another business about which the average man is so ignorant, and moreover the nature of the business is such that it continually tempts the legislator to use the insurance funds as a source of revenue, for he is seeking the easiest sources of additional revenue for the increasing state expenditures. It has large funds, accumulated from many different sources, and the apparently small tax rate which is usually levied on the gross premiums yields a large revenue. Being an indirect tax widely distributed as to payment, the real burden is not easily perceived.

What has been previously stated in reference to the historical development of insurance refers in the main to legal reserve insurance. It is often called old line or level premium or scientific insurance. Old line, legal reserve insurance is insurance sold by a company for a premium or premiums fixed in amount during the length of the policy, or for a limited period, the premiums being such amounts as will accumulate a sinking fund or reserve which together with future premiums will meet all obligations of the company. We have now to describe the development of two other kinds of life insurance, viz. assessment and industrial.

The Development of Assessment Insurance. — The general plan of assessment insurance is to collect sums from each of the members of the society as the claims fall due; but there have been many modifications of this plan. In some cases the same amount was collected from each member, regardless of the age at entry or attained age. In other cases there has been an attempt to adjust the amount collected to the age, but in practically all cases the amount collected was arbitrarily decided without much reference to scientific plans. Frequently the plan called for the payment of the same amount to each beneficiary upon the death of the insured, although this amount might differ from time to time.

In Europe the assessment plan preceded the level premium plan, naturally enough, for it seemed to supply cheap protection upon an equal basis. In the United States, however, the assessment plan did not develop until the level premium plan was well established. The early settlers brought with them the prevailing ideas of insurance in England, and this was the level premium plan.

Two kinds of assessment companies must be distinguished: (a) the business assessment companies, and (b) the fraternal assessment organizations. In 1867 the first important business assessment company was organized in the United States, and in 1868 appeared the first important fraternal assessment company, the Ancient Order of United Workmen. This association is yet in existence.

Explanation of Popularity of Assessment Insurance. — It may be difficult to explain completely the causes for the rise of assessment insurance in the United States, but the following reasons go far in the explanation: (a) The disappointing practice of the early level premium companies in accepting notes of the policyholders for the premium upon the supposition that the large anticipated dividends would equal the face of the notes. These notes were charges against the policy and bore interest. The large dividends promised were not earned and the policyholder was in the position of having less insurance and an increasing amount to pay as interest. Now the policy in the earlier years of insurance in the United States was a whole life policy contract with level premiums payable as long as the insured lived. None of the present-day benefits, such as a cash surrender value in case of failure to pay the premiums, a loan, or paid-up insurance, were provided in the contract. If the policyholder ceased to pay his premiums, he had no insurance, and previons payments were the property of the company. Many policyholders were unable to keep up the payments when the large dividends did not accrue and when their interest debts increased. Many were forced to give up their insurance, and since the policy did not provide for any cash surrender value, many felt that they had been robbed. The managers of the companies, most of which were on the mutual plan, had not understood insurance and were deceived by the low death rate in the earlier years. They were led to promise these large dividends which the inevitably higher death rate of the later years made impossible.

(b) In the second place the policyholder perceived that the companies had accumulated, particularly in the earlier years, sums far in excess of the demands made by death claims, and they could not understand the necessity of this reserve fund. They were paying more than was necessary and getting nothing when they ceased to be a member of the company, so they reasoned. This violated all their ideas of mutuality, the plan of all for each and each for all. It was not unnatural, then, that the assessment plan became very popular, and when the hard times of the seventies came, this accelerated the movement towards assessment insurance. Hundreds of business assessment companies were formed in the seventies and eighties, but to-day these have largely passed out of existence, and those in existence are conducted on somewhat different plans from those of the early societies. The first societies started on the plan of collecting the same amount from each member regardless of age. Soon, however, this unfair plan was changed for the one in which a member was charged a sum at entry on the basis of his age. If the death rate at 25 is 7 per 1000 and at 50 it is 10 per 1000, then they erroneously reasoned the monthly payment of a man at the former age should be one twelfth of $7 and at the latter age one twelfth of $10. This made the mistake of not taking into consideration the increasing age of the members in the latter history of the company. This mistake was sometimes recognized later, and an effort was made by some of the companies to correct it by accumulating a fund by an addition to the ordinary assessment. This in practically all cases proved an entirely inadequate fund to meet their obligations.

Fraternal Insurance and the Assessment Plan. — The assessment idea, as applied to fraternal societies, has had quite a different history. It must be stated, however, that all fraternal insurance of the present is not on the assessment plan. Some of it is on the level premium plan which has already been described as that of the old line companies, and what we now have to state refers to fraternal insurance on the assessment plan. It has been stated that the first fraternal order was that of the Ancient Order of United Workmen, founded at Meadville, Pennsylvania, in 1868. Two stages in the development of fraternal societies may be noted. The first stage in which they were conducted on the unscientific plan of the earlier assessment orders, and the second stage of transfer to the scientific plan of reserve insurance, based on the mortality experience of fraternal societies. It is not intended that the reader shall infer that all fraternal societies have passed through this period of transformation and are now on a scientific basis, for many of them are struggling to solve this difficult problem, and doubtless many of them will not be able to solve it. No further description is necessary of the first stage, since what has been said of business assessment societies equally applies to fraternal assessment societies on this plan.

The most important fact in connection with the fraternal societies, and the one which differentiates them from the business assessment companies, is the fraternal idea which characterizes the former. It was this alone which made possible a transfer to a scientific basis. This idea of brotherhood, a willingness to share each other's burdens, that all might have protection, induced the members in some cases to pay the necessary higher premiums called for when the society undertook to correct the errors of the old plan by accumulating a reserve. Rates were adjusted in some fraternal societies and are being adjusted in some others by this appeal to the fraternal instinct. Members have continued in the societies long after they would have withdrawn from the business assessment societies. Then, too, the state has interfered very little with the conduct of fraternal insurance. The societies have been left largely free to organize and conduct their business as they pleased. Whether this has been an ultimate advantage has been questioned, but in any event it has left them free to adopt their own plans of transfer to scientific insurance, and the members have felt that whatever they have done has been done of their own volition and for their own good. These societies in time came to use a mortality table based upon their own experience. This table has a lower death rate than the table used by the legal reserve companies; and this, coupled with the fact that the expense of securing members and conducting the insurance business in connection with their other fraternal activities is lower than in the legal reserve companies, makes the transfer easier.

The Strength of Fraternal Insurance. — Fraternal insurance needs no defense for its existence. Mistakes have been made in the past, and errors, as in all institutions, are yet present. The pure assessment plan has been the source of disappointment to thousands. Many have made years of sacrifice from which their dependants have received no benefit. Doubtless some have been induced to take out regular insurance after having held a policy in assessment societies, but the unfortunate experience of many persons in assessment societies has caused many others to refuse to buy any kind of insurance. Nor is it a complete justification for the existence of the pure assessment plan to maintain that at least some of the intended beneficiaries have benefited from these small inadequate collections. Some do benefit, but many others lose so that paradoxically as it may seem the most successful assessment society is, from one point of view, the least successful. It is a small temporary benefit in exchange for a large future injustice. The present movement by insurance commissioners and state legislators to compel fraternal societies now on the assessment plan to operate upon a plan such as will insure the meeting of all future demands by the accumulation of an adequate reserve may well be encouraged and will certainly come to pass in time.

The Development of Industrial Insurance. — Industrial insurance is that form of ordinary level premium insurance in which the premiums are paid weekly to the agent of the company and in which the amount of the insurance is adjusted to the premium. The premium

D

is 5 cents weekly or the multiples of 5 cents. This form of insurance originated in England in 1849 by the formation of the Industrial and General Insurance Company. The business of this company was assumed by the Prudential Insurance Company of the same country in 1854 when Industrial Insurance as now known was begun. The business has attained enormous proportions in the United States, although over 90 per cent of the business is done by three companies — the Prudential of New Jersey, organized in 1875; the Metropolitan of New York, organized in 1875; and the John Hancock of Massachusetts, which began writing this kind of business in 1879.

Among other important industrial companies are the Life Insurance Company of Virginia, organized at Richmond, Virginia, in 1887, and operating chiefly in the South; and the Western and Southern, organized at Cincinnati in 1888, and operating chiefly in the Middle West. The chief purpose of industrial insurance is to provide burial funds for members of the family. Every member can be insured. As its name implies, it is insurance for the industrial classes, the wage earner, who either cannot from his small net wage save enough to carry ordinary insurance or who will not, from lack of foresight and thrift, save enough when his wage would make this possible. This statement suggests one of the chief values of this form of insurance, viz., that it is a powerful factor in inculcating habits of thrift, saving, and industry. Large numbers of those who first carry industrial insurance may later carry regular insurance. Not only does it enable the family to en-

joy a higher standard of family life and meet the unexpected obligations incurred as a result of sickness and
death, but it also has a direct value to society in that it
relieves it of the expense of meeting these obligations.
It indirectly benefits society by benefiting the units
of which it is composed — the family.

Industrial insurance may be compared in one sense
with ordinary insurance by describing the former as
insurance at retail and the latter as insurance at wholesale. The price of goods and services on the retail plan
is higher than on the wholesale plan and just so is the
price of industrial insurance higher than ordinary insurance. The expense of collecting weekly from door to
door these small sums from so many different people
is enormous, which added to the increased office and
accounting work explains in great part its higher price.
The premiums are based on the same principles as are
those of ordinary insurance and the insurance is as scientific as the latter. The average weekly premium paid
in this country is about 10 cents. The greatest problem
in industrial insurance is to reduce the expense of its
transaction so that the numerous classes which it serves
may secure the benefits of insurance without incurring the
risk of undermining habits of industry and thrift by any
public form of charitable relief. The fuller discussion of
workingman's insurance is deferred to a later chapter.

The following table, exhibiting the insurance carried
by the old line regular life insurance companies and by
the assessment life associations and fraternal orders,
shows that assessment insurance is still an important
factor in the competition for life insurance.

LIFE INSURANCE AGGREGATES, JANUARY 1, 1914

(United States Companies. New York Insurance Department)

No. of Companies	Kind of Insurance	No. of Policies	Amt. of Insurance in Force	Average Amount of Policy
229	Old Line (Ordinary)	8,774,638	$16,587,378,943	$1890 +
31	Old Line (Industrial)	29,431,756	3,977,091,002	135.12
509	Fraternal	8,058,317	9,622,276,590	1194.
96	Assessment	730,359	400,701,350	548.63
5	Stipulated Premium	13,426	12,758,530	950.28
	Total	47,008,496	30,600,206,415	

REFERENCES

Yale Readings in Insurance, Vol. I, Chaps. III, V, VI.

Annals of the American Academy of Political Science, Vol. XXXVI, pp. 181–190, 308–316.

The Insurance Year Book (Life). The Spectator Company.

Dawson, Miles M. The Business of Life Insurance, Chaps. III, XXIX, XXX.

Fricke, W. A. Insurance, pp. 355–401, 442–452.

Henderson, C. R. Industrial Insurance in the United States.

Brown, Benjamin F. The Brown Book of Life Insurance.

Walford, Cornelius. Cyclopedia of Insurance.

Annual Reports of the State Commissioners of Insurance.

Insurance Guide and Handbook, Fifth Edition, Chaps. I, III, VIII, and XX.

An Introduction to the History of Life Insurance. A Finland Jack.

Transactions of the Insurance and Actuarial Society of Glasgow. Second Series, pp. 190–217.

CHAPTER II

THE THEORY OF LIFE INSURANCE

The Theoretical Basis of Life Insurance. — We have now to consider the theory upon which life insurance is based, and in its most important aspects it may be treated under the two heads: (*a*) Rate of mortality, and (*b*) Rate of interest. Insurance is the assumption of risk by a group in order that the individual may be protected. The theory of risk, as applied to insurance, needs to be explained; and to do this the doctrine of chance and the law of probability must be introduced.

The Theory of Chance. — As we observe phenomena we are continually making generalizations from the data collected by the examination of single cases. We speak of a chance happening, meaning by this that a certain result has been brought about from unknown or unknowable causes. However, most of the results or phenomena which we ascribe to chance pure and simple become knowable and understandable after observation is made over longer periods and of a greater number of events. Order comes out of chaos. We come to perceive aggregate regularity amidst individual irregularity. For example, it is a fact that the age at which any one of a group of 1000 children will die is unknown, but continued observation of the life history of such groups of children will disclose a regularity of deaths at succeeding ages. Or, again, if a perfectly constructed coin is spun in the air, it may fall heads or tails, the chance of a head or tail appearing being one half. However, if it is spun a great number of times, the number of times that heads and tails will come up will approach equality. That is to say, order begins to appear as we increase the range of our observation. It is not true that this irregularity as to individual instances is complete, for in every case it has definite limits. For example, it is absurd to conclude that the average length of life is uncertain, because we cannot foretell when an individual child of the 1000 will die. It certainly will be considerably under 125 years, just as the coin will come up either head or tail.

Bernoulli's Propositions. — Bernoulli has summed up the above facts in the two propositions: (a) that the probability of events happening in numbers proportionate to their respective chances in a single trial is greater, the greater the number of trials or observations; (b) that the number of observations or experiments may be so determined that the deviation from this stated ratio approaches certainly as closely as is wished, or concisely: "In the long run events will tend to occur with a relative frequency proportional to their objective probabilities." The tossing of the coin and the tendency to secure an equal number of heads and tails as the number of tosses is increased illustrate the first theorem; or, again, if the births of 10,000 children are known and 1000 die the first year, the chances of any one infant living during the first year is $\frac{9}{10}$. As the number of children under observation increases, the actual results, that is, the deaths, will closer and closer approximate the calculated ratio of deaths. That is to say, order gradually emerges out of disorder, and a definite and recognizable uniformity is disclosed. This uniformity, however, has certain conditions, without which it will not apply. There must be a sufficient number of incidents to disclose it, and the observations must be confined within definite periods.

Life Insurance and Bernoulli's Theories. — That is to say, in the practical application of the principle to life insurance, a large number of lives must be observed within definite periods. Owing to advances in civilization, to improvements in living conditions, to changes in ideas of life and the employments of man, the average duration of life changes. It is certainly now longer than it was 100 years ago and doubtless its duration will be different 100 years from now. It may be longer or shorter either from necessity or choice. All that is necessary for successful scientific insurance is that the uniformity through any period be known, even though the uniformity be subject to secular changes. We therefore assume in life insurance that the conditions determining the length of life are fixed, and that we have a fixed limit — the average duration of life — within which or towards which the individual length of life is tending. It is true, indeed, that just as there are " runs of luck," as when in tossing a coin, heads may come up continuously for several times in succession, so, too, in life insurance there may be an unusual number of deaths within a short period, or the number of deaths may be far below what is normally expected and calculated. But these abnormal experiences will so counteract each other in the long run that the total result will be in harmony with the uniformity previously observed.

The practical effect of this in life insurance is that those who live longest pay into the general fund a more than proportionate share in order to balance the less than proportionate payments of those who die earliest, that is, die before they have experienced the average duration of life. The factors which influence a particular individual's length of life are too numerous and too generally well known to need enumeration. What we need to realize is that the interaction of these numerous forces upon numerous individuals produce a general uniformity which is the first principle upon which the practice of insurance is based. We need not attempt to assign to each agency affecting the length of life its respective force. All we need to know in applying the theory of probability to the duration of life is that certain major forces operate upon large groups of individuals of a given age for considerable periods of time with the same or equally increasing degrees of intensity. The minor forces may operate now positively, now negatively, thus counteracting each other. An example of a major force would be climatic conditions, and an example of the minor force, the character of the occupation.

How Uniformity in the Phenomena is Secured. — In order to secure a greater uniformity in experience, insurance companies endeavor to secure a homogeneous group. That is to say, they exclude individuals affected with diseases, such, for example, as tuberculosis. This is done because these individuals bring into the group, agencies affecting the length of life, whose force cannot with any degree of accuracy be calculated. If, indeed, the number of individuals afflicted with any particular disease were sufficiently numerous, a certain uniformity might be disclosed so that the average duration of life of the group being known, the insurance principle might be applied. However, practical difficulties, not only as to sufficient numbers, but also as to determining the influence of external and internal forces, would be so great as to preclude in most cases any scientific application of the insurance principle. Such rapid advances are being made in the control of contagious diseases, the ignorance about inherited diseases is being so rapidly dispelled, that even supposing accurate data for a homogeneous abnormal group, if such a group can exist, could be collected, it would not be true of the succeeding generation of this description. The rate at which 10,000 consumptives now die would not be the rate at which 10,000 with the same disease would die ten years from now. The group to which insurance is to apply must, therefore, be fairly homogeneous. Indeed, the more homogeneous the group, the more scientific the insurance, and hence the more equitable will the principle work to the individual members of the group. The force of this is seen in the increasing demand that insurance companies tabulate the experience or life history of the various classes of members composing the society and adjust the charge for insurance on the basis of this experience.

Insurance is Concerned with the Group. — It must not be forgotten, however, that insurance does not concern itself primarily with individuals as such, but with groups of individuals. Insurance is a combination of risks, and while the total risk for the company is, generally speaking, the sum of the individual risks, yet that part of the risk borne by an individual of an insured group is less than the risk borne by a similar individual not insured. Insurance is interested in learning what happens to that fictitious person, the average member of the group. It does not assume that any particular individual will live any definite number of years. The individual may be the victim of chance. It assumes irregularity as applied to individuals of the group, but regularity as applied to the group. That is to say, of a large number of individuals, certain numbers will die at certain periods, the numbers living beyond the average lifetime balancing those that die before this period. Insurance has therefore been defined as a mutual contract among those who so dread the consequences of the uncertainty of life that they will employ the aggregate regularity to neutralize the individual irregularity. From one point of view some gain, others must lose. It is from one viewpoint an individually unfair arrangement which is collectively fair.

Insurance and Gambling. — Theoretically there is scarcely any limit to the application of the insurance principle. All that is necessary is to have a relative homogeneous group exposed to a risk, the probability of which can be calculated with some reasonable degree of accuracy. Such practical difficulties are, however, in the way that not infrequently we witness attempts to apply the principle which are little less than a gamble. The theory of all insurance is based upon the regularity of predictable events, and upon the fact that it is possible to fix a rate sufficient to accumulate by periodic payments a fund adequate to meet the losses incurred by the happening of these predictable events. Each risk is insured by the plurality of the other risks, and not by a company, when one exists, for the company as such is only the means or agency through which the system of insurance operates. The risk exists for the individual regardless of whether he unites with others in a mutual association or in a company for protection. The company can neither increase nor decrease the risk except in so far as it, through its officials, incorrectly or wisely applies in practice the exact theory of insurance. Herein is suggested the real distinction between gambling and insurance. In gambling individuals expose themselves to the risk of an unnecessary loss, while in insurance the risks are present and by their combination and assumption by the group, the individual is freed in part from the evil results of the happening. In the one case a risk is created, in the other an existing risk is decreased by its distribution among a group. The object of the gambler is gain, while the end of insurance is protection against a possible loss. No method of computation can predict the result of a gambling transaction. The motives which impel a man to engage in gambling and in insurance are diametrically opposed. The one seeks excitement, the other security. In insurance it is a desire for regularity. In gambling it is the fascination of the irregularity which results from the uncertainty of the game.

The Risk in Life Insurance. — From the foregoing discussion it must be clear that the insurance company knows, not only the total sum that must be collected, but also the parts of the sum which will be paid out by it each year. It is, therefore, able to determine the amounts necessary to be collected each year. Disregarding for the present the compound interest accumulations, it may be said that the amount to be collected is determined by the risk, and the risk is measured by the probability of payments demanded each year. The risk is the difference between the amount the company has obligated itself to pay and the amount which it has reserved from the payments made by the individuals to whom it promises to pay. It is evident that the amount at risk in the early years of the company's existence is absolutely large, since it has reserved from its policyholders' payments only a small per cent of the amounts which it has obligated itself to pay. However, the risk is relatively not great, for the company has assumed in its calculation a certain death rate among its members and certain additions to the sinking fund or reserve from interest accumulations. Manifestly, if it should be called upon immediately to pay the face value of all its policies, it could not do so. We shall see later that there is even less chance of a large number of demands being made on the insurance company than upon most other financial institutions. Nothing could cause this large demand for the face value of the policies other than a great plague.   Nevertheless, the amount at risk is a question which demands consideration in its practical bearing.   That is to say, the character and amount of the individual risks as such determine the character of the total risk and therefore affect the soundness of the company.

The Risk and the Death Rate. — In insurance more than in most kinds of business whatever affects unfavorably the parts, affects the whole.   For example, if a company insured at normal rates a great number of under average lives, that is, individuals who did not experience the average lifetime, it would find itself in the position of having to pay obligations before the time calculated upon.   It would be in a position similar to an individual borrowing money to build a factory or to finance a crop and being called upon to repay the loan before his factory was placed in operation or before his crop had been harvested.   Or, again, if a company should insure for very large sums an undue proportion of individuals who died within a few years, this would tend to impair the soundness of the company and in any event would reduce the surplus.   In this connection the subject of suicide in its effect upon the risk arises, and the influence is readily perceived. Most companies will not, therefore, pay the face of the policy if suicide occurs within one or two years from the date of issue of the policy.

The Risk and Investments. — Another practical problem .in connection with the risk was suggested, viz., that of investments.   The company has made its contracts, not only on the basis of having a certain mortality experience, but also on the basis of being able to earn a certain interest on its invested funds. The actual mortality experience may, as we shall see later, vary from the calculated, but care should be taken to keep the actual mortality well within the expected. Likewise the actual earnings may vary from the expected, but care must be taken to keep the funds invested so continuously and so profitably and so safely, that the investment part of the business contributes its aid in maturing all obligations of the company.

Insurance has to do with a great number of future happenings, the occurrence of which can be predicted with sufficient accuracy to determine the present action. It deals with probability and average. If, for example, the amount of the risk is widely distributed, both the probability of a general deviation of the final result from the average result and marked single fluctuations are lessened. The same principle is applied, not only in the number of insured lives, but also in investing the funds. No company would, for example, invest all its funds in railroad bonds, however good the investment might be at any one time. The effect on the amount at risk is similar in each case, that is to say, an effort is made to secure continuous and stable results throughout the period of the contracts. No specific rule can be laid down as to the limit of the risk on individual lives or the number of such large risks which a company may safely write. It is the practice of many companies to limit the amount of insurance which is written on an individual life, the maximum in general tending to be greater, the greater the total amount of insurance on the books and the wider the distribution of risks both as to territory and kinds of contract. It can be seen, however, that other factors, such as the amount of the surplus accumulated, enter into the problem, for the range of fluctuation is a resultant of many variable factors.

The Limit **of the** Risk. — A prominent authority has summed up the problem as follows: " In the first place the limit of the risk is not one which at present has to do chiefly with the solvency of the companies, for the legal reserve companies are too substantially founded and operated to cause much concern on this point. In its immediate effects it is a problem of whether the company will be able to distribute its dividends or fix its premiums at the point or below the point of those in the past." Again, the limit of the risk in the early history of companies should be very moderate, and this for two reasons: first, because there has not yet been accumulated a sinking fund or reserve of any large amount to meet assumed obligations, and if single policies of large amounts should fall due, it would place a strain upon the general resources of the company and especially affect the dividend rate; and second, the benefits from compound interest have not yet had time to be realized. After a time when the business has expanded, both as to area and number and kind of policies, and the addition to the reserve has become large from the compound interest source, the limit of the single risk may be raised.

The reader will understand that the large risk is from one point of view a special risk which may have somewhat the same influence upon the most successful operation of the company as do substandard risks or an underaverage life. If sufficient numbers of these risks could be secured to thus make up a homogeneous group, no particularly difficult problems would be presented, for a normal experience could be deduced from the individual experience which deviated positively and negatively from the normal. This statement must, however, be considered in connection with the amount of surplus which the company has accumulated. It is a question to what extent these large and unexpected claims will reduce this surplus. Certain other aspects of the risk, such as the methods of dealing with special risks, are reserved for a more detailed discussion in later chapters.

The Risk and the Annual Premium. — Insurance organizations are usually operated upon the assumption that payments, called premiums, will be paid each year by those who hold policies. Only a small number of policyholders will die or suffer a loss each year out of all those who pay these premiums. There will therefore be a surplus of payments which invested at interest will accumulate additions to the insurance fund. These annual payments for life insurance, as will be shown in a later discussion, are in the early years of the policy in excess of the actual cost of the protection for those years and hence a large interest-earning reserve fund for future payments is accumulated. The excess payments of the early years are made on the theory that the policyholder is usually more able during his productive years to pay larger sums for insurance, the practice thus making possible a payment in the later years of the policy less than the actual cost of the protection. There is ordinarily no change in the amount of the premium which he pays during the length of the policy, but since the chance of death increases with age, the cost of the protection would, if expressing this fact, gradually increase with age.

Compound Interest Calculations. — This reserve of excess payment is the sinking fund accumulated out of premium payments for the purpose of meeting obligations as they fall due. Since the life insurance contract is a monetary obligation extending over a long period of time, this interest accumulation is a very important part of the principle upon which the companies operate. It is these interest accumulations which determine in part the premiums to be charged. The rate to be earned in the future is necessarily a subject for estimation, and great care must be taken in fixing a conservative rate which can be attained in experience.

The most important point to understand in connection with the interest accumulations is that it is not a simple interest accumulation. That is to say, the yearly interest earned on a premium paid in is not only added to it and draws interest the second year, but at the beginning of the second year another principal — the premium — is added and with the original principal draws interest. For example, $100 invested for one year at 4 per cent yields $104. If the principal sum the second year is the original one plus the interest, it becomes at the close of the third year $112.48, whereas at simple interest the sum would merely be $112. A

E

continuation of the calculation would show that the difference between simple and compound interest grows greater with time, so that, for example, at the fortieth year the difference between the two interests for $100 is $220.10; that is, $110 at compound interest would amount to $480.10, while at simple interest it would amount to $260. But the above illustration does not represent the actual facts in regard to the finances of an insurance company, because each year it receives from the policyholder another premium which is added to the previously received premiums and their interest accumulation. This, then, constitutes a new principal upon which interest is earned.

If $100 is paid each year and invested at 4 per cent on the plan that each year's payment with its interest accumulation becomes a new principal, with the new annual payment of $100 added to it, then the true results of compound interest as it operates in insurance calculations are seen. The $100 payments made in this manner amount at the close of the fourth year to $446.13, whereas the interest on an original and single payment of $100 with its interest accumulations compounded amounts only to $116.98. If 1 be invested for a year at a rate i, the amount at the end of the year is $(1 + i)$ and if any other sum, P, is invested at the same rate, the amount at the end of the year would be $P(1 + i)$; likewise the amount in n years will be $P(1 + i)^n$. If this accumulated amount is expressed by the letter S, the equation for the calculation of the sum for any year is:

$$S = P(1 + i)^n$$

and from this formula any one of four unknown quantities may be calculated, the remaining three being given. For example, suppose $382.88 will be paid in five years for $300 paid now. At what rate of interest can this be done? The rate of interest

$$i = \left(\frac{S}{P}\right)^{\frac{1}{n}} - 1$$

$$= \left(\frac{382.881}{300}\right)^{\frac{1}{5}} - 1$$

$$= 1.05 - 1$$

$$= .05$$

Likewise from $S = P(1 + i)^n$ can be derived
$$n = \frac{\log S - \log P}{\log (1 + i)}$$ and from this formula the time in which any sum doubles itself may be calculated. In this case $P = 1$ and consequently $S = 2$. Therefore

$$n = \frac{\log 2 - \log 1}{\log (1 + i)}.$$

By using the natural logarithm to the base 1 and neglecting the small value of i in the formula, the general rule from this formula for finding the time in which money doubles itself is: divide 69 by the rate per cent.

A company must not only know that it can accumulate funds at a certain rate, but also what sums it must collect upon which interest is to be accumulated. That is to say, knowing from the mortality table that a certain number of deaths will occur each year and knowing, therefore, that the total payments to be made are the sums named in the policies of those dying, it must know what sums invested at a certain rate of interest will amount to the total face value of the claims made.

The application of this principle will be explained when the subject of premiums and premium calculation is considered. We thus see that the science of life insurance is based upon calculations involving mortality statistics and compound interest earnings. It is a combination of the theory of probabilities with certain principles of finance.

REFERENCES

Pearson, Karl. Chances of Death, Vol. I, Chap. I. Grammar of Science, Chap. IV.

Jevons, Stanley W. Principles of Science, Chap. X.

Bowley, A. L. Elements of Statistics, Part II, pp. 261–355.

Venn, John. The Logic of Chance, Chaps. I, II, III, IV, XV.

Willett, Allan H. Columbia University Studies in Economics, History, and Public Law, Vol. XIV, Chaps. I, II, III, IV, V, VI.

Yale Readings in Insurance, Vol. I, Chaps. I, IV, VII.

Principles and Practices of Life Insurance. The Spectator Company, Publishers.

Insurance Guide and Handbook, Fifth Edition, Chap. IX.

Notes on Life Insurance. Edward B. Fackler, Chaps. I to V.

Insurance and The State. W. F. Gephart, Chaps. I to III.

Practical Lessons in Actuarial Science. Miles M. Dawson, Vol. I, pp. 38–60.

Insurance Science and Economics. Frederick G. Hoffman, Chaps. I and II.

CHAPTER III

MORTALITY TABLES

IF the reader seeks to understand the principles upon which life insurance is based as well as the practical application of these principles in the actual conduct of the business, the significance of the mortality table must be understood. The mortality table is the expression of the theory of probabilities as applied to life insurance.

Mortality Table Defined. — A mortality table is a table which shows the number of persons remaining alive at each age out of a given number and also the number dying during each year of age. It is " the instrument by means of which are measured the probabilities of living and dying." The table does not show the actual individual experience of the group at each age, but an average with the deviations reduced. The number upon which the experience is based, usually 100,000, is called the radix of the table. A table may commence at any age, but usually begins at 10 with the upper limit at 100 years. The sources of the data from which such tables are constructed are usually either general population statistics or statistics of insured lives. We therefore have the two chief classes of tables, the general or population tables and the select tables of mortality. Manifestly the early tables were of the first kind.

53

Mortality Table as a Life Table. — The table may be considered either a Mortality or a Life Table, although such tables are usually called Mortality Tables. That is, if a large number of children could be placed under observation throughout life, and the number dying each year could be tabulated, there would be remaining each year the number living; or on the other hand there could be tabulated the number living out of the group at the beginning of each year, thus accounting for the number dying. Such a method of constructing a Life or Mortality Table is manifestly impossible and therefore other methods to be described later must be used. Life Insurance is based upon the principle that the number of deaths occurring each year among a large group follows a definite law of average and is not dependent upon chance. This law forms the basis of calculating the sums which are to be paid to the policyholders or their beneficiaries.

Development of Mortality Tables. — The duration of life was long a subject for speculation, and the ability to predict with accuracy its duration with respect to large groups of individuals represents one of the greatest accomplishments of the human intellect. There were many stages in the collection of facts about life, but even after a large number of such facts had been collected, it was a long time before these facts could be interpreted and applied in the form of a mortality table. There were many early estimates and speculations of the duration of life and the causes of that duration. It was an early custom to record the ages at death, and many early efforts were made to discover a law limiting the duration of life. Under the Falcidian Law of 44 B.C. which sought to prevent a testator from leaving more than three fourths of his estate in legacies, annuity calculations had been made, but these were very erroneous. Ulpian, the Roman jurist, later drew up annuity tables to correct these, and this table was certainly one of the first measures of life, graduated according to age. It was a life table, and not as present tables are, both life and death tables; nor did it take into consideration interest accumulations. It was a simple and rough estimate of the expectation of life if measured by the standards of the present annuity tables. But inaccurate as this table was, it was the best one available up to the close of the sixteenth century. The doctrine of probabilities or chance received little attention, or at least little development, before the seventeenth century. The simple statement of this doctrine is, that if an event must either happen or fail to happen, and a are the chances of its occurring and b the chances of its failing, then the probability of its happening is represented by the fraction $\frac{a}{a+b}$ and the probability of its failing by $\frac{b}{a+b}$. Upon this simple formula the theory of life contingencies is built up. However, the relation of the duration of life to this doctrine, or that the duration of life could be expressed in terms of this doctrine was for many years not perceived.

De Wit's Table. — The States General of Holland in 1671 decided to raise funds by sale of annuities, and directed the prime minister, John de Wit, a mathematician and pupil of Descartes, to prepare a plan. He constructed some hypotheses from the data available, dividing life into the four periods: 3 to 53, 53 to 63, 63 to 73, and 73 to 80. He assumed that life during the first period was most vigorous and that death was equally distributed over each six-month period. It is interesting to note in this connection that in many insurance calculations at the present time this distribution of loss is used. De Wit's calculations called for a high charge for these annuities, and as this was not favorable to their sale, the government repressed these calculations, which were lost for one hundred and eighty years. His estimates did not include the value of an annuity for each age, but only for one age.

Halley's Tables. — In 1693 Dr. Halley, the Astronomer Royal, read before the Royal Society a paper entitled "An Estimate of the Degrees of Mortality of Mankind drawn from curious Tables of the Births and Funerals at the City of Breslau with an attempt to ascertain the price of Annuities upon Lives." This was the real basis of the first tables of mortality, although Bills of Mortality were found in England as early as 1538 and regularly in London from 1603. All mortality tables preceding the Carlisle Table of 1815 were constructed from the record of deaths, supplemented in some cases by statistics of yearly births, but with no accurate knowledge of the number of the population. For an accurate and complete mortality table there need to be statistics of births, deaths, and population. The limitations of this Breslau Table were well recognized by its originator. Its chief value consisted in the principle which it devised for the calculation of an annuity. This was, that the true value of annuity is to be found by taking the present value of each yearly payment which according to the Mortality Table can ever be received and by reducing each of these sums by the respective chances — as shown by the Mortality Table — of the life surviving to receive it, the present value being the sum of all these separate calculations.

De Moivre's Tables. — In 1725 De Moivre published his tract on Annuities and Reversions, in which the following advances were made in mortality calculations. First, he showed how one annuity value could be calculated from another, and second, he originated the famous De Moivre Hypothesis. This hypothesis was, that there were equal decrements of human life which proceeded regularly for at least short intervals of time. That is, the number expressing the living at different ages in a mortality table are in arithmetical progression, the annual decrements of life being equal; or that out of a given number of persons living at any age an equal number will die every year until all are extinct. This did not represent the actual facts, but it did mark an important advance, and from this time the development of the science of life contingencies was very rapid. Thomas Simpson in 1742 wrote on Annuities and Reversions and showed the value of joint and single lives. He also constructed a table of mortality based on the mortality statistics of London.

In 1746 Deparcieux published his Essai sur les Probabilities de la Durée de la Vie Humaine, in which he constructed twenty-two tables. This work did much to advance the science on the continent. Deparcieux was the first to demonstrate the superiority of female lives.

Northampton Table. — In 1771 Dr. Price published his Observations on Reversionary Payments in which was included the Northampton Table of Mortality. This was the first table that was used for calculating premium rates for life insurance. The table was based on the number of deaths during a period of forty-six years, from 1735 to 1780. He used a radix, 10,000 lives and erroneously assumed that the population was stationary. In 1778 Charles Brand, the Registrar of the Amicable Society, published the seventy-two years' experience of that society, which was the first collection of data of this character. When Francis Bailey in 1810 published his great work, " The Doctrine of Life Annuities and Assurance," most of the foundation of the science of life contingencies was laid.

Carlisle Table. — In 1815 Milne constructed the Carlisle Table, which was based on the data of the general population of two parishes in Carlisle during the eight-year period, 1779–1787. Milne, by a rough graphical method, graduated his data, but owing to the limited number of lives under observation and to the broad generalizations in it, the table was far from accurate. It was, however, the best table constructed up to that time.

Gompertz Calculations. — In 1820 Gompertz showed in the first of his three papers presented to the Royal Society, that if in a mortality table the intervals of age be very small, a series will be formed which for a short period is very nearly in geometrical progression. In 1825 in his second paper he showed that this law was true for equal long periods. He suggested that death may be a result of two coexisting causes, one of which was chance, which was constant at all ages, the other being a continual increasing deterioration of vitality. In 1861 in his third paper he showed how to adapt his formula to the variations which mortality tables indicated, that is, variations of the actual deaths from the results shown by this simple mathematical formula. The technical details of applying this formula to a mortality table are of little importance to other than those interested in actuarial science. Makeham later modified the work of Gompertz by showing that the probabilities of living a year increased — or diminished — in a constant ratio from a series whose logarithms are in geometrical progression.

Other minor modifications and extensions have been made to the science of life contingencies, but the preceding include the most important stages in the development of this science. Upon the basis of these investigations a large number of mortality tables have been constructed. Among others may be mentioned the following:

Other Tables. — (a) The Seventeen Assurance Companies' Table, constructed in 1843 from the data of seventeen insurance companies of England and Scotland. Since the data were collected and arranged under a Committee of Actuaries, it came to be called " The Actuaries Table." By the Life Insurance Companies Act of

1872 in England it received statutory recognition, although it has been little used in England. In fact only a few copies of the table for private circulation were ever published. In the United States it has had considerable use, owing in part to the early use and emphasis placed upon it by Elizur Wright, the first Insurance Commissioner of Massachusetts.

(b) The Twenty Offices Table, constructed in 1869 under the direction of the Institute of Actuaries of England and Scotland. This table is known as the Combined Offices Experience Table. It was based upon the experience of ten English and ten Scottish Insurance Companies. This table differs from the Seventeen Offices Table of 1843 in that it was based upon lives and not upon policies as was the Seventeen Offices Table. These lives, totaling 160,426, were divided into four sections, the Healthy Males (Hm), Healthy Females (Hf), Healthy Males and Females (Hmf), and Diseased Males and Females (Dmf), thus making four separate tables of mortality.

(c) The American Experience Table was constructed by Sheppard Homans and published in 1867. This table was based in large part upon the experience of the Mutual Life Insurance Company of New York. This is the table in general use in the United States, although the Combined Experience or Actuaries Table is used in some cases.

Insurance had been transacted in the United States for many years previous to this date. The English tables of mortality had been used, for there were no American vital statistics adequate for constructing a mortality table. Some cities had published death records, but these were not reliable. It was very naturally assumed that the duration of life in the United States corresponded with that of the countries from which most of the people had come, and especially with that of England. The companies in the United States therefore generally selected the Carlisle Table, for they observed that the English companies had had a favorable experience under it, especially such companies as the Equitable and Amicable of England. The actual rates adopted were, however, not those shown by the Carlisle Table, but rather the rates established by some of the English companies which probably represented a modification of the Carlisle Table, that is, rates derived either from their actual experience or as a result of an applied theory of the officers of these early English companies.

(d) In 1881 there was published the Thirty American Offices Table, based upon the experience of thirty insurance companies of the United States and extending over the period of thirty years, ending with 1874. It was based, like the Seventeen Offices Table, upon policies.

(e) There are also the English Life Tables, of which there are five in number, each of which is based upon the data from the English Registrar's office. These tables are population tables and were published in 1843, 1853, 1864, 1885, and 1897. In addition there may be mentioned such other important mortality tables as The French Actuaries Tables, The Twenty-three German Offices Table, as well as special tables such as Impaired Life Tables and Select Life Tables. Mention may also be made of The National Fraternal Congress Table.

N. F. C. Table. — (*f*) This N. F. C. Table is a result of the work of the committee on statistics of the National Fraternal Congress, which published in 1899 the result of its investigations of the mortality experience of persons insured in fraternal societies. The rates of mortality of this table are much lower than the rates in the American Mortality Table. For example, the mortality rate in the N. F. C. Table at age 20 is 5 per 1000 lives and in the American Table 7.81; at 40 in the former table it is 7.17 and in the latter 9.79; at 60 in the former 22.75 and in the latter 26.69. The fraternal orders can conduct the business of insurance more cheaply than the commercial companies only by making a better selection of lives, by earning greater interest, or by doing business at a lower expense. Of these possibilities only the last is a probability, and this in its highest realizations is often not sufficient to equal the difference in the mortality rate upon which the premiums are based.

Errors in the Early Tables. — Many of the early tables were unreliable not only on account of the fact that there was not sufficient data, but also because the science of contingencies had not been developed sufficiently to know how to use the available data in order to secure the best results. Since, however, the science of life contingencies is based upon the law of averages and in order to have this law applicable, large numbers are necessary, the greatest shortcoming of these early tables was the paucity of the data. The chief reliance of these early tables was upon death statistics, but the ages at death were often erroneously stated. Even now in many parts of modern nations, vital statistics are not taken with sufficient care and resultant accuracy to serve as a basis for the deductions found in a really scientific mortality table. The element of error was much greater in these early times when the practice of taking vital statistics had scarcely begun. There are so many variable factors which affect the birth and death rate in a population, such, for example, as movement of population, occupations, sex and age composition of the group, misstatement of age, that great care is needed in deducing general principles.

As soon as life insurance companies were formed, their tabulated experience on insured lives supplied the data for constructing more accurate mortality tables. The common errors in population statistics are almost entirely absent in the statistics of insurance companies, for among other advantages, the company knows the ages of those taking out insurance, and the ages at death. They are thus able to have under continual observation a great number of individuals at various ages, and when the observation of several companies is combined, the data are more accurate.

Tables in Use. — The tables now in general use are the Actuaries or Combined Experience Table in England and the American Experience Table in the United States. The American Experience Table is the one prescribed by the laws of most states as the basis for the valuation of policies issued since January 1, 1901. Most policies issued previous to this date are valued on the Actuaries Table. The American Experience Table represents with considerable accuracy the experience of insured lives after the benefit of selection has passed, that is, after the lower death rate, due to a recent medical examination, has passed. It is assumed that this benefit disappears after about five years.

Such a mass of information regarding vitality is being collected and such improvements are being made in collecting vital statistics, that we may expect new and more accurate life tables to be supplied from time to time. Such in brief is the history of mortality tables, and it is now our purpose to show in a general way how the tables are constructed and to describe the actual experience under them.

Select Tables. — When mortality tables are calculated, showing the benefits of this medical selection during each of the five years, they are called Select Mortality Tables in contrast to Ultimate Mortality Tables, which are those from which the experience of the first five years has been eliminated. The term " Select Tables " is used in two other senses: (*a*) a table based upon the experience of insured lives, since these may be considered as constituting a select class; and (*b*) a table based on the specific experience of groups of the same age at entry and duration of insurance. This last is simply a greater degree of selection in that the intermixing of the different rates of mortality of different ages and duration of insurance is avoided. If sufficient numbers for each age could be secured, this would make possible the most scientific insurance.

With the increasing accuracy of vital statistics in modern nations and the increased experience of insurance companies, both as to numbers of lives insured, different ages of policyholders represented, duration of insurance, and increased amount of insurance taken, more accurate mortality experiences of different classes are being obtained.

A comparison of the data of the various tables may be made from the following tables in which are shown the number surviving at the decennial ages according to the important tables and also the expectation of life at various ages:

TABLE I

SHOWING THE NUMBER ALIVE AT THE END OF EACH TENTH YEAR UP TO AGE NINETY OUT OF ONE THOUSAND LIVES ACCORDING TO VARIOUS TABLES OF MORTALITY

Age	10	20	30	40	50	60	70	80	90
De Wit, 1671	1000	824	649	474	298	164	67	oo	oo
Breslau, 1693	1000	905	803	673	523	366	215	62	oo
De Moivre, 1725	1000	868	737	605	474	342	211	79	oo
Deparcieux, 1746	1000	925	834	747	660	526	352	134	125
Northampton, 1771	1000	904	773	641	503	359	217	83	8
Carlisle, 1815	1000	943	873	786	681	564	372	148	22
Equitable, Davies, 1825	1000	951	879	786	681	536	361	169	23
Equitable, Morgan, 1834	1000	928	961	784	692	559	360	140	13
17 Offices Experience, 1843	1000	933	863	787	695	560	358	133	13
English, No. 3, Males, 1864	1000	943	863	771	661	517	324	116	14
Institute, Hm, 1869	1000	962	899	823	727	589	381	139	15
American Table, 1867	1000	926	854	781	698	579	385	147	8

F

TABLE II

EXPECTATION OF LIFE AT DECENNIAL AGES ACCORDING TO VARIOUS
TABLES

Age	10	20	30	40	50	60	70	80	90
Ulpian's, Circ. A.D. 250	30	30	25	20	10	7	5	—	—
Breslau, 1693 . .	40.50	34.26	27.93	22.33	17.03	12.23	7.35	3.72	—
De Moivre, 1725 .	38.	33.	28.	20.	18.	13.	8.	3.	—
Deparcieux, 1746 .	46.83	40.25	34.08	27.50	20.42	14.25	8.67	4.67	1.75
Northampton, 1771	39.78	33.43	28.27	23.08	17.99	13.21	8.60	4.75	2.41
Carlisle, 1815 . .	48.82	41.46	34.34	27.61	21.11	14.34	9.18	5.51	3.28
Equitable, 1825 .	48.83	41.00	33.98	27.40	20.83	15.06	9.84	5.38	2.65
Equitable, 1834 .	48.32	41.37	34.53	27.40	20.36	13.91	8.70	4.75	2.56
17 Offices, 1843 .	48.36	41.49	34.43	27.28	20.18	13.77	8.54	4.78	2.11
English, No. 3, 1864	47.05	39.48	32.76	26.06	19.54	13.53	8.45	4.93	2.84
Institute, 1869 . .	50.29	42.05	34.68	27.40	20.31	13.83	8.50	4.72	2.36
American, 1868 .	48.72	42.20	35.33	28.18	20.91	14.10	8.48	4.39	1.42

The Medico-Actuarial Investigation. — A survey of
the development of mortality tables, however brief,
would not be complete without some reference to the
recent Medico-Actuarial Mortality Investigation published in 1915. This was made by a joint committee
of The Association of Life Insurance Medical Directors
and the Actuarial Society of America, with Mr. Arthur
Hunter, Actuary of the New York Life Insurance Company, as Chairman. Forty-three life insurance companies of the United States and Canada coöperated
in the investigation, which included, among other important subjects, the following:

(a) Occupational hazards.

(b) Medical impairment.

(c) Female mortality.

(*d*) Negro mortality.

(*e*) Height and weight in its relation to mortality.

(*f*) Indian, Chinese, and Japanese mortality in the United States and Canada.

(*g*) Regional mortality.

The chief purpose of the investigation was " to obtain a set of mortality ratios which approximately represent the average experience by *policies* of companies in the United States and Canada with sufficient accuracy to be used as a standard for testing the degree to which the mortality of the various classes differs from the average combined experience of the companies on policies."

Mortality under Fifty. — The investigation indicates that the greatest improvement in mortality has been at the ages under fifty. This is shown by the following table, adopted from Mr. Henry Moir's address before the Actuarial Society of America in 1915.

Age	American Experience Table	Medico-Actuarial Investigation
20	7.80	
25	8.06	4.70
30	8.43	4.90
35	8.95	5.10
40	9.79	5.70
45	11.16	7.50
50	13.78	10.00
55	18.57	15.80
60	26.69	24.00
65	40.13	39.00
70	61.99	61.70
75	94.37	91.90
80	144.41	137.20
85	235.55	203.70

Purpose of the Investigation. — Many other very valuable facts were shown by this investigation, which represents the high-water mark of vital statistic studies in America. The rates deduced are not intended to be used for the calculation of premiums, reserves, or other monetary transactions of life insurance companies. Partly as a result of this investigation and partly as a result of the general belief that the American Table no longer represents the actual mortality of insured lives, there is projected an investigation which will result in a new American Mortality Table. The present table was constructed in 1867, since which time there has been made available a large body of data on insured lives. The mortality curve of modern American experience of insured lives is undetermined, and it is the purpose of the proposed investigation to derive this curve. The results may or may not be used by insurance companies in their business. If the new table should show a lower death rate, it would not necessarily follow that the cost of insurance would be reduced. The death rate actually experienced, and not the rates shown by the table, ultimately determines the mortality cost. Nor is it probable that a new mortality table with lower death rates would result in lower reserves. It is more probable that reserves would be higher.

While a mortality table is both a life and a death table or a picture of a generation passing through life, it is impossible to observe such a generation and record the deaths as they occur. The actual methods of constructing the table now need to be described. There are several methods which may be used to construct such a table.

Method of Constructing a Mortality Table. — *First,* by hypotheses, such as De Wit's Presuppositions, De Moivre's Hypothesis, or Gompertz's Law. These have been previously described.

Second, from the records of deaths alone, as was done by Halley in constructing the Breslau Table.

Third, from the records of a certain number alive at specified ages compared with the number dying at each age, as was done in the English Life Tables, the Actuaries and the American Table. In this case the vital statistics may be derived from the general population or from selected groups, as, for example, insured lives. The advantage of a mortality table based upon the general population is that statistics of both sexes, of a great variety of ages, and of population in different sections of the country are secured. In a select table of mortality as compared with such a general population table, there is the disadvantage of having only a comparatively few lives at middle and old ages. A select table has, however, the great advantage that the data are more accurate. There may be, for example, some errors in the ages at which individuals are insured, but there is very little chance of error in the life statistics after the individual enters the company. However, the element of error in the statement of ages is likely to be less at the ages at which the individuals are insured than at the earlier or later period of life.

Since a large number of lives cannot be individually observed in order to secure the data to construct a mortality table, it is necessary to apply the doctrine of probabilities to arrive at the same results. It is only necessary to know the relative number at each age in comparison with the number alive at the preceding age.

The table is constructed by recording the ages of as great a number of persons as possible at a specified time and then tabulating opposite each age the number who live to that age, the deaths being placed opposite the ages at which death occurred. The probability of death at a patricular age is obtained by dividing the number of deaths at that age by the number living at that age. If, then, the number living at the age in which the table begins, is multiplied by the probability of dying at that age, the result will be the number of deaths. Then, subtracting this result from the number living at the age, the number of survivors is obtained. This multiplied by the probability of dying in the next year will give the deaths, and so the calculations are continued to the end of the table. Symbols are used in the calculations. Age is represented by x, the number reaching the age by l_x; the number who die between x and $x + 1$ is represented by d_x, and the number reaching the succeeding age one year later by l_{x+1}. Since the number living of the group constantly decreases with age,

$$d_x = l_x - l_{x+1}$$

and

$$l_x = l_{x+1} + d_x.$$

Likewise the deaths over any number of years are the sum of the annual deaths, and therefore

$$l_x - l_{x+2} = d_x + d_{x+1}.$$

Applying these simple formulas to the mortality table at the close of the chapter, the probability of dying or living can be calculated.

Calculating the Probability of Living and Dying. — Taking age 10 and the radix 100,000, which is an assumed number, — for the laws of mortality apply to any number, — the probability of dying between ages 10 and 11 is 749 — the number dying in the year divided by 100,000 — or .00749. Likewise the probability of living at age 11 is .99251 — the number living at that age divided by 100,000 — or .99251. The probability of living a year is represented by p_x and the probability of dying is expressed by q_x. If therefore the general law of probability is expressed in terms of mortality, since either death or life occurs in any one year, the equation stands

$$p_x + q_x = 1$$
$$p_x = 1 - q_x$$
$$q_x = 1 - p_x$$

which, expressed as a general formula, becomes

$$p_x = \frac{l_{x+1}}{l_x},$$

from which any one of the three unknown values can be calculated.

The probability of living any number of years is n_{px} and therefore

$$n_{px} = \frac{l_{x+n}}{l_x}.$$

In the actual construction of a table, a usual method is to calculate the probabilities of living at each age and, assuming a stated radix of the table, to multiply the values of l_x by the succeeding values of p_x. Having the values of p_x, the values of l_x can be secured, since

$$l_{x+1} = l_x \times p_x$$

and l_x is any convenient radix which has been adopted. Thus obtaining l_{x+1}, the values of l_{x+2}, l_{x+3} are easily obtained, since

$$l_{x+2} = l_{x+1} \times p_{x+1};$$

likewise for succeeding values of l_{x+3}, l_{x+4}, and so on for further values of those living at later ages.

Graduation of Tables. — After these calculations are completed, the numbers calculated as dying and living each year are found not to correspond exactly with the law of mortality. To correct the results to correspond with the facts and therefore secure an actual mortality table, a process called Graduation is applied to the data. This is done either by mathematical formulas, as originated and applied by Gompertz, Makeham, Woolhouse, Hunter, and others, or by the Graphic Method, which was used by Milne in the construction of the Carlisle Table and which has been refined by Sprague and other actuaries. The object in either case is to smooth out the irregularities in the curve represented by the crude mortality calculations.

As has before been intimated, the insurance companies do not derive the mortality tables which they now use from the population statistics of the general census, but from the experience of insurance companies. The data from the last-named source are more accurate, since they make greater efforts to secure the correct age at entry, and know definitely the age at death. However, the principles of procedure in using the data are the same.

Purpose of Mortality Tables. — The specific uses to which mortality tables are put by insurance companies are: first, the calculations of charges or premiums which individuals must pay to secure stated benefits; and second, to calculate from time to time the valuation of the liabilities under these contracts. They are also used to calculate what sums can be paid to those of the insured group who withdraw from the organization; also what dividends or overcharges can be returned to policyholders with respect to the mortality actually being experienced by the company.

Expectation of Life. — A mortality table usually has five columns, representing respectively the age, the number living, the number dying, the probability of dying, and the probability of living. Frequently there is added another column showing the expectation of life. The meaning of this phrase should be clearly understood, for it is often carelessly and erroneously used both in insurance discussion and by those not informed on insurance matters. It does not mean the number of years which an individual can expect to live after a given age has been reached. It has no relation to the time when any individual is likely to die nor to the time when death is most probable. The laws of mortality can tell nothing with respect to the life contingency of an individual. These laws refer to groups and not to individuals of the group. Expectation of life simply means the average number of years which *persons* of a given age will survive. It is neither the most probable lifetime, nor does it disclose when the individual has an even chance of surviving. It would, for example, be erroneous for a person at age 40, when the expectation of life according to the American Table is 28.18 years, to conclude that his probable age at death will be 68.18. The expectation of life is found by adding the numbers living at all ages subsequent to the age for which the expectation is to be calculated, and dividing this sum by the number living at that age and adding one half or .5. The one half is added because each person besides completing a certain number of years may be expected to live a fraction of another year, some living a large fraction of the year and some a small fraction, so that, on the whole, all may be considered to live one half the year. Reference to the preceding table will show the difference in the expectation of life as derived from the various tables of mortality. The chief value of expectation of life consists in using it to make an easy comparison of the death rates in different mortality tables, since it is but slightly affected by graduation. No actuarial calculations for financial purposes are based upon it, since it applies not to individuals, but to a group of persons of the same age.

Most Probable Lifetime. — Another phrase used in connection with mortality statistics is " the most probable lifetime." This is found by referring to the mortality table and locating the age at which the largest number of deaths occur. The age thus located is the age at which death is most probable, and the difference between that age and the age of the individual is the most probable lifetime. Under the American Table at age 30 the most probable lifetime is 43 years, while the expectation of life at that age is 35.3 years.

The Probable Lifetime. — Another phrase is the "probable lifetime" or the *vie probable*. This is simply the number of years that an individual has an even chance of living. It is found by observing at what age beyond the specified age the number then living is reduced one half. For example, the number living at age 30 is, by the American Table, 85,441. At age 68 there are living, 43,133, and 40,890 are living at age 69. Therefore, the probable lifetime of a person at age 30 is between 38 and 39 years, which is over three years greater than the expectation of life at age 30.

Even after a rate of mortality has been found, either from general population statistics or from the experience of insured lives, the actual mortality of the insured group does not usually correspond to this rate in any single year. It has been particularly difficult to derive a table in which the actual mortality closely corresponded to the calculated mortality in very early and very late life. This in no sense invalidates that general law of mortality which is expressed in the mortality tables. These tables have been graduated as has been described, by which the accidental irregularities have been smoothed out. The important practical consideration of this fact is expressed in the questions, How many lives need a company insure in order to secure these average results of a mortality table, how wide a fluctuation can be permitted, and how can it improve the personnel of its membership in order that it may

continue a solvent concern? If it is to be called upon
to pay a larger number of claims before it had calculated
that they would fall due, it may fail, both because the
principal sum already collected will probably prove
insufficient and in addition the force of compound
interest has not had time to produce its contribution
to the resources of the company.

Calculating the Number of Lives to be Insured. —
The first problem, that of the number of lives necessary
to be insured in order that the actual number of claims
by death may be confined within certain limits of the
expected, is solved as follows: If the probability of an
event occurring at a single trial is d, it will probably
happen in m trials dm times. It has been proved that
the probable magnitude of the deviations from dm
can be expressed by the following formula:

$$\sqrt{\frac{2}{\pi}\,mdp}$$

in which π equals 314,159, m the number of trials or
lives under observation, p the chance of surviving one
year at the given age, and d the probability of dying
during the year. An application may be thus made.
In the American Table assume there are 20,000 lives at
risk at age 41, where d is .01, the expected percentage of
survivals being therefore .99. The probable extent
to which the actual result would differ from this is
obtained from the formula thus:

$$\sqrt{\frac{2}{3.1416}\,20{,}000 \times .01 \times .99}$$

which equals 11.2. That is to say, the deviation of deaths from the expected 200 would probably be 11.2, the experienced mortality varying between 189 and 211. Equally simple is the problem of calculating the number necessary to be under observation in order to keep the actual experience within a certain percentage of the expected.

Actual and Expected Mortality. — The reader must have realized that a number sufficient to display average results must be secured. Insurance deals with the law of average as applied to a considerable group. It would be absurd to attempt to conduct the business with a score or more of members, and doubly absurd if they were of the same age, sex, and occupations. In actual practice the companies expect to have a favorable mortality experience; that is, they make such calculations and allowances as they think will procure for them an actual mortality well below that shown by the table for the respective ages and groups. From this source come what are called mortality savings. In companies writing policies the holders of which receive dividends based on the earnings of the companies, this saving is one of the sources of the fund from which dividends are paid. These dividends, as we shall later see, are not dividends in the ordinary sense in which this word is used, but are, so far as this mortality savings is concerned, simply the return of overcharges. The difference between the expected mortality on the net amount at risk and the actual mortality less the reserve thereon is the mortality saving. In determining the expected mortality for a given calendar year, the old business is assumed to be exposed for the full calendar year; the new issues of business of the calendar year are assumed to be exposed on an average for only one half the year; the cancellations of the old business are assumed to be exposed for one half the year; and the cancellations of the new business are assumed to be exposed for one fourth of the year.

Statistics for the past ten years of the ordinary legal reserve industrial companies show the following facts: In the case of thirty-two of the most important ordinary legal reserve companies the average mortality was 75.43 per cent of the expected, varying, however, from 52.24 per cent to 92.52 per cent. Thirteen of these thirty-two companies experienced a mortality saving of over 30 per cent. In the three leading industrial companies the average for the past ten years of the actual to the expected mortality was 104.05 per cent. Only one of these companies, and this the least important, had an actual experience below the expected. In the fifty leading ordinary companies the percentage of the actual to the experienced mortality in 1909 was 72.16 per cent.

TABLES OF MORTALITY

At Age	Actuaries or Combined Experience Table of Mortality Number Surviving	Deaths	American Experience Table of Mortality Number Surviving	Deaths	At Age	Actuaries or Combined Experience Table of Mortality Number Surviving	Deaths	American Experience Table of Mortality Number Surviving	Deaths
10	100,000	676	100,000	749	55	63,469	1,375	64,563	1,199
11	99,324	674	99,251	746	56	62,094	1,436	63,364	1,260
12	98,650	672	98,505	743	57	60,658	1,497	62,104	1,325
13	97,978	671	97,762	740	58	59,161	1,561	60,779	1,394
14	97,307	671	97,022	737	59	57,600	1,627	59,385	1,468
15	96,636	671	96,285	735	60	55,973	1,698	57,917	1,546
16	95,965	672	95,550	732	61	54,275	1,770	56,371	1,628
17	95,293	673	94,818	729	62	52,505	1,844	54,743	1,713
18	94,620	675	94,089	727	63	50,661	1,917	53,030	1,800
19	93,945	677	93,362	725	64	48,744	1,990	51,230	1,889
20	93,268	680	92,637	723	65	46,754	2,061	49,341	1,980
21	92,588	683	91,914	722	66	44,693	2,128	47,361	2,070
22	91,905	686	91,192	721	67	42,565	2,191	45,291	2,158
23	91,219	690	90,471	720	68	40,374	2,246	43,133	2,243
24	90,529	694	89,751	719	69	38,128	2,291	40,890	2,321
25	89,835	698	89,032	718	70	35,837	2,327	38,569	2,391
26	89,137	703	88,314	718	71	33,510	2,351	36,178	2,448
27	88,434	708	87,596	718	72	33,159	2,362	33,730	2,487
28	87,726	714	86,878	718	73	28,797	2,358	31,243	2,505
29	87,012	720	86,160	719	74	26,439	2,339	28,738	2,501
30	86,292	727	85,441	720	75	24,100	2,303	26,237	2,476
31	85,565	734	84,721	721	76	21,797	2,249	23,761	2,491
32	84,831	742	84,000	723	77	19,548	2,179	21,330	2,369
33	84,089	750	83,277	726	78	17,369	2,092	18,961	2,291
34	83,339	758	82,551	729	79	15,277	1,987	16,670	2,196
35	82,581	767	81,822	732	80	13,290	1,866	14,474	2,091
36	81,814	776	81,090	737	81	11,422	1,730	12,383	1,964
37	81,038	785	80,353	742	82	9,694	1,582	10,419	1,816
38	80,253	795	79,611	749	83	8,112	1,427	8,603	1,648
39	79,458	805	78,862	759	84	6,685	1,268	6,955	1,470

	Actuaries or Combined Experience Table of Mortality		American Experience Table of Mortality			Actuaries or Combined Experience Table of Mortality		American Experience Table of Mortality	
At Age	Number Surviving	Deaths	Number Surviving	Deaths	At Age	Number Surviving	Deaths	Number Surviving	Deaths
40	78,653	815	78,106	765	85	5,417	1,111	5,485	1,292
41	77,838	826	77,341	774	86	4,306	958	4,193	1,114
42	77,012	839	76,567	785	87	3,348	811	3,079	933
43	76,173	857	75,782	797	88	2,537	673	2,146	744
44	75,316	881	74,985	812	89	1,864	545	1,402	555
45	74,435	909	74,173	828	90	1,319	427	847	385
46	73,526	944	73,345	848	91	892	322	462	246
47	72,582	981	72,497	870	92	570	231	216	137
48	71,601	1,021	71,627	896	93	339	155	79	58
49	70,580	1,063	70,731	927	94	184	95	21	18
50	69,517	1,108	69,804	962	95	89	52	3	3
51	68,409	1,156	68,842	1,001	96	37	24		
52	67,253	1,207	67,841	1,044	97	13	9		
53	66,046	1,261	66,797	1,091	98	4	3		
54	64,785	1,316	65,706	1,143	99	1	1		

REFERENCES

Newsholme, A.   Vital Statistics, Chaps. X, XI, XII, XIII, XIV, XV.

Yale Readings, Vol. I, Chap. VIII.

Graham, W. J.   Romance of Life Insurance, Chap. VII.

Dawson, Miles M.   The Business of Life Insurance, Chap. II. Practical Lessons in Actuarial Science.

Reports of the Twelfth Census, Parts I, II.   Mortality Statistics, 1909.

Report on National Vitality, Parts I, II of Vol. III.   Senate Document No. 676, Sixtieth Congress, Second Session.

Farr, William.   Vital Statistics, Part V, pp. 443–494.

The Principles and Practice of Life Insurance, Seventh Edition. The Spectator Company.

Bowley, A. G. Elements of Statistics, Second Edition, Part I, Chaps. V, VII, X, Part II.

Institute of Actuaries' Text Book, Part II.

Proceedings of the International Congress of Actuaries.

Proceedings of the Actuarial Society of America.

Insurance Guide and Handbook, Fifth Edition, Chaps. II, X, XI.

Practical Lessons in Actuarial Science. Miles M. Dawson, Vol. I, pp. 60–122.

System and Tables of Life Insurance. Levi W. Meech.

Journal of Insurance Institute, Vol. III, p. 351.

Medico-Actuarial Mortality Investigation. Five volumes.

CHAPTER IV

THE SELECTION OF LIVES

THE description given in the preceding chapter of the principles underlying the mortality of lives and the facts which the experience of insurance has disclosed might lead the reader to conclude that the actual conduct of insuring lives is very simple. However, the first problem which confronts the officials of an insurance company is that of securing a body of individuals whose life experience as insured persons will be in harmony with the principles which have been discussed in connection with the mortality table. Great care must be continually exercised in insuring lives in order that the actual experience will be within reasonable limits of the calculated. It is even more true of the insurance business than of other kinds of business that it should be able to be conducted on the plans laid down before entering upon the actual business. In almost every business adjustments can be made from time to time to bring the original plan in harmony with unexpected changes in the nature of the business; but in insurance the contracts are not only made for long periods, but also with great numbers of individuals. Therefore, adjustments can be made only with great difficulty.

Selection Defined. — The first problem, then, in placing the principles of insurance in practice is to select suitable lives for insurance. By selection is ordinarily meant that examination of applicants by competent physicians in order to exclude all whose present or prospective physical conditions or mental characteristics are below the standard required by the insurance society. This medical examination is, then, one of the methods devised to prevent adverse selection, that is, the conscious or unconscious attempt to secure insurance by persons who are undesirable risks. Another method used by the company to prevent adverse selection is the incorporation of certain protective clauses in the contract; such, for example, as the suicide clause, which frees the company from liability if the insured commits suicide within a certain period, usually one or two years. Adverse selection is again illustrated in the tendency of individual poor risks to select the cheaper plans of insurance, and again in the case of those seeking to defraud the company. Anything which adversely affects the company's interest in so far as it is interested in securing a group of individuals who will experience the normal experience is adverse selection. That is to say, the effort on the part of the company is to secure a group of persons who will have equal chances of risk and benefit from insurance.

Benefit of Selection Defined. — The lives thus chosen by the company through its agents, who are supposed to exercise good judgment in soliciting applicants, and the medical examiners, who carefully examine them, are called select lives. It has been found from long experience in insuring lives that the rate of mortality among the recently insured is lower than among the general population or among a non-insured group of equal ages which has healthy and unhealthy individuals among it. Not only is this true, but it has been found that an insured group recently selected has a lower mortality rate than a group of insured lives of equal age but of longer duration of insurance. For example, 1000 individuals insured at 30 years of age would show for a period of about five years thereafter a lower mortality than the mortality shown for the next five years of 1000 individuals, insured at 25 years of age, but now 30. This temporary advantage to the company is called the benefit of selection. This advantage enables a company to use as expenses or as dividends, which may be used to reduce the premiums, the funds thus saved, since this selection means the actual losses will be below the calculated. This favorable mortality on recently insured lives also explains why newly formed companies or companies which are increasing their numbers rapidly have frequently such a low percentage of actual to expected mortality.

Rate of Mortality and Duration of Insurance. — The rate of mortality is a resultant not so much of the age of the insured as it is of the duration of the insurance. During the first two or three years of the insurance the mortality is very light. It then increases among insured lives for a considerable period of the insurance, becoming in the later years somewhat lower. These changes in the mortality experience of insured groups are due to this effect of selection which can operate either against the company or against the insured members by acts of the company. The former result occurs when members withdraw from the company or permit their policies to lapse. The latter situation is brought about when the company rejects, rates up, or refuses an application for insurance. To a less extent the same results occur when the applicant is permitted to select or is refused a special type of policy or a particular method of using his dividends. That is, if a poor risk is permitted to have a long-term policy with a decrease in his premiums by the use of his annual dividends, the company has less funds to pay the death claim in the event that the policyholder dies early in the life of the policy because the policyholder has paid in a very small per cent of the total sum which his beneficiary receives. This results in a selection against the company. Conversely there may be a selection by the company against the policyholder, if he is compelled to select a high-priced policy which is likely to mature before the indicated impairment in his life is likely to prove fatal.

Duration of Benefit of Selection. — There is some difference of opinion among actuaries as to the length of time to which, from the standpoint of the company, this " benefit of selection " extends. The elimination of all lives in actual bad health at the time of making application for insurance exhausts within a comparatively short time a large part of the benefit of selection. There remains, however, another portion of this benefit of selection which results from refusing to insure persons of intemperate habits and those who have an unfavorable family history. This part of the benefit of selection is of a kind which is not likely to show itself within a short period of five or ten years.

Nor is it true that all lives show the same ratio of increase of mortality with the increasing years of insurance. For example, the rate of increase of mortality among young lives is likely to be higher than that among lives of middle or older ages. The benefits of selection therefore are likely to endure longer among older than among younger lives. It does not follow, however, that an insurance company with all or a large per cent of its members over forty years of age is better than one with groups of lives at various average ages. The laws of mortality previously discussed should protect the reader from any such erroneous conclusion, and further the excellence of any company as compared with another depends upon a great variety of circumstances.

Effects of Benefit of Selection. — The important effects of the benefit of selection have been stated by the actuary, Dr. Sprague, as follows: " The medical examination and the other precautions taken have the result of eliminating from the general body of persons whose lives are proposed for insurance almost all those individuals who are suffering from a disease likely to cause early death as well as persons whose habits are so intemperate that they are likely to die prematurely." The effect of this is, that the rate of mortality among recently insured lives is greatly below the normal mortality corresponding to their ages. The difference is greatest in the years immediately following the date of the insurance and becomes gradually less in each succeeding year until after a lapse of time, variously estimated, it disappears and the normal rate is attained. It seems probable that a similar effect will be found to exist whenever a body of lives is chosen according to any law, that is to say, any group selected according to a principle with no additional new lives taken into the group. The American Experience Mortality Table is regarded as a safe ultimate table, the benefit of selection being assumed to extend for five years. The mortality rates during these first five years in the select and ultimate American Experience Table bear the following ratios: In the first year after admission the benefit of selection amounts to 50 per cent of the ultimate mortality; in the second year, 65 per cent; in the third year, 75 per cent; in the fourth year, 85 per cent; and in the fifth year, 95 per cent. The ultimate mortality thereafter experienced is assumed to be that shown by the American Experience Mortality Table.

The explanation of the causes of this lower mortality among recently insured lives is largely in the fact that chronic diseases have not had time to develop and produce their results. The deaths are chiefly due to accidents and to those acute diseases which rapidly produce death. Then, too, acute diseases developing in the early period often become chronic with fatal results at a later period. The rate of mortality, then, among insured lives is, all other things being equal, a result of the age at entry and the duration of membership. The following table clearly illustrates the above facts regarding the mortality at different ages and different duration of insurance.

ANNUAL MORTALITY RATE PER 1000 IN PERIODS OF INSURANCE

AGES IN QUINQUEN-NIAL GROUPS	UNDER 5 YEARS' DURATION	5 YEARS AND UPWARDS	UNDER 10 YEARS' DURATION	10 YEARS AND UPWARDS	TOTAL PERIOD OF LIFE
25–29	6.60	10.	7.30	9.20	7.30
35–39	8.30	11.	9.30	11.70	9.70
45–49	11.70	14.40	12.50	15.20	13.60
55–59	18.10	24.70	21.	25.20	23.50
65–69	36.30	50.60	43.50	51.10	49.

The rate of mortality for those who have not been insured five years, column 2, is less than those who have been insured less than ten years, column 4, and still less than those insured for more than ten years, column 5. A study of this table will disclose additional important facts regarding the effect of introducing new lives in the different quinquennial periods.

The Annual Rate of Mortality. — The annual rate of mortality at any age is found, as we have shown in the previous chapter, by dividing the number of deaths occurring in the year following this age by the number of thousands exposed to death at the beginning of the year.

Many adherents to the assessment plan of insurance have depended upon the introduction of new blood to keep down the increasing death rate. It will be observed, however, that the benefits are of a decreasing character as the original group becomes older, for the new entrants at the older ages are accumulating at a geometrical ratio, and the number of new lives necessary to keep the mortality experience down to that of the earlier ages would have to be very great; so great, in fact, that in actual experience no company on the assessment plan has been able to secure sufficient numbers to keep its mortality experience to that of the earlier years. It is not to be understood, however, that the entrance of young lives does not favorably affect the mortality, but rather that this method cannot be relied upon to correct the errors of unscientific plans of pure assessment insurance. It must also be evident that if lives were insured on the basis of mortality tables constructed on the experience of insured groups at different ages, the individual who insured at an advanced age would pay relatively a larger premium than those who insured in earlier life. That is to say, the benefit of selection is less at very advanced ages than at earlier ages. The premium for young lives is established on the expectation that there will be a continual infusion of new blood and these young lives thus receive through many years the benefit of selection from many groups.

Self-selection. — There is another kind of selection in insurance which may be called self-selection, that is to say, a selection not made by the insurer, but by the insured. This has been instanced in the case of an applicant selecting particular forms of policies. If it is a poor risk and the applicant is conscious of his impaired life, he is likely to select the policies with low premiums. If he intends to defraud the company, he will make the same selection. It is, therefore, necessary for the company to make its selections as accurate as possible;

that is, it must require medical examination, and take precaution to discover the true facts about the applicant. It is true, indeed, that in certain forms of compulsory insurance of foreign countries for the wage earners no medical examination is made, but in these cases the insurance is required of all members of the group, and since the group is homogeneous to a large degree, selection has already been made. Average results are for these two reasons secured.

Significance of the Medical Examination. — In the early history of insurance there was no medical examination, but this did not imply that there was no selection. No evil consequences were experienced from this absence of medical examination, for the applicant was recommended to the company by a responsible person. He was often questioned by the officials of the company as to his physical condition; insurance was in general taken out only by the better classes; competition for business was not very extreme; and lastly the mortality tables used had a wide margin of safety. The actual process of selection now made by an insurance company is usually as follows. The agent seeks the applicant, who may be asked to answer certain questions regarding his physical condition and family history. If the facts disclosed by these answers are decidedly unfavorable, that is, if he is ill or has recently been ill or belongs to a family which has had numerous members who have been afflicted with certain very fatal diseases, such as tuberculosis, the applicant is not sent to the medical examiner; otherwise, he is. The latter asks him more detailed questions regarding his physical history and that of his family, and in addition makes a thorough physical examination. Efforts are also made to secure information as to the use of alcohol and narcotics. The medical examiner makes a complete report of his findings to the medical department of the company at the home office. Efforts may also be made by the company through independent inquiries and references supplied by the applicant to discover the personal habits of the applicant, his financial responsibility, and other facts which will supply information to decide the desirability of the risk.

The mortality table assumes that all members of the company enter it in good physical condition, and premiums are based on this assumption. It is the duty of the medical department to make the actual facts correspond to the assumed facts. If all the information elicited is satisfactory, a policy is granted. If the amount applied for exceeds the limit fixed by the company on a single life, the company may accept the application and reinsure a part of the risk in another company. That is, it takes out a policy payable to itself in another company for the amount in excess of what it cares to insure a single life.

Classification of Risks. — Insurance has become increasingly popular, due to a better general understanding of its benefits and to the aggressive competition of the companies. As a result many applications for insurance are made by those who do not possess normal physical vigor. These lives belong usually to one of three classes: (1) those whose medical examination indicates symptoms of some organic disease; (2) those who have an unsatisfactory family history; (3) those who are engaged in occupations where the risk of death is above the normal. In order to grant insurance to these classes insurance companies have devised methods of adjusting charges which take into consideration the added hazard of the risk; that is, since insurance assumes to protect against the one and the same risk of death, the company in justice to all its members is bound to equalize as nearly as possible the risk against which protection is granted. Otherwise there would be groups enjoying protection at the expense of other groups.

A convenient classification of risk for purposes of discussion, but one which has no legal sanction in the case of ordinary insurance companies, is as follows:

(a) Preferred risks. These are risks which when not affected by the occupation are insurable under any plan of insurance. The individuals composing this class have good physical conditions, weight and height within the standard established, correct habits, good family history, which means a low mortality under 70, and freedom from constitutional and hereditary diseases.

(b) Ordinary risks. These applicants are frequently required to take that form of policy which will bring the premium-paying period within 75 per cent of the life expectation. This is done in order that the possible large claims due to a high mortality will not overbalance the sums paid in by this class and the accumulations on it. Individual members of this class must be in first-class physical condition when insured, but there may be a tendency in the family to certain diseases; they may be persons who have lost a limb, persons of mixed races; persons who have had remote attacks of such diseases as asthma, inflammatory rheumatism, pneumonia, and in some cases, blood spitting, if not recent, provided the family history is good. The preferred and ordinary risks include the vast majority of insured lives, and it is these classes upon which insurance calculations are chiefly made.

(c) Doubtful risks. This class includes a great number of individuals and for a great many various reasons. One of the most important classes is overweights, and another underweights; another class is those who are addicted to the use of alcohol or narcotics, although if the amount of either used is in excess of a certain quantity, such persons will not be accepted as risks on any plan of insurance. It is not only because the use of alcohol and narcotics undermines the physical constitution, thus making the individual more subject to disease and less able to resist its attacks, but also because to such individuals fatal accidents are more likely to happen at those times when reason is dethroned on account of the excessive use of the alcohol or the narcotic. In other words, it is a question to what extent the shorter duration of life of those who use alcohol is due to the destructive effects of the alcohol and to what extent it is due to their careless mode of living, of which the use of alcohol is the tangible evidence. Underweights and overweights ordinarily demand special treatment. The companies use a comparative table of height and weight: For example, applicants 5 feet 10 inches in height between 30 and 39 should weigh by the table between 134 and 200 pounds, the normal weight being 167, which thus makes a provision for a deviation of about 20 per cent. However, if it can be shown that the abnormal weight is a family characteristic, the variation is of little importance, all other things being equal.

Adjusting the Charge for Underaverage Lives. — The chief methods of making adjustment for an impaired or underaverage life are as follows:

(a) Charging the regular premium for a higher age.

(b) Writing the policy applied for at the regular premium, but with a proviso that if the insured die within a certain period, such as five or ten years, the face amount of the policy is reduced. This is the lien method. `

(c) Charging a higher premium.

(d) Granting the insurance applied for, but on a policy different from that applied for; as, for example, issuing an endowment policy when the application was for an ordinary life policy.

(e) Issuing the policy on premiums based on impaired life tables.

Rating-up Age. — The first method, that of charging the regular premium for a higher age, has been followed extensively by the European actuaries. It is simply to charge an applicant, for example, at age 40 the premium at age 45, thereby assuming that his impaired physical condition practically makes his chance of death that of the average person of the latter age. This assumption, that impaired physical condition will cause the risk to increase at an increasing proportion, is not true in all cases. It is doubtless true that tendencies to certain diseases do increase or are constant with increased age, but there are other tendencies to disease which decrease with age. If, therefore, the tendency either increases or decreases, there should be an adjustment of the premium. The method of thus treating substandard lives is so easy of application from the standpoint of practical administration, and its success in the past has been so great, that it continues in great favor. Then, too, since from the standpoint of the company it protects the company, not only for the extra risk at the time, but also in the future, the company is able to insure applicants on plans of insurance such as the limited payment policies which otherwise it would not be able to do. This makes it satisfactory to many of the applicants, for in many cases no policy could be sold unless it was the same as some friend of the applicant had. Especially is this plan satisfactory in these days of popularity of the limited-payment policies. Few individuals care to be restricted to buying an article which most of the people do not want. The addition to the age is usually under ten years, and while the extra yearly amount in the early years is not great, if the individual lives long, he pays a considerable extra sum. If the substandard life is at age 30 and is rated up to age 40, the excess premium is not great for several years at least, but if the substandard life is rated up from 50 to 60 and enjoys the average expectation of the normal individual at age 50, he pays a sum considerably in excess of what he otherwise would have paid. It will not be forgotten, however, that these individuals do not, as a class, enjoy the normal expectation of life of standard lives at their age.

Some policyholders naturally object to paying a higher price for the same policy which a friend has, for most persons are unwilling to admit that they are inferior to others. Lapses are not infrequent under the plan of rating up lives, although much depends upon the education of the people as to the particular method of treating substandard lives. There are other objections to the above method, but, as has been stated, it seems to have worked in Great Britain, where the people have been educated up to this method.

The Lien. — The second method of treating substandard lives, namely, that of placing a lien against the policy, has become very popular in recent years with some American companies. This is the plan under which the substandard risk is accepted at its actual age for the premium at that age, but the full face of the policy is not paid in case of death within certain periods. The deduction from the face decreases as the insured survives beyond the stated periods, until the amount agreed to be paid by the company is the full face value of the policy. This plan was devised to meet the objections urged to the plan of charging a higher premium. It is also an aid in selling insurance, since the policy on the impaired life can often be sold to the person who feels that he is getting the same policy as his neighbor and paying the same price for it. Then, too, few individuals are willing to admit that they are substandard, not only as to longevity, but as to most characteristics, and thus the vanity of the applicant is satisfied. The applicant has confidence in his ability to live the average length of life, and if he does, his personal judgment has been vindicated without any extra premium, and if he dies, he has no judgment to be vindicated. The beneficiaries will probably be favorably disposed in their judgment of a contract from which they benefit. It must be recognized, however, that given a substandard life with this lien imposed upon it, which disappears completely, say after ten years, there is no assurance that the experience of the companies on this class of lives will necessarily be favorable on account of using this method of treatment. It may well happen that at the time the lien disappears the impairment of the life has so progressed that the individual is almost at the point of death; or the tendency to the disease, on account of which the lien was imposed, may have completely disappeared.

The Objections to the Lien. — The liens do increase the desirability of the insurance, but in a manner not really appreciated by the insured at the time of purchasing the policy. In the actual practice of companies these liens are often not nearly equivalent to what the additional premium would be if the plan had been followed of rating up in years the substandard risk. The method of rating up lives by liens, as has been stated, has more to recommend it as a policy of practical administration than as one of scientific value. Other objections to the plan besides that of not rating the life up sufficiently and hence burdening the ordinary policyholders unduly with a more than proportionate contribution to the insurance fund are, that a policy with a lien cannot be offered as collateral for loans, and, lastly, if such a policyholder dies soon after taking out the

H

policy, his family receives little benefit from his insurance.

Determining the Amount of the Lien. — A method of determining the amount of the lien is as follows: If an applicant, aged 30, shows the diminished prospect of the life of an average individual of a group at age 40, the difference between the premium at age 30 and 40 is multiplied by the number of years of expectation of life at the actual age. If death occurs the first year, the face of the policy is diminished by this amount. If the insured die the second year, the lien is decreased by one year's difference in the premiums. At age 30, suppose an applicant has the diminished expectation of an average person aged 40. The net premium in the American Experience Table with 3 per cent per $1000 on the whole life plan for age 30 is $18.28 and for age 40 is $24.75, the difference being $6.47. The expectation of life at age 30, the actual age, is 35.33 years. This expectation multiplied by $6.47 would give a lien of $224.59 for the first year. Theoretically the lien should be annually decreased, and even then it would not by this method be equivalent to insuring the life at age 40, but in practice the lien period is only for a fixed number of years. Another method is to have the number of years of loading imposed on any life arbitrarily fixed by the chief medical examiner.

The method of charging an extra premium has been sufficiently described in connection with the second method to indicate some of its objections.

Charging a Higher Premium. — The plan of charging a higher premium, especially if it is on the policy applied for, has little to recommend it, either from the standpoint of scientific accuracy or practical business operation of the company, unless it is based upon data collected from experience of impaired lives of the class to which the applicant belongs. If the higher premium is collected because the applicant is granted a higher premium policy, as, for example, an endowment policy, when the application was for an ordinary life, the applicant is likely to be dissatisfied. Difficulty may be encountered in delivering the policy, and even after delivery, lapses are likely to occur on account of dissatisfaction.

Moreover, the plan does not often give adequate protection to the company. If, for example, an applicant shows tendencies to tuberculosis and is granted a twenty-year endowment policy when he applied for an ordinary life, the assumption is that he shows the expectation of the average healthy life of the group at that age. But the life is admittedly substandard, and an abnormal death rate produces loss to the company, regardless of the plan of insurance. It is true that the company gains the difference in the reserve between the endowment and the whole-life plan, but this amount in such cases is often insignificant.

Adjustments in Premium for Occupations and Regions. — It has become increasingly the practice of companies to write policies free from any conditions as to change of occupation after the policy is granted, although the practice is not yet uniform, especially as to compelling an adjustment of the charge of premium in the case of extra hazardous occupations, such as military and naval service in time of war. Nor is it to be inferred that insurance companies will grant policies to individuals with good family history and normal lives, but engaged in very hazardous occupations where the known mortality rate due to the occupation is high.

In reference to additional charges for regional mortality, that is, residence in certain districts of a country, such as the southern parts of the United States, the practice of the companies has become in general very liberal, owing to the advances in sanitary and medical knowledge and the improvement in the conditions of living in most districts of civilized countries. Restrictions in policies are still to be found for residence in tropical countries or in frigid regions as well as in certain districts known to have a high mortality rate.

Difficulties in Determining the Charge for Substandard Lives. — The plan of insuring substandard lives on impaired life tables depends upon the applicability of the tables. If it is based on the Institute of Actuaries' Impaired Life Table, it may not have very close application to risks in America or Australia. It is difficult to devise any method entirely satisfactory for the reason that there is introduced a known abnormal life into a group of normal lives, the degree of abnormality being impossible to determine. It is the same difficulty which always arises when devising principles and rules to govern a homogeneous group and then have introduced into it heterogeneous individuals. It is an attempt to make a rule for the exception.

Sex Mortality. — As to sexes it may be said that women as a class show a lower death rate, in the later years, than men do. The statistics of insured women seem to indicate a higher mortality for married women during the childbearing period than for men or unmarried women of the same age. The practice of companies in insuring women is not uniform. Some.accept women at all ages on the same terms as men. Some require an extra premium; some accept them after the childbearing age has passed; many accept them only when they are self-supporting in order that there may be no question as to the insurable interest in their life. With the growing freedom of the sex, doubtless there will be more demands from women for insurance on the same terms as men. It is urged that there is more of a hazard in the case of women than in the case of men for the reasons that: (*a*) there is more of a tendency on the part of women to understate age in the early years; (*b*) that a certain delicacy on the part of women, as well as the medical examiner, prevents as thorough a medical examination as in case of men; (*c*) that childbearing introduces an extra hazardous factor; (*d*) that the possession of dependent children also may bring in the question of moral hazard in the case of the widow who is anxious to secure protection for her children in case of her death.

Sex mortality for all ages is indicated in the following table, taken from Newsholme's Vital Statistics and referring to the *population* of England during 1891-1895.

MEAN ANNUAL RATE OF MORTALITY PER 1000 OF EACH
SEX

	MALES	FEMALES
Under 5	62.1	52.0
5–10	4.5	4.5
10–15	2.5	2.7
15–20	4.0	4.0
20–25	5.3	4.9
25–35	7.2	6.7
35–45	12.2	10.3
45–55	19.8	15.3
55–65	36.3	29.8
65–75	71.9	62.8
75–85	149.9	136.1
85 and up	290.6	263.8

It will be observed that this table indicates an especially favorable mortality for females in later life.

The Medico-Actuarial Investigation affords the most recent and complete statistics of mortality of women. The statistics available up to the time of this investigation seemed to justify the common practice of insurance companies of charging women an extra premium or placing them in a separate class as regards dividends on their policies. However, the accumulated experience of insurance companies which had insured women on the same terms as men during the ten-year period ending with 1914 had shown a satisfactory experience. The following statements are, therefore, to be understood as referring to the mortality of insured females as distinguished from female mortality in general. The investigation shows that when female risks are solicited by agents, thus securing a selection, the experience has been satisfactory. The data are based upon the mortality of insured females between the years 1885 and 1908, and refer to the following classes: spinsters, married women with the husband as beneficiary, married women with the beneficiary other than the husband, and widows and divorced women. The general results are indicated by the following table:

Ages at Entry	Actual Deaths	Expected Deaths	Ratio of Actual to Expected Deaths
			Per Cent
15-29	3975	3481.34	114
30-39	4438	4258.40	104
40-49	3431	3498.22	98
50-59	3040	3034.41	100
60 and over	623	699.04	89

The mortality among women is higher than among men at young ages at entry and lower at ages of entry at 60 and above. The mortality is decidedly heavier in the early policy years at ages of entry 15-39 than among men. The adverse selection against the company is thus especially prominent in the early policy years of the earlier age groups.

The deductions from the mortality experience of the special classes are as follows. As regards spinsters:

(a) The mortality is much more favorable than among men.

(b) There is no greater adverse selection than among men.

(c) The mortality in comparison with men decreases with advancing age at entry.

As regards married women:

(*a*) The mortality is distinctly higher than among men.

(*b*) In comparison with men the relative mortality decreases with advancing age at entry.

(*c*) Married women who insured as married show much higher mortality than those women who insured as spinsters.

(*d*) There is a well-defined adverse selection against the company in the first and second policy years.

(*e*) The experience on women with the husband as beneficiary is slightly less favorable than where some one other than the husband is named as beneficiary.

As regards widows and divorced women:

(*a*) The mortality experience is between that of spinsters and married women.

(*b*) The increase of the mortality by policy years is of the same nature as that in the case of spinsters.

(*c*) There is no more adverse selection than in the case of men.

The following tables from the Medico-Actuarial Investigation show the mortality experience of the different classes of women both on the basis of policy years and ages at entry.

RATIO OF ACTUAL TO EXPECTED DEATHS BY THE
MEDICO–ACTUARIAL TABLE

Policy Years	Spinsters	Married Women, Husband Beneficiary	Married Women, Husband not Beneficiary	Widows and Divorced Women
▾	82	146	135	104
2	72	143	133	106
3	81	129	117	108
4–5	85	127	115	107
6–10	81	111	106	104
11–24	80	108	104 .	102
Ages at Entry				
15–24	100	150	158	210
25–29	83	147	144	129
30–39	73	129	123	109
40–49	70	109	102	104
50–62	68	98	100	103

Race Mortality. — The hazard due to races can be
determined with increasing accuracy as the vital statistics of races become more accurate. In the United
States the vital statistics of the registration area show a
higher mortality among negroes than among whites.
The causes for this condition are too well known to need
description. The greater ignorance of the negro race,
not only as to sanitary living, but also as to their correct
age, adds another element to the normal hazard. Some
companies practically refuse to accept negroes. This is
done in various ways, such, for example, as not giving
the agent any commission for writing the policy; others
discriminate against them in the examination. Many
states enacted laws after the Civil War requiring com-

panies to accept negroes on the same basis as whites in
the belief that they were thereby enforcing the spirit
of the fourteenth amendment, but in practice such laws
can easily be evaded.

The Medico-Actuarial Investigation affords some
reliable statistics of mortality experience of negroes,
Chinese, and Japanese, residing in the United States,
and Indians. Negroes were divided in the investigation into two classes, (a) ministers, teachers, and other
professional men, and (b) all other colored men.

In Group (a) the ratio of the actual to the expected
mortality was 137 per cent, and in Group (b) the ratio
was 147 per cent.

The mortality of negroes was at all ages higher than
among the white, but relatively higher at ages of entry
under 30.

Relation of Height and Weight to Mortality. — In
the Medico-Actuarial Investigation the relation of
height and weight to mortality was studied. It was
shown that at the younger ages tall men were less
desirable risks than short men, while at the older ages
the short and medium-sized men were poorer risks than
the tall men. This conclusion was reached on the basis
of the number of pounds departure from the average
weight, and not to the percentage over or under weight.
If measured by the percentage over or under weight, the
advantage of the tall, elderly entrants diminishes rapidly
with increasing weight and disappears altogether at the
greater degrees of overweight; tall men at all entry
ages where there is overweight by more than a moderate
percentage have proved worse risks than shorter men.

Height and weight were also investigated in connection with tuberculosis. Among other conclusions the following may be noted. In the case of tuberculosis of one parent it was found: (a) that the mortality was high at the younger ages at entry among the light-weights; (b) that tuberculosis in one parent seems to be of comparatively little importance except at the younger entry ages; (c) that the mortality at the older ages at entry was good except in the overweight group; (d) that at entry ages under thirty a record of tuberculosis appears to be of more consequence in the case of a brother or sister than of a parent.

In the seven southern states of Alabama, Georgia, Texas, Louisiana, Florida, Mississippi, and Arkansas, it was found in the Medico-Actuarial Investigation that the death rate from typhoid fever was about one and a half times the standard, and from malaria about seven times the standard. The actual death rate varied from the expected in these seven states from 114 per cent to 127 per cent, but it must be remembered that "the mortality would vary with the proportions in which the business was issued in different sections of the state, and such proportions may have differed widely in the two periods."

The warning that vital statistics of different age and sex groups should be interpreted in the light of all attendant circumstances cannot be too carefully observed.

Occupation Mortality. — In the Medico-Actuarial Investigation a careful analysis of occupation mortality was made. The data included one hundred and ninety-nine occupations, and from these the following selections are made to indicate the relation of the occupation to mortality:

Occupation	Ratio of Actual to Expected Mortality
	Per Cent
Army — commissioned officers, excluding chaplains, physicians, surgeons, and paymasters	131
Bakers (journeymen)	98
Glass industry — bevelers, grinders, engravers, cutters	146
Breweries, excluding clerks, managers	152
Rolling mill employees	117
Coal miners (anthracite)	191
Coal miners (bituminous)	132
Locomotive engineers	160
Structural ironworkers	168
Bricklayers	108
Janitors	112
Plumbers and steam-fitters, journeymen	99
Undertakers and embalmers	95
Veterinary surgeons	80
Woolen mill operators (men)	113

Conservation of Life. — A movement which has attracted considerable attention within the past few years, and one which affects the insurance of lives, is that of the conservation of human life. The movement seeks to preserve, to broaden, and to extend life. It is well known that the advance in the medical and sanitary science has been very remarkable within the past several decades, and while the general public has received much benefit from the advance made in this science, yet it can hardly be claimed that these many new discoveries in hygiene are known and acted upon by the general public. What is needed is a vigorous campaign to educate the people in better ways of living.

The most marked effects of what has been done in the past reflect themselves in the lives of the two classes, the dependents and defectives. The children and the aged are better cared for, and hence more children grow to maturity. The defectives, such as the feeble-minded, the deaf, and the blind, are also much better cared for than they formerly were. It must be admitted, however, that these classes are objectively and temporarily a burden on the productive classes. It may be possible, as some believe, to secure a class of old people who retain their mental vigor sufficiently to be of great value to the other members of society who do not have that wisdom which comes alone from age and experience. Least attention, however, has been given to the productive classes, the men and women of adult and middle life, who are the chief factors in determining the efficiency and worth of a civilization.

The movement has for its purpose the lengthening and broadening of life at all ages, and the effect on the insurance business is readily perceived. Insurance of lives is based to a large degree upon a mortality table or rate of deaths among a selected group of the population. Such a movement would, if successful, affect the death rate by lowering it. It would extend the productive years of the insured's life; it would add to his efficiency while he is a producer; it would create a finer sense of his obligation to take insurance. We have seen that a mortality table is drawn up on the assumption that it is subject to secular and temporary

changes, and this movement would favorably affect
both changes. By thus lowering the death rate, it
would lower the greatest single cost of insurance, namely,
the mortality cost. The movement if most successful
would prevent untimely death, so that a smaller sum
could be charged as a premium, but it would be as sufficient as the larger sum now collected because it would
secure greater additions from its compound interest
accumulations. It would increase the expectation of
life. Not only the average length of life would be
affected, but also the breadth of life, for life is nar-
rowed by morbidity. The length of life is usually only
extended by controlling sickness, so that the prevention
of sickness is the primary object of the science of hygiene. If it is true, as has been stated, that " one
third of the deaths are preventable, that is, postponable,"
and that " it is within the power of man to rid himself of
every parasitic disease," then the significance of any efforts
which seek to extend and broaden life is very important.

Methods of Conserving Life. — The particular
methods by which these results are proposed to be
brought about are in general as follows: First, by
affecting heredity. This may be done by creating such
public opinion as will consider with disfavor the marriage
of the physically and mentally unfit and the propaga-
tion of their kind. This result may be aided by legal
restrictions on marriage. Second, by hygienic laws and
the activities of the federal, state, and local governments; such, for example, as by quarantine regulations,
pure food laws, pure water supplies, milk inspection,
regulation of hours and conditions of labor, and instal-

lation of safety devices. Third, by semipublic hygienic activities. This includes medical research and instruction, which results in the discoveries of preventive medicine, of antiseptics, and especially making public property the knowledge thus acquired. It is only within the past few years that the medical profession, as such, has done much to educate the public in the proper care of the body. Semipublic institutions, such as hospitals, sanitariums, and asylums are doing much in this connection. The public schools are beginning to give more attention to the health of the pupil, and much good can be expected from this source. Fourth, by activities of private associations, such as societies to prevent the spread of contagious diseases, corporations seeking to care for the health of their employees, and life insurance companies. Fifth, by the practice of personal hygienic habits as a result of the activities of such associations previously mentioned and a better realization of their importance.

The conservation of life depends, not only upon the collective activities of all on a wide scale to prevent contagious and other unnecessary diseases, but also upon the care with which an individual looks after his daily health. That is to say, length of life is a personal and an impersonal matter. The individual must help himself and be helped by his fellows. He has a right to expect that his fellows will not necessarily expose him to disease, but his fellows also have a right to demand that he will not so injure his vital powers by acquiring improper habits, and by lack of exercise, that he will become an easy prey to disease.

Life Insurance Companies and Conservation of Life. — The question arises, To what extent is the insurance company justified, if at all, in taking part in this movement to conserve life? It calls for an expenditure of money, and an insurance company has no money other than that which it receives from its policyholders. It is a trustee of these funds whether it be a stock company with its self-chosen officials or a mutual company with its officers chosen by the many members of the company. It is urged that precedents are found for life insurance companies in the case of fire insurance companies, which have spent large sums of money in various ways to reduce the fire hazard; also in the activities of liability and accident companies, which spend considerable sums in inspection work and in devising protective devices of various kinds to which they call the attention of employers and their insured members. It is admitted by all that the insurance organizations are chiefly business and not philanthropic organizations. Is such an organization justified in making any expenditure which does not directly effect a saving for its members?

A particular activity of an insurance company need not, however, for this reason benefit only the members of the insurance group. It may benefit the general public as well. But ought not the activity to benefit the insured lives in particular and the general public only incidentally? Then, too, even assuming that the monetary benefit of activities to conserve life is clearly shown, there yet remains a very great practical objection. Would other companies coöperate in a general action for this purpose? If one or several companies should undertake this expenditure, it might unfavorably affect their expense ratio as compared with other companies; for assuming the justification and benefits of such a movement, the policyholders of other companies would equally benefit.

A number of the large insurance companies have engaged in various forms of educational activities to preserve and promote the health of their members. This has taken the form of pamphlets and other literature on health preservation and in some cases the establishment of sanatoria for the insured members. There are, however, certain practical difficulties in the way, such as securing the coöperation of other companies for any wide plan for the expenditure of insurance funds — the property of the policyholders — with a view of improving the lives of insured individuals.

REFERENCES

Harbaugh, C. B.   The Selection of Risks by the Life Insurance Solicitor.

Roche, J. F.   A Method of Handling Impaired Life Risks.

Stillman, Chas. F.   The Life Insurance Examiner.

Fricke, William.   Insurance, pp. 278–310.

Yale Readings, Vol. I, Chap. XXI.

Report on National Vitality, Parts III, IV of Vol. III, Senate Document No. 676, Sixtieth Congress, Second Session.

Bowley, A. L.   Elements of Statistics, Part I, Chap. VI.

Insurance Guide and Handbook.   Fifth Edition, Chaps. XV, XVI.

Proceedings of Association of Life Insurance Medical Directors of America, 1913–1915, pp. 4–76.

Transactions of the Faculty of Actuaries, Vol. II, pp. 57–90, 195–205, Vol. I, pp. 49–70.

Journal of Insurance Institute, Vol. XII, p. 87; Vol. III, p. 401; Vol. VIII, p. 99; Vol. II, p. 383; Vol. IX, p. 13.

CHAPTER V

LIFE insurance organizations may be classified upon the basis of the systems of insurance under which they operate, upon the character of the control of the organization, and upon the character of the policy written.

Classification of Companies. — According to the systems of insurance there are the Old Line or Regular Organization, the Assessment Organizations, the Fraternal Organizations, and the Stipulated Premium Organizations. The Old Line Organizations may be subdivided into those which write ordinary insurance and those which write industrial insurance.

According to the character of the control by the members of the insurance organizations there are the Stock Companies, the Mutual Companies, and the Mixed Companies.

On the basis of the kind of policy written, there are the organizations which write participating, that is, those under which the policyholder shares in the surplus earnings of the company and those which do not, that is, non-participating. It must not be inferred, however, that each of the classes is mutually exclusive. The distinction among them is based partly upon the different character of the insurance transacted and partly upon the difference in the laws governing their operation.

114

Level Premium Companies. — The " old line," " regular," or " level premium " companies are those which sell policies of insurance for a premium fixed in amount during the length of the contract, and which accumulates a sinking fund or reserve to meet all claims upon the company. The word " old " has no reference whatever to the length of time that the company has been in business, since the youngest company organized under the plan is as " old " as any other in existence. Without anticipating the later discussion of the premium, it may readily be seen from what has been said of the risk that the necessity of reserve is the effect of not collecting an increasing premium for the increasing risk of death. More than the actual cost of carrying the individual risk is collected in the early years of the policy in order that less than the actual cost may be collected in the later years of the policy, and thus the absolutely small charges of the earlier period and the excessively large ones of the later period are equated into a moderate charge for the whole period of the policy.

The insurance under this plan may be from year to year, in which case the premium increases with each year, but it is still a fixed and known premium. However, it is usually for a fixed term of years with an unchanging annual charge, reducible only by any surplus which may be distributed by the company among its policyholders. This is the " ordinary " " old-line, level premium " insurance. There is also the " industrial " " old-line, level premium " insurance which is purchased by the wage-earning classes in small amounts by weekly or monthly payments. A single insurance organization may sell both kinds of this " old-line " insurance, keeping each business distinct in its book-keeping, but with its agents and officials selling and administering both classes of policies. There are, however, but few organizations which transact both kinds of business. The Prudential, the Metropolitan, and the John Hancock Insurance companies in the United States are the most noted examples of companies which sell both of these kinds of policies.

Assessment Companies. — The second general class of insurance organizations is the Assessment companies. These associations had a very early beginning in the various organizations, formed for a variety of purposes, but with the especial object of aiding its members at time of death by levying some sort of a charge or assessment upon the members. At different times they have been called guilds, friendly societies, funeral societies, and a variety of other names. Their chief characteristic is the voluntary charge or assessment which is paid and which usually varies in amount from year to year in accordance with the number of deaths and the amounts which are paid to the beneficiaries of the deceased members.

Early Plans of Assessment Insurance. — The assessment system of life insurance is, therefore, that one under which theoretically the cost of the insurance is annually collected from the members by assessing on them the costs. In practice there have been so many modifications of this theory that it is difficult to characterize the assessment plan; but the essential idea of this system is that no full reserve is collected. In no plan of assessmentism is the policyholder guaranteed a level premium. In its earliest form an assessment or a collection was made from each member upon the death of a member. Later a definite sum was promised in each case of death, and each member was charged a certain sum at entry, but it was not at first based upon his age at entry. Age at entry was later taken into consideration, but it was soon perceived that the persisting old member was paying the same sum as the young entrant. Whatever of equity there had been at the beginning of the company soon disappeared, so that with the increasing death rates of the later years, the healthier old members tended to withdraw on account of the high cost. It was but natural that at the end of each year, as the assessments increased, a number of healthy members would refuse to pay the higher assessments. This would further increase the assessments required, since those remaining in the organization would not only be smaller in number, but also of inferior physical vigor. Other young and healthy lives would be deterred from entering on account of the increasing costs. The effect was therefore cumulative. The sums collected were usually arbitrarily fixed without reference to mortality tables. It was an attractive plan to many because it seemed that men paid for their insurance as they got it. The present plan in some such companies is to charge a sum at entry, based upon the age at entry and on a contract which provides that such additional assessment may be levied from time to time, as the needs of the company demand. This sum is frequently in excess of the current cost of the insurance during the early years of the organization and thus affords for a time a fund. In some cases a membership fee is collected, which also aids in establishing a fund.

However, in practically all the plans of pure assessment insurance the premiums collected are not sufficient premiums as required by the most reliable mortality table. The plans are too often devised to make it appear that the buyer of the assessment insurance is getting it cheaper than he would old-line insurance. Insurance, like any other commodity, has its price, and no visionary plans can make it cheaper. Indeed, insurance costs are more definite than most costs, for they have a limited range. The stern fact of certain death and a fairly definite rate of dying confronts all those who sell the commodity — insurance. No such reductions or fluctuations in cost from year to year are present, as in the case of the production of material goods on account of the use of improved appliances or other changes. Only the very gradual improvements in conditions of living, better care of the sick, more successful surgical operations, and more secure and better investments can cause permanent reductions in the cost of insurance. It is not a difficult matter to determine whether the premiums collected by assessment companies are sufficient, since mortality tables and interest calculations will disclose the fact.

Assessment Insurance in America and England. — Assessment companies have had an unusual development in the United States and Canada as compared with Europe. In England the Friendly Societies became important, but these differ somewhat from the American Assessment Societies in that the latter frequently employ agents to solicit insurance and in other ways prosecute their business in much the same manner as a regular insurance company. Most of the Friendly Societies also made regular, periodical collections of fixed charges on premiums and also accumulated a reserve for future payments. In the United States assessment insurance has had its greatest development since the Civil War, that is, since 1870. Such organizations were formed before this date, but life insurance in general in the United States originated and had its early development as regular life insurance on the basis of specified charges or premiums collected in advance. These early organized regular companies were as a whole very successful. They had a low mortality. Their premiums, based on the modified Carlisle Table of mortality, the many restrictions in their policy contracts in favor of the company, and the management of the companies each operated to this end. Between 1870 and 1880, however, many of these regular companies failed for reasons previously described. The failure of these regular companies, their high premiums, the restricted policies, and the early success of the first assessment societies, due largely to the early low death rates, all contributed to the organization and popularity of the many assessment societies which were formed after 1870. A large number of such societies were formed, in fact many thousand, Pennsylvania alone having at one date two hundred and fifty. Some of them confined their business to a single state or even to adjoining counties, while others soon developed business in many states and even in some foreign countries.

Many of these companies were organized by adventurers and promoters for their own selfish ends. Many were organized by honest men, but unfortunately they were not informed as to the principles of insurance. As a result, the life of such organizations has been brief, except in those cases where the officials and members later recognized the inadequacy of the payments which they were collecting and were able to transfer them to a thoroughly scientific insurance basis. This has occurred in a relatively small number of cases, and most of these companies organized between 1850 and 1900 have failed. Some are yet in existence, operating upon an inadequate basis, while others are endeavoring to transfer their business to sound insurance plans.

Fraternal Insurance. — Fraternal Insurance organizations were synonymous in their period of development with assessment companies, having had their important origin and development in the United States since the Civil War. They employed in their early history the same insurance system, viz. the assessment plan. Many of them yet operate on the assessment plan, although an increasing number have adopted definite rates of charges on the basis of the National Fraternal Congress Table of Mortality. Like the assessment societies, many at first charged a flat rate upon entry, regardless of age. Later a charge based upon age was collected as well as a special entrance fee. The chief difference between the early Fraternal and Assessment companies was that the former employed no agents to solicit business, but depended upon their members to secure other members. In the latter days, however, many of the fraternal- societies employ members who are to all intents agents. Fraternal insurance organizations are also to be distinguished from the assessment societies in that insurance was only one of the purposes of the organizations. All members of the fraternity or lodge may not be eligible to membership in the insured group on account of physical condition, although it is frequently true that a life rejected by an ordinary or regular life insurance company will be insured by the fraternal insurance organization. This fraternal spirit binding together the individuals in a lodge and insurance society has been a very great factor in making it possible for many of these fraternal societies to transfer from unscientific and inadequate insurance rates to proper charges for their insurance. Where, in the assessment society, the member would often refuse to pay the higher assessment, the member of the fraternal organization would be constrained to do so by this mutual fraternal feeling of a desire to preserve the organization and make it possible for it to fulfill all its obligations. These fraternal organizations exist in large numbers at present. As they now operate, their insurance is transacted either on the assessment basis, in which case the rates are in practically all cases inadequate to meet the incurred obligations, or they are societies with fixed charges, usually established on the basis of the National Fraternal Congress Table of Mortality.

Assessment Insurance and Public Regulation. — Such companies have been in the past relatively free from the compulsory valuations required by state departments of old-line companies, and it is for this reason alone that many of them have been able to continue in business. The fraternal assessment companies especially have been considered purely voluntary and private associations, and it has been difficult and in most cases impossible to bring them under the regulation of the state. It has been argued that they are not organized for profit, and they have always had sufficient representation and political influence in the state legislatures to defeat regulative legislation. As a matter of political expediency the party in power has often hesitated to oppose them lest future votes might be lost. The evils of the purely business assessment system have become so generally recognized, however, and the activity of the state along the line of protective legislation has so increased that uniform laws, recommended by the association of state insurance commissioners, seem likely to be adopted in many states. The fraternal assessment societies themselves have accepted the principle of the recommendations, and while the adoption of them will not completely rectify the errors of the past, yet it is a long forward step and in the end will result in placing assessment insurance on a scientific basis.

No well-wisher of insurance has any desire to force fraternal insurance companies out of business, for they have much to recommend them in addition to the lower cost at which they may transact insurance, as compared with the old-line insurance company. It is unreasonable to suppose, however, that the people of the twentieth century, with their increasing care for system in organization of business, will much longer permit such a blot in the insurance business as the old unscientific and practically dishonest assessment company. So far as the plans of fraternal companies are the same as the unscientific assessment plan, so far are they unable to meet their obligations, and no specious appeal to the sentiment of fraternity should be permitted to conceal the injustice of the plan. What more elementary requirement is there about fraternity than that brothers should meet their obligations? What more fundamental characteristic of real fraternity should be observed than honesty in making a contract and fidelity in carrying it out? If fraternity is not to be a farce, those who are responsible for the millions of fraternal assessment insurance now in force must make adequate provision for the meeting of the obligations now unprovided for. Much of the fraternal insurance of the assessment character now held has not been paid for. In many cases less than one third is paid for; that is to say, for every $1000 of insurance in force $600 of it is a worthless promise to pay. The National Fraternal Congress Table of Mortality is much lower than the American Table, and certainly no rates lower than those called for by the former table should be permitted. The death rate in some of the fraternal organizations is now in excess of the rates of the Fraternal Table and even in excess of the rates of the American Mortality Table. A number of states prohibit the organization of any insurance society on the old assessment plan or the organization of any new company on any other plan than one which will absolutely guarantee the collection of a premium which with safe and wise investments will meet all future demands. It is a kind of dishonesty, which, although often originating in laudable motives, has been all too prevalent in the past.

Stipulated Premium Insurance. — A brief description may be given of the fourth type of insurance organizations, based upon the system of insurance. These are the stipulated premium companies which are at present of very little importance. These were formed upon the basis of charging the smallest possible premium but with a safety clause in the contract which protected them against insolvency in times of financial and industrial depression. This clause granted to the company the right to charge any deficiency in their assets in respect to their obligations to the policyholders, who either had to pay this additional charge or have his insurance reduced by its equivalent. That is, the face of the policy or the amount promised to be paid to the insured was an uncertain sum. This resembles in some respects the practice of regular companies when, on account of a substandard risk, the amount to be paid during a period of years varies with the attained age of the insured, gradually approaching the face of the policy. Special laws were enacted in some states to govern the operation of these stipulated premium companies, under which they were required to charge a premium equal at least to the costs indicated by the rate of mortality for a single year and in addition a certain sum to cover expenses and contingencies.

The One System of Insurance. — There is, then, but one system of life insurance. There can be but one system from the standpoint of premium collections, and that is one under which such a premium will be collected as the rate of mortality and rate of interest show are sufficient. All these other so-called systems of insurance should be classed with the gambling contracts of the early developmental stage of insurance. The only difference is that in assessment insurance there was not always an intent to deceive, while in the gambling contracts this intent was either always consciously present, or it was a purchase and sale of mere chance. However, if in last analysis, injustice results, it makes little difference to the bearer of it whether the original purpose was good or bad. The penalty of ignorance, both in written and unwritten law, is no less severe than that of knavery, and it is the concern of society to protect itself from its well-meaning but ignorant members no less than from its dishonest members. As has been well said, "assessmentism has merited a sentence of legal death and fraternalism a suspended sentence."

The second general classification of companies as previously outlined is Stock, Mutual, and Mixed organizations.

The Stock Company. — The stock company is one organized by private individuals who purchase the shares of stock with the expectation of receiving dividends. The amount of the stock may be the minimum established by law or it may be such larger sums as the promoters may think it possible to sell or to earn dividends. Often in the sale of the stock an effort is made in both pure stock companies and in mutual companies to distribute the stock widely among prominent men in the territory in which the company expects to operate with the purpose of aiding the company in securing business. The stock company is owned and controlled by the stock contributors who select the officials to operate the company with a view of serving the ends of the stockholders. The securing of this end does not mean that policyholders in a stock company have any less liberal policy provisions than those in mutual companies, but since the stock company has issued its shares as an investment, like any other stock corporation, it must endeavor to pay dividends on them. All the profits in the pure stock companies go to the stockholders, and all policies are issued on the non-participating plan. If a company organized as a stock company issues policies which share in the surplus earnings of the company and also permits policyholders to have some part in the management of the company, then such a company is properly called a mixed company.

Claims for the Stock Plan. — It is claimed for this kind of a company that the self-interest of the stockholders will guarantee fidelity to their trusteeship in caring for the policyholders' funds and that competition of other stock and mutual companies will guarantee a fair cost of insurance to the policyholder. It is also argued that the stockholders have every interest in selecting the most efficient officials, and this they are free to do without any interference from the uninformed policyholders who theoretically can dominate the policy of strictly mutual companies. The stock company was the first to develop both in England and America because the capital was a partial guarantee of the contracts in the early days of insurance when the mortality tables were not known to be sufficiently accurate to assure solvency from the annual contributions by the members of mutual companies. It is assumed under the stock plan that a small addition is made to the actual net premium, and this becomes the fixed premium to the policyholder. Any losses are borne by the stockholders and any profits go to them as payment for the risk incurred. The element of risk, however, so far as it is one of mortality rate, is not great, for such a mass of experience is now available that there is little excuse for any insurance organization not collecting sufficient premiums for the actual mortality to be experienced.

The Mutual Plan. — In a strictly mutual company there is no capital stock and hence no stockholders. The company is the policyholders, who select their officials and control the management of the company. The older mutual companies have no capital stock and the newer ones in most cases only a nominal capital. It is often provided that those who advance the capital necessary to start the company shall receive a certain interest, say 10 per cent, for the risk up to the time at which the capital may be retired when a reserve and possibly a surplus has been accumulated. The policyholders in a mutual company pay a premium in excess of the actual mortality premium demanded and also in excess of the premium for the same kind of a policy in a strict stock company; but whatever of this premium is not necessary, as the future experience of the company shows, is returned to them. The return of this overcharge is called a dividend and hence the policy in a strictly mutual company is said to be a participating policy.

Claims for the Mutual Plan. — It is claimed for this form of company that it has no dividends to pay the stockholders and can manage its affairs in such a manner as the policyholders decide is proper. Some mutual companies, however, issue policies at such a rate that the contract does not entitle the holder to share in the dividends, that is to say, his future overcharges are supposed to be discounted in the form of a lower premium. If a surplus is accumulated in addition to the reserve, this is also the property of the policyholders. This surplus is accumulated for emergencies; that is, for higher mortality claims or to enable the company to give its policyholders the same general dividends or returns that it has been making in the past, or to cover any depreciation in assets.

The Mixed Plan. — In the mixed plan there are stockholders who receive dividends on the capital which they have advanced. A certain rate of interest is fixed to be received by the stockholders, and all surplus earnings are then distributed to the policyholders. In some cases no limitation is fixed as to the amount which the stockholders are entitled to receive and they may take what they please, although they are compelled by the participating policy contracts to make some distribution to such policyholders. Some states require the retirement of the stock and fix the maximum interest to be paid, while others have no special requirement. Most of the companies now organized have capital stock because most states require a guarantee capital for the organization of a company.

We have thus stated the theoretical basis of the different kinds of companies, but in actual practice there are some points of difference. At first the stock company was the rule, but soon the mutual company came in vogue. The large dividends paid by many of the mutual companies attracted the attention of certain investors inclined to speculate, and stock companies were organized in larger numbers. Later the mixed company became the rule.

The Control of Mutual and Stock Companies. — It must be pointed out, that in actual practice the difference between stock and mutual companies is more apparent than real. The ordinary reader could not determine from the rate books of two such companies which was a mutual and which was a stock company. It is true that there is a general tendency for stock companies to sell only non-participating insurance. The late investigations of the insurance business by New York and other states resulted in laws requiring either that a company should confine itself to writing participating or non-participating policies, or should keep separate accounts of the two classes of business. This was done in the belief — whether or not justified by the facts — that the company's earnings on participating policies were used to make lower rates for the

K

non-participating policies. It does not necessarily follow because there are stockholders who receive dividends that the net cost of the same kind of a policy to the insured in a stock company will for this reason be higher than the net cost at the end of a contract in a mutual company. The net cost of an insurance policy to the holder is a function of so many variables that an excess at one point in the cost may be balanced by a saving at another point.

Nor does the distinction based on the fact that in one case the company is controlled by the stockholders and in the other case by the policyholders amount to very much in real practice. The management of a mutual as well as a stock company is controlled by very few men. We have seen that a stock company sometimes permits its policyholders to vote, but in neither this case nor in the case of a mutual company does the average policyholder ordinarily exercise this right. Few of the policyholders could attend in person the meeting, and even if they did, they are not ordinarily well enough informed upon the subject to vote intelligently. In most companies the proxy system is followed. Under this system the policyholder, either at the time of purchasing a policy or later upon invitation from the officials of the company, when a notice of a meeting of the officials is sent, gives his proxy or right of voting to the president of the company. This system permits the company to be directed by the board of directors and its chosen executive officials, who doubtless are in position to pass most intelligently on the questions which come up for decision.

It is urged as an advantage of mutual companies that the policyholder has an opportunity in times of crises in the company's affairs to express his will and thus correct evils. This is a power more theoretical than actual, for the history of insurance affords no clear-cut case when this has accomplished any great reform. The competition of other companies, both mutual and stock, and the knowledge of this final power resting in policyholders, together with the supervision of the state, are the really protective forces for the policyholder in securing honest and efficient administration of the company. It was thought by some that the mutual company would afford a means of educating the people to an understanding and appreciation of insurance. Some efforts have been made to organize the policy-holders into local associations which could make their will known to the home office, but such attempts have not been successful. The average policyholder knows little about even the policy he owns and still less about the insurance business and with the protection afforded by the state there is no immediate prospect that he is going to make much effort to inform himself on the subject. Efforts must be made by the company to educate him to a more intelligent appreciation of in-surance, supplemented by the work of educational institutions. The apathy of the average policyholder is surprising, even when it can be shown that the cost of his insurance is to be affected, as in the case of ad-verse legislation. He is too busy, as he thinks, in his business and professional work, to give attention to insurance. There is, then, in the actual conduct of the business, little difference between a stock and a mutual company so far as the question is concerned as to what individuals shall direct the affairs of the company. In either kind of a company it is a few men and not the rank and file of policyholders.

Tendency to Mutualization of Companies. — There is some tendency for insurance organizations to become mutual in character. Several companies in the United States, including the Prudential and the Metropolitan, have been mutualized and others are discussing plans looking to the same end.

It is suggested that this is a tendency which should be encouraged, and if necessary by legal enactment, if life insurance is to continue a business for private enterprise and not one for state conduct. Is insurance by its very character a business from which individuals should be permitted to take profit in the economic sense of the term? Or is it a business of such social importance that its costs to those whom it serves should be prime costs? That is, should the outlay for the service be limited to wages for those who are employed to conduct the business of insurance?

Whether it is or not a suitable business for profit must be determined largely by two considerations. First, to what extent is the individual free to deal in the commodity or service? Second, to what degree is the element of risk present whereby unusual skill, foresight, and great ability are under our present economic system supposed to justify one in taking or receiving a large return in the nature of a profit, risk interest, wages of management, or whatever we are pleased to call this unusual fund?

Profit from Insurance. — As to the first point, we have but to consider again the nature of insurance. It is but a method of combining and distributing necessary risks to which every one is in some manner exposed. The fact that many do not avail themselves of the insurance principle does not prove that they are essentially free to choose. Indeed they have chosen. The risk remains whether or not they choose to admit its existence. Their failure to reduce the risk by joining with their fellows in applying the insurance principle means that their social mind lacks development, and it means further that their fellows ultimately bear a large part of the risk. The loss of a life is usually a loss to society, not only because of the potential value of the life itself, but also because of the withdrawal of protection from those dependent upon that life for support and preparation for efficient living. The loss of property falls immediately upon the owner, but it is also a destruction of so much social capital. The loss of time by sickness or accidents means that so much less of the work of the world is done, or perhaps it is shunted upon shoulders already heavy with work. The individuual ought not to be free to choose whether he shall increase social well-being by using the insurance principle, even though it be true that insurance *per se* gives but a very indirect benefit to the individual. Its first and fundamental characteristic is mutuality, the principle of each for all and all for each. If, then, the idea of profit to the insured is excluded by the very nature of insurance, and if it is a method of reducing necessary risks and if the value resulting is distinctly a social value, should individuals be permitted to receive a profit from administering it? Paradoxical as it may appear, it is the insurance officials who often argue for this view. This is most clearly shown in the taxation laws of the various states. The greater number of insurance officials, especially those connected with the life insurance companies, oppose the taxation of insurance on the ground that its character does not justify the tax. It is called by them a " tax on thrift," yet the legislators make insurance a source of considerable revenue for the state.

The Risk as a Basis of Profit. — As to the second point, viz. whether there is such a risk present in conducting the business as would justify the taking of a profit. This question has been answered in part by the consideration of the basis or principles upon which the business is conducted. These principles have been in most kinds of insurance long known and well understood. The results of many years' application of the principles are known. The data are available, and in most cases are organized or capable of being organized, so that no great element of risk is present. This is not to state that perfection has been reached in applying these data, but certainly with our present knowledge there is no excuse for dangerous experiments. Mortality and morbidity statistics are available and are becoming more accurate. The costs of insurance are well known, or at least we know that a certain minimum amount must be collected. How much less might be sufficient is a debatable question. In short, the application of the insurance principle presents no great difficulties or risks.   It is not a venture upon unknown seas.

Participating and Non-participating Insurance. — The third general classification of insurance organization, viz. those writing participating and those writing non-participating policies, has been described in connection with the other classifications.   It should be understood that this classification has more significance in reference to policies than to distinct organizations. The stock companies for many years wrote both participating and non-participating policies.   In some states they are yet permitted to do so, although they are generally required to keep the two kinds of business separated in their accounts.   This was made a legal requirement because there was some evidence to show that in the case of some companies one class of policyholders was benefited at the expense of another class or that the stockholders themselves were permitted unusual returns by this mingling of the accounts of the two types of policies.   In theory the stock company should write only non-participating and the mutual company only participating policies.   Actual practice is rapidly conforming to this theory.

Methods of Organizing a Company. — The organization of a life insurance company, whether on the stock, mutual, or mixed plan, requires several stages. In addition to the general laws governing the organization of all corporations, practically all the states have special laws which govern the organization of life insurance companies.   In many states the minimum number of persons who may organize such a company is fixed by the statute. These several persons agree to advance certain sums of money for the initial expenses, for even if it is a purely mutual company — a kind now seldom organized — a certain amount of capital is required for the initial expenses.

The interested persons hold a meeting to decide the kind of a company which is to be organized and the amount of capital stock which is to be issued. The officials of the company are also chosen. Since most of the states require a certain minimum of capital stock for even the ordinary mutual company, in most cases the capital stock must be paid in. This minimum capital is required as a deposit fund, held by the state in invested securities, the income of which goes to the company. This deposit fund is supposed to give greater security to the policyholders, but if the company is operating on scientific plans and its transactions are carefully supervised by the state, the necessity for such a deposit is not evident.

The Charter. — After the above requirements have been met, the interested persons apply to a state official, usually the secretary of state, for articles of incorporation, which are usually called a charter. The state official makes an examination of the terms upon which the company proposes to organize and do business in order to discover whether the proposed plans violate the state constitution or state laws. Certain matters may be referred to the chief law officer of the state, the attorney-general, and certain other matters, having to do with the financial security, to the insurance commissioner. If, then, the state official, empowered to grant articles of incorporation to insurance companies, is satisfied with the terms proposed, a charter is issued. The charter does not, however, grant a right to do an insurance business. It merely grants the right to proceed with the organization of the company, and it frequently happens that several years elapse after a charter is granted before a company begins writing business. It also happens in some cases that the company is not able to effect an organization and never applies for a license to write policies. The next important step after securing a charter is to dispose of the stock.

Evils of Promotion. — A well-marked evil has developed in connection with the organization of the numerous new companies since 1905. This consists in the very large commission given to agents by proposers of a new company for selling the stock of the new concern. Not infrequently have these stock salesmen been permitted as high as 20 per cent commission, and when it happens that the officials of the new company are also the stock salesmen, the evil is particularly glaring. Sometimes shares of stock are either given or sold at a large discount to influential men in a community in order to capitalize their name, and thus sell stock in their community. This last evil is doubtless difficult to correct, but the former can be remedied by limiting the commission permitted to sellers of the stock of new companies. This has been done in some states. The expenses of such sales do not vary considerably in different sections of the country, but this variation can be taken into consideration by each legislature in establishing the limit. There should be no place in the insurance business for the professional promoter. In order to control the organization of companies more carefully, some states have given to the insurance commissioner control of the activities of companies immediately after a charter is issued; that is, during the period of formation. After the stock has been sold and other details of the organization have been worked out, the company applies to the insurance commissioner for a license to do business. The insurance commissioner then makes an examination of the company's condition, and its transactions since it received its articles of incorporation, and the plans under which it proposes to do business, the policies it proposes to issue, and other matters to see that the laws governing the operation of insurance companies are not violated. Particular attention is given to the financial condition of the proposed company. If he is satisfied on all these points, a license is issued to the company, and this marks the time of the real beginning of doing an insurance business.

Expenses of Organizing a Company. — It must be evident that the expenses incident to the establishing of a new company in the insurance business are very considerable. In addition to the usual expenses of establishing an ordinary business, such as rent, office equipment, and salary of higher officials, the very difficult problem of securing a working force — that is, agents to sell the policies — must be solved. There are not, as in most kinds of business, a number of workers waiting for positions. The insurance agent should be a skilled workman. It usually requires a certain amount of training to be able to sell insurance. The new company must, therefore, either induce agents to leave other companies or train the inexperienced man. The successful agent of the established company is ordinarily not anxious to connect himself with a new company for, all other things being equal, it is easier to sell insurance for an established company than for a new company. Consequently the new company often is compelled to make an offer of a higher commission in order to induce him to become their agent. But it is entirely too expensive to thus purchase all its agency force; so the new company endeavors to secure a certain number of trained men, who then build up an agency force by training new men. There is in the insurance business, as in all businesses, a certain number of " floating " workmen, but they are not a class upon which a company can depend for substantial results.

The charter and the license granted to the company in a particular state do not confer the right to do business in any other state. It must be admitted to do business by the authorities of each state in which it seeks to do business. However, by the operation of state comity the entrance into other states is usually a simple matter. Some companies do business in all the states; some confine themselves to certain sections of the country. The new company gradually organizes its business in other states, usually in the adjoining states first, but entering as quickly as possible the states of dense population.

The Regulation of Fraternal Insurance. — The process of organizing a fraternal insurance company is somewhat different from that of the ordinary stock or mutual company. It has been stated that efforts have been made for several years to bring this class of companies under more strict control as to their organization and operation. The officials of such companies and the national associations of insurance commissioners have agreed upon a bill which has been enacted into law in some states and which is pending in other states.

The chief provisions of this bill are as follows: (a) a definition is given of fraternal benefit societies; (b) the reserve for extended and paid up protection and withdrawal equities must be accumulated and maintained under a table of mortality not lower than the American Experience Table on a 4 per cent basis; (c) membership is limited to persons between 16 and 60 years of age who have been examined by a legally qualified physician; (d) no society can be incorporated in or admitted to the state in the future which does not provide for stated periodical contributions sufficient to provide for meeting the mortuary obligations when valued upon the basis of the National Fraternal Congress of Mortality or any higher standard with interest assumption not more than 4 per cent; (e) the investments of funds must be in such securities as are permitted for the investment of the assets of regular life insurance companies; (f) there must be at least seven incorporators of the proposed company; (g) the organization must be completed within a year, during which time a bond is held by the insurance commissioner and a certain minimum amount of insurance must be written; (h) annual reports must be made to the state commissioner of insurance, and beginning with 1914 a report of the valuation of policies must be sent to each beneficiary; (*i*) if the valuation of the certificates on December 31, 1917, shall show that the present value of future net contributions together with the admitted assets is less than 90 per cent of the present value of the promised benefits, the deficit shall be reduced at a certain rate at each succeeding triennial valuation until it is removed, and in case of failure, proceedings for dissolution of the organization shall be instituted. By the preceding provisions and others, fraternal insurance is brought under more careful control with a view of assuring that all the obligations will be met. Exemptions are made in the case of certain societies.

Internal Operation of a Company. — The internal operation of the company after once organized is much the same as that of any other corporation which has to do with collecting, investing, and disbursing sums of money. The board of directors has complete general supervision of the company. It chooses the president and the other principal officers. The board divides itself into various standing committees, which usually act for the board as a whole. The number of committees varies in different companies, but there is usually a committee on death claims, one on agencies, one on accounts, one on finance, and an executive committee. These committees meet as often as is necessary. They listen to reports from the heads of the departments over which they have supervision. At stated intervals the whole board meets to ratify the action of committees, to discuss general policies of management and other matters which pertain to the business of the company. The board of directors delegates very large powers of an executive nature to the president. At most it lays down policies or adopts them upon the suggestion of the president and then intrusts the details of execution to the principal officers. The president of an insurance company is, therefore, an important official. He needs to be well informed on financial matters, and at least well enough informed in the work of the other departments to make intelligent recommendations to them and interpret the results secured. He is a counselor for the board of directors, a director for the subordinate officials, and a protector for the policy holders.

Officials of a Company. — There may be several vice presidents, each of whom may be at the head of a department, the work of which is to be described later. The treasurer is responsible for the prompt collection and safe-keeping of all funds and the oversight of all investments. The investments are not made by the treasurer, but by the committee of the board of directors or the president acting for or with the board or with the committee. The secretary has supervision and charge of the records of the company and the correspondence. The actuary has charge of all the subjects which pertain to premiums. He prepares premium tables, tables of loans and surrender values, calculates the reserves and dividends and the mortality experience of the company. Many special calculations are annually required in a large company as to premiums, results secured on past policies, and the preparation of gain

and loss exhibits.   All this work is done by the actuary.
He is the one indispensable official to guarantee that
the business is scientifically conducted.   His recommendations may not always be followed, but if they
were, it would go far towards guaranteeing safe insurance.   The medical director has charge of the force of
medical examiners.   He selects the physicians to act as
the company's examiners and is the final authority on the
desirability of a risk from a physical standpoint.   All examinations made by the local examiner are submitted
for his final approval.   He advises the officers and board
of directors on all matters pertaining to his department.

Departments of a Company. — The work of an insurance company may be divided into the following departments: executive, medical, actuarial, legal, financial,
and agency.   Additional departments, such as accounting, statistical, and investment, may be found.   The
work of some of these departments has previously been
described sufficiently, but others demand a more detailed consideration.

The legal department concerns itself with the conduct
of cases before the courts, arising out of contested claims,
foreclosures of mortgages, clearing titles to property,
and a wide variety of other subjects.   It must also see
that bonds are properly drawn up, that the security
supporting them is good, that the policies state pre-
cisely what is intended, and that notes are properly
drawn.   It keeps the officials informed as to the character of old and new laws enacted by the legislatures
affecting insurance.

The statistical department not only tabulates the

varied experiences of the company on insured lives and on its investments, but it also interprets these statistics in order that the future conduct of the business may be improved from the experience of the past. The deductions made are of especial value to the executive and actuarial departments.

The agency department is one of the most important of all departments, for it is the one which secures the business for the company. At the head of this department is a superintendent of agents, who is sometimes a vice president of the company.

The Agency Force. — Several plans of organizing the agency force are in vogue: (*a*) the general agency system; (*b*) the direct agency system; (*c*) the cashier and branch office system; (*d*) the brokerage system. It was the early practice of insurance companies, in England and America, to pay certain commissions to any one who induced a person to insure with the company. A class of persons was thus encouraged to enter the business, who considered the interests neither of the company nor of the policyholder, and very grave evils developed. No dignity was given to the work, and insurance suffered undeserved criticism on account of the irresponsible and dishonest persons who sold it. Some improvement was made when the companies employed persons, either on a fixed or contingent salary, who should appoint agents to solicit insurance on a commission or a salary; but this did not solve the problem, because the local agent was not definitely controlled by the company and the general agent was often not adequately rewarded.

The General Agency. — The general agency system is established by giving exclusive control of a territory to a general agent. He organizes the business of soliciting insurance in his field, by appointing agents for whose conduct he is responsible. He is often required to produce a certain amount of business. He receives a commission on all business written in the territory as well as a renewal commission on the business, that is, a certain per cent of each premium when it is paid to the company. There is a tendency among companies, however, to permit a general agent to write business in any territory, and where exclusive territory is granted, it is usually of a small area. The objection to the general agency system as it developed in the past was that the general agent with the exclusive territory was often tempted not to develop the business after he had secured an income from past business. If he is required to make each year a percentage increase in business, the results secured may be quite as good as under any other system. The direct agency system is that in which the agents are appointed directly from the home office, are directed from it, and report to it. The merit of this system is in the centralization of authority at the Home Office. In this system exclusive territory may or may not be assigned.

The Broker. — The brokerage system, which has come to be of less importance in life insurance, is also one of direct contracts and no exclusive territory and no renewal commissions. The cashier and branch office system is the one in which branch offices are established at different points in charge of a manager and a cashier.

The manager secures local agents upon terms over which he usually has some discretion, but all contracts with local agents must usually be approved by the Home Office. The manager is allowed a certain sum for office expenses. All payments on policies in the territory of the branch office are made through it, or if sent to the Home Office by the policyholder, are credited to the account of the particular branch office.

The Commission. — The agent is paid either on a commission basis, that is, a certain per cent of the cost of the policy to the insured person, or upon a salary, or upon a combination of these two methods.

The commission may be a percentage only of the first year's premium, or it may be in addition a certain less percentage of several succeeding years' premiums. The latter is called a renewal commission. In the earlier contracts which agents had with the companies this renewal commission extended over a long period of years. It is now commonly limited to the first seven years of the policy. The commission also varies with the kind of policy. That is, the larger the cost per thousand dollars of insurance the less the rate of commission. This does not mean that the commission varies with the age of the insured, but that there is an attempt to equalize the commission to the agent on the different kinds of policies which he sells. Concretely, this means that usually an agent will receive no more for selling one policy costing $50 to an individual, age 30, than for selling another policy costing $35 to another individual age 30. This is done by varying the rate of commission, and has for its special object the prevention of the agent selling policies wholly for the sake of the commission, since the best policy for an individual is that one which is in harmony with his family obligations and his financial ability.

Selling Insurance. — A brief discussion may be made in conclusion about the business of selling insurance. We have seen that the old type of agent was simply interested in bringing a prospective purchaser to the company, which then insured or rejected him. The agent was a solicitor. He accepted the contract as made by the company and did not concern himself with its terms. He knew little about its terms and cared less. He was simply interested in getting his commission. A new type of agent has largely displaced this earlier type. He is not only familiar with the terms of the contract, but very frequently knows considerable about the insurance business. He also feels a personal responsibility to the company to produce for it desirable business, and to the policyholder to sell him honestly a policy suited to his economic and social position. He takes a legitimate pride in his work, for he comes to appreciate its immense social value. He is continually appealing and urging men to do their known duty. His work is, speaking generally, no longer to convince men of the desirability or excellence of insurance, but rather to persuade them to purchase what they need. However, the most successful agent is not necessarily that one who writes the greatest number of policies, but rather that one who sells to the greatest number of individuals, policies which are suited to them. Doubtless many agents have not yet acted up to their responsibility in this particular, but no young man who expects to build up an enduring insurance business can adopt a safer plan than that of determining that he will be completely sincere in his honest efforts to place the kind and amount of insurance where it is needed. The characteristics required to become a successful salesman of insurance are not entirely peculiar to this business. He must above all be energetic. He should have the qualities of originality and leadership to a considerable degree. He should be a good judge of human nature and be able to express clearly his thoughts in a concise and forceful manner. He needs to have sufficient analytical power to determine the significance of the terms of his company's contracts and those of his competitors. He should thoroughly believe in the business and the excellence of his company. As the knowledge of insurance and its practices become more widely diffused, a higher type of agent will be necessary, for there is no immediate prospect that men will voluntarily purchase insurance without the activity of the agent. For the young man who has these qualities, the insurance business offers a most excellent present and future field, not only from the standpoint of remuneration, but also because it is a business which brings satisfaction to the conscience of the individual. In many cases in old age is a man led to consider the character of his life work, and few find greater satisfaction than the man who has spent an honest life in the insurance field. His work has been constructively social.

Insurance Organizations. — Agents and officials of companies have formed various organizations for the purpose of mutual benefit and for the education of the public on the subject of insurance. The best known of the agency organizations is the National Association of Life Underwriters, which has done and is doing a splendid work, both in securing an improved *esprit de corps* among agents and also in various public activities, such as engaging in educational campaigns to secure on the part of the public a better understanding of insurance. Among other organizations of insurance officials may be mentioned the Association of Life Insurance Presidents and the American Life Insurance Association. Annual meetings are held, at which matters of general interest are discussed. An organization which has done much to further scientific insurance is the American Actuarial Society.

In concluding this chapter a brief discussion may be given upon that much-mooted question of how' to compare companies. This question frequently arises, especially in connection with the discussion of the merits of stock and mutual companies. It may at once be stated that in the present condition of insurance knowledge on the part of the public an attempt to decide the merits between two particular companies is usually an impossible task for the average person. The old maxim that " a man is judged by the company he keeps " may be reversed and profitably used by the average purchaser of insurance in the form of a general rule that an insurance company and its policies may be roughly judged by the men it keeps, that is, its agents. No amount of investigation of the most detailed character will enable the conclusion to be drawn that a particular company is and has been the " best " company. There is no best company any more than there is any best policy.

There are, however, some general criteria which may be applied in judging a company.

How to Compare Companies. — First, as regards the size of a company If a company has in force that volume of business which is sufficient to prevent marked fluctuations in the rate of mortality and investments, no great importance need necessarily be attached to the size. In many respects the business of insurance is peculiarly subject to the law of decreasing costs; that is, additional units of supply or business can be produced with a decreasing cost per unit. This is due chiefly to the character of the fixed expenses. That is, for a company to do any business it is necessary to have an office, an office force, and an agency force. With a given volume of business, there are certain expenses, and this volume of business might well increase twice without expenses increasing twofold. There may come a time in the increase of business when expenses will increase at a more rapid rate than business.

However, with the advance which has been made in business organizations during recent years, the point at which a large insurance company's expenses necessarily begin to increase more rapidly than the volume of business is doubtless very remote.

It must be remembered, however, that the favorable results from the operation of the principle of decreasing cost with increasing units produced arise frequently from the side of bargaining gains rather than from the lower specific producing costs. There is little in the operation of an insurance company which corresponds to the bargaining aspect of an industrial organization, producing goods for sale. A very large insurance company cannot secure its agents any cheaper than a moderately large company. Nor can it secure any more profitable investments for its funds. Nor does it operate under a different mortality experience. Whatever advantage it may have will arise from a more complete utilization of its equipment or organization; that is, the plant is more nearly operated to its maximum capacity. Nevertheless, there are certain potential economies for the smaller company. The close personal supervision possible in a moderately large company may result in a low unit cost in producing the service. After all due allowance is made for the remarkable progress which has been made for improvements in business organization, the fact remains that to secure this potential efficiency in large plants it is necessary to have, as the directing administrative officials, men of unusual ability. Such men are not common, and a man of less ability may well secure an equal or greater efficiency in a smaller company. It is therefore impossible to be dogmatic as regards the respective advantages in costs of the large and small company. If the data were available for a complete analysis of the cost to policyholders in very large and in moderately large companies, it would probably show that low cost could not be predicated exclusively either of large or small companies. In insurance as contrasted with industrial concerns there are no large number of new plans, processes, or inventions to be discovered and put into operation. It is largely a question of good judgment, skill, and foresight in applying ideas known to all competitors. The personal factor, therefore, is all important in administering an insurance company, as it expresses itself as a factor in costs of the commodity.

Second. The character of the business and the expense of placing it on the books is more important than mere size. If under the stress of competition and the ambition to make a strong showing of early success, a company insures a large number of poor risks for which it pays a high cost, the results are certain to show themselves. In life insurance it is especially true that " the business which pays is the business that stays." This is true both from the standpoint of the policyholders and the stockholders.

Third. Emphasis is often laid in comparing companies upon the respective assets. As an insurance company grows older and increases its business the assets become larger. A strong young company may be as strong or stronger than an old large company. No deduction can safely be made simply from the amount of the assets. It will later be shown how a company makes advance collections in its premiums, and these remain in trust with the company. A company, therefore, with a decreasing rate of new business might have increasing assets.

Fourth. Much emphasis, especially in former years, was placed upon the amount of the surplus which one company had as compared with another. This surplus in a life insurance company represents the excess of accumulated collections over future obligations. The chief interest of a prospective policyholder in a company is in the payment of the face of the policy, and if a company ,has funds according to the mortality table and the prevailing interest rate to do this, he is not particularly interested in this surplus. Indeed, he might interpret this large surplus to the disadvantage of the company that he is comparing with another. He might inquire in case it is a mutual company why it was not returned to the policyholders, since it resulted from overcharging them for their insurance. If it is a stock company, he may consider it a proof that the company is overcharging on its policies and that the stockholders have had and are enjoying large dividends.

There is very little reason for a company, either stock or mutual, to accumulate a large surplus. The chief justifications for it are found in that it may be used to equalize dividends to stockholders over a series of years, or to equalize the so-called dividends or returns to policyholders. Its accumulations may be to make up for any unexpected losses from unfavorable investments and for any unusual mortality, the last being, however, a contingency that is very remote in the present days of accurate mortality knowledge.

Fifth. There is often an attempt to compare companies by dividends or returns of annual sums which are made to policyholders. Great care needs to be exercised in making such a comparison in order that the amount of the two premiums, the length of time the policy has been in existence, and the benefits of the two policies may be on a parity. In this connection great care is needed in comparing the " actual cost " of a participating and a non-participating policy. It is not a valid comparison to deduct the total dividends received from the company by a policyholder under a participating policy from the total amount he has paid in and compare this amount with the total amount paid in under a non-participating policy. The interest accumulations on the dividends paid by the company must be considered. If dividends are taken by the individual, they are potentially interest bearing, and if left with the company, they increase the face of the policy to be paid upon its maturity.

The Gain and Loss Exhibit. — Sixth. The Gain and Loss Exhibit. This is perhaps the most generally used method of comparing companies, although, as has often been shown, it is capable of being so interpreted as to confuse rather than to enlighten. This Gain and Loss Exhibit is a statutory requirement in many states. It purports to show the profits and losses on each kind of business for the year which affects the surplus. As usually prepared the exhibit has four columns. First, the percentage of expenses incurred to the loading in the premiums; second, the percentage of net interest earned to the interest required to be earned; third, the percentage of the actual to the expected mortality; and, fourth, the percentage of reserves returned on Surrenders and Lapses of Policies. The first percentage is affected by the rapidity of growth of the company, its age, the character of its business, whether participating or non-participating, the plan upon which its policies were written; and several other factors. The second percentage is affected by the basis upon which the business is written; that is, whether it has business on a 3 per cent or 4 per cent interest accumulation basis. The third percentage depends somewhat upon the age of the business, the recently organized company always having a low actual, as compared with its expected mortality since it is enjoying the benefit of selection. The fourth percentage is also affected by the age of the business and its character. It must also be understood that any one year's Gain and Loss Exhibit is a dangerous method of comparing companies, since fluctuations in the respective percentages from year to year among a large number of companies are likely to be very marked.

For the average policyholder who is not versed in insurance matters the easier methods of comparing percentages of expense to premium income or to total income, the average rate of interest earned by two companics, and the distribution of their investments, the character of their officials and agents, together with the character of the state laws of the two companies, is the only safe method to use.

REFERENCES

Dicksee, L. R., and Blain, H. E.   Office Organization and Management.

Annals American Academy of Political Science, Vol. XXVI, pp. 192-203, 243-255.

Graham, William J.   The Romance of Life Insurance, Chaps. VI, XIII.

Report of Joint Committee of Assembly of New York, pp. 358-362, 388-393.

The Story of Life Insurance, Chaps. V, VI, VII.   Burton J. Hendrick.

Journal of Insurance Institute, Vol. X, Vol. VII, p. 267.

CHAPTER VI

THE POLICY

The Policy Defined. — The policy is the written agreement or contract between the insurer and the insured. It is an offer made by the insurer and accepted by the applicant, who thereby becomes the insured. The medical and inspection departments of the company, after investigating the physical and financial condition of the applicant, certify their findings to the executive department of the company, which then offers to insure the applicant on such terms as the previously disclosed findings warrant. Ordinarily the contract is not completed until the policy has been delivered to the applicant, accepted during his good health, and the first premium paid by him. In some cases at the time of securing the application a binding receipt is given for the premium then paid. This is an advantage to the applicant in that the policy is in force as soon as issued, although it may not be in the possession of the applicant. It is an advantage to the company in that the applicant cannot refuse to accept the policy, since he has already paid the first year's premium.

Parties to the Contract. — There are usually three parties interested in the contract: the insurer, the one who assumes the obligation to pay the insurance;

the insured, the one upon whose life the insurance is written; and the beneficiary, the one to whom the insurance is payable. The beneficiary may be, under some forms of the contract, the insured. The state is also interested in seeing that the terms of the contract are fair and that both parties observe' its terms.

General Classification of Policies. — Life insurance policies are apparently of so many different kinds that beginning students of the subject are likely to be confused; further study of insurance, however, discloses the fact that the seemingly large number of different kinds of policies can all be reduced to a few simple forms. The contracts seem to be numerous because of the many combinations of the simple forms.

Policies may be classified, first and most fundamentally, according to the manner in which they mature. First, life policies, that is, policies which mature only upon death and whose premiums are ordinarily paid annually throughout life.

Second, limited-payment life policies, which mature at death, but the premium-paying period is completed at the end of 10, 15, 20, 25, or 30 years.

Third, term policies, which provide temporary insurance, that is, insurance payable only if death occurs during a specified period, which is usually 5, 10, 15, or 20 years. Term policies may be renewable for successive equal periods, or they may be non-renewable. A yearly renewable term policy is frequently issued with increasing premiums and hence becomes a natural premium whole-life policy. Renewable term policies may be renewed without a medical examination at the close of the period. Term insurance may be for increasing amounts, as in the return premium feature when in case of death within a certain period the company agrees to pay the premium up to the time of death in addition to the face of the policy. Term insurance may be for decreasing amounts, as when taken out to cover a mortgage, which is reduced year by year. The insurance decreases with the amount of the mortgage. In order to secure funds for expenses, companies may write a regular policy on the preliminary term plan, that is, make a twenty-payment policy a one-year term policy, followed by a nineteen-payment life policy. This subject will be discussed further when we treat of the premium and the reserve.

Fourth, endowment policies, which mature in case of death during a specified period, or in case of survival to the end of that period. This policy is a combination of a term policy and a pure endowment policy, the latter of which pays only in case of survival. Endowment policies are usually for quinquennial periods of 15, 20, 25, 30 years or mature at quinquennial ages, such as endowments at age 50, 55, 60, 65, etc. A double endowment pays, for example, $2000 in case of survival or $1000 payable in case of death, and a semi-endowment pays $500 in case of survival or $1000 payable in case of death. Endowment policies may be paid for by annual premiums until the end of the endowment period or they may be paid for by a limited number of premiums, that is, by ten premiums, fifteen premiums, or twenty premiums. In this event they are called, for example, a ten-payment twenty-year endowment policy.

Policies may be classified in the second place on the basis of dividends, that is, participating policies, those that share in the earnings of the company, and non-participating policies, those which do not share in the earnings of the company and therefore have a lower premium than the participating policies of the same kind and for the same age. The participating policies may participate annually, quinquennially, or at longer periods, although the longer periods have been forbidden in many states. The dividends may be used to reduce the premium, to buy additional insurance, to hasten the endowment, to shorten the premium-paying period, to accumulate interest with the company for the policy-holder, or they may be taken in cash.

In the third place, policies may be classified on the basis of the kind of premium, that is, those in which the premium is a natural premium, a single premium, or the level annual premium. In this classification, the first is of least importance, for few policies are written on this plan. Policies in assessment societies may be written with premiums below or above the natural premium, although this premium in theory is the basis of the assessment plan of insurance. Some policies are written with a comparatively low premium for the first five years and a larger premium thereafter; others are written with a large premium to begin with, and the premium is reduced by fixed amounts at stated periods thereafter.

Again policies may be classified on the basis of the character of the settlement. That is, the policy may provide at maturity for a cash settlement, for installments, for bonds, for annuities, or for continuous installments. It must not be understood, however, that it is intended to convey the idea that each one of these plans is mutually exclusive of all others. As a matter of fact, they are not. For example, one may purchase by a single premium a twenty-year endowment policy, the settlement of which may be in cash, in installments, or in annuities.

Again any ordinary form of policy may be purchased on the non-participating plan. Many other different combinations of the previous classifications may be made.

The most important classification of policies is that of life, term, limited-payment life, and endowment policies. This is the classification ordinarily meant when a person speaks of the different kinds of policies. The many different classes of policies are usually some form of these four kinds of policies.

Special Policies. — Some of the more important special policies may be described. One of these policies which is becoming of decreasing importance is the joint-life policy. The face of such a policy is paid upon the first death — that is, of either husband or wife. Or a joint policy may be purchased by partners in business which is payable at the first death of one of the partners in the business. There are very decided objections to this policy, both from the standpoint of the company and the insured. Companies usually prefer to write single policies on each life of the persons desiring protection. In the case of husband and wife, if the latter die first, the husband may not then be insurable at this latter date, and yet he may have obligations, such as young children, which would demand that he have insurance. If each had carried individual policies, all the benefits from a joint policy would have been realized and in addition the children would be better cared for in the event of the death of the husband, subsequent to that of the wife. In the case of partners in business, the death of any partner terminates the insurance, — the protection, — but if there are more than two members in the firm, there still exists a reason for insurance as a firm asset. If a partner withdraws from the firm, there is no reason for the further existence of the joint partnership policy, whereas if there had been individual policies, the withdrawal of a member of the firm would have simply involved the change of the beneficiary.

Joint-life Policies may be written as a Whole-life, a Limited-payment Life, a Term, or an Endowment Contract.

Corporation Insurance. — Another special policy which is increasing in number and importance is the Corporation Policy. This is an extension of the protection of insurance from that of a family protection to that of protection to business. It is a form either of partnership insurance or of corporation insurance. In the latter case the corporation takes out a policy on the life of its president or some other valuable officer or employee from whose death the organization would suffer considerable loss. A successful business is often dependent upon a manager who has organized and directs it and the loss entailed by his death corresponds

M

somewhat to that occasioned by a fire destroying the physical plant except that it may be more permanent in its results. The proceeds of the insurance policy give to the corporation a fund which enables it to make good any losses due to the death of the skilled manager during the succeeding period of readjusting its organization. The cost of these corporation policies is paid from the funds of the corporation, since the policy is the property of the company and not of the individual who is insured. The policy may be used as a basis of loans, either from the insurance company or as a form of collateral for loans from other sources. There is little doubt that this form of insurance will continue to increase in importance as the relation of insurance to business is understood, for the complexity of business organization and its dependence upon credit become continually greater.

Group Insurance. — Another special form of policy which is of recent and increasing importance is the Group Insurance Policy. This form of insurance is an outgrowth of the modern industrial system and the increasing disposition of employers to aid their employees. Under this policy the employer may pay a part of the premium, as, for example, one half, or he may pay none of it or all of it. The insurance company usually prefers the last-named arrangement and insists in all cases that the employer at least be interested in the plan and have some control over his employees. The policy is usually written on the one-year renewable term plan and may be for a level amount on each employee or for an amount of insurance increasing with the length of service of the employee. A medical examination may or may not be required. The group insured may include all the employees of a firm if there is no great difference in the hazards of their employment, or it may be confined to a more homogeneous group. In any case the group must be sufficiently large for the law of averages to work. It has been stated with considerable presumption of validity that any large number of individuals selected at random, as for example those passing a particular point on a much-traveled street, could be insured, and the results would approximate those of an insured group selected by the medical examination. It must be apparent that in any large group of employees in a modern industrial plant there has been a certain kind of selective process which may safely be accepted for insurance purposes except in so far as the hazardous character of the employment interferes with the working of the normal law of mortality. The ignorant and physically inferior lives either have not secured the employment or have been eliminated, so that continuous employment gives proof of a normal bodily and mental vigor. Experience under this form of insurance is too recent to make dogmatic statements as to the results, but what evidence is available shows that the mortality results are supernormal. There are marked economies in writing such policies, especially where there is no medical examination. There is little or no soliciting expense, no medical reports, a saving in book-keeping, postage, and in many other administrative expenses, all of which makes it possible to write the policy at a per capita rate less than for an ordinary single policy upon the same individual. This fact becomes of especial importance to the employee in those cases where the employer pays a part of the premium. These policies should not be confused with the ordinary accident insurance policies or with the various forms of workmen's compensation and employer's liability insurance. They are the regular life insurance policies and perform the double function of protecting the families of the employees and rewarding efficient and continued service. The policy as written contains most of the provisions of the regular policy, such as disability benefits and a conversion clause; that is, benefits in case of permanent disability and provision by which it can be converted into a regular individual policy in the event, for example, that the worker leaves the particular employment. Changes in the number of employees in the business are provided for in the group insurance policy by a provision for the readjustment of the premium paid or due.

There is also a return premium policy in which not only the face of the policy is paid, but also a certain portion or all of each premium is returned if death occurs within a specified time. This manifestly calls for an extra premium, and the objections to such a policy are evident. There are many other forms of policies, but the more important of them will be considered in the discussion of the method of settlement of policies in the latter part of the chapter.

Analysis of the Policy. — In attempting an analysis of the policy contract it is difficult to make statements which apply in all cases to the different policies now in force. This difficulty arises from the fact that the insurance business is a subject for regulation by the numerous states and not the national government, and consequently the policy contract is theoretically and actually in many cases what the various legislatures choose to make it. Much has been done in the way of state uniformity, but much yet remains to be done. In many particulars little of state comity has been recognized. The characteristics of the state legislation as pertaining to the policy contract were so changed after 1905, as a result of the insurance investigation, that a description in general terms of the policy provisions previous to that date and an outline of the chief requirement adopted since 1905 as they apply to the contract are given. Let not the reader forget, however, that we are attempting to state what is true of different and independent states' regulations and also what is true of several times that number of insurance companies, for the policy contract is in part what the different legislatures say it shall be, and in part what the different companies wish it to be.

Early Form of the Policy. — The policy contract in the early history of insurance had what now seem very harsh provisions. The insured had practically no privileges. The contract was a whole-life policy contract which was absolutely null and void, not only for failure to pay premiums, but also for changes in place of residence and occupation. Companies could easily avoid payment of the policies because warranties and not representations were the rule, with the consequence that many of the insured lost the result of their payments for many years, since warranties must be absolutely true and representations need be only substantially true. Partly as a result of the harsh terms of this contract the whole-life policy as a form of insurance came into an ill repute from which it has not yet recovered. This form of policy deserves greater popularity and will certainly have it when the purchasers of insurance learn to appreciate its merits. The average agent frequently does not make much effort to sell this policy at present because he often does not recognize its value, and also because it is usually easier to sell some other form of a policy and because his commission is in some cases larger on the larger premium policies.

The historical development of the form of the policy was a whole-life policy, a limited payment life policy, and an endowment policy. In time there was developed a form of policy which provided for an annuity to the beneficiary only after the death of the insured. But this had the shortcoming that the beneficiary might die first and the insured would have paid premiums, — as he erroneously argued, — on which nothing was given in return. This caused the installment plan to be devised, under which the proceeds of insurance policies are paid during a stated period of years, usually from five to twenty. This form was later modified so that not only the installments certain were paid during the period provided, but also payments of equal amounts were made to the beneficiary if the beneficiary lived beyond the period named in the installment clause.

The Group Justice of the Policy. — When it is stated that the insurance contract is an unfair one because the insured is not bound to continue as a party to it while the insurer is so bound, it must be remembered that the insurer has laid down in the contract the conditions — or has accepted the conditions as fixed by the state — under which alone the insured may discontinue as a party to the contract. Life insurance contracts, like all other contracts, are construed by the courts against those who frame them, on the theory that the makers of the contract have drawn them in their own interests. If there is an apparent conflict between clauses in the body of the contract and clauses attached or written, the latter takes precedence over the former. It is customary for the contract to contain a clause which specifically states that the company is not bound by statements of the agent; that the printed contract is the sole contract between the company and the insured. Undoubtedly some purchasers of insurance have been deceived or misled by the statements of agents, but recourse does not ordinarily lie in an action against the company for statements made by the agent. It is the duty of the buyer to acquaint himself with the terms of the contract before he accepts it. It may well happen that the buyer of legal reserve insurance will not get what he wants, but there is little danger that he will not get the worth of his money in these days of competition among the old-line insurance companies and the state regulation of their business. Less than 1 per cent of the claims against insurance companies are contested in the courts by the companies. It is also significant that the companies win more than 75 per cent of these contested claims, for no company will contest a claim on trivial grounds.

Age Limits. — While it is not a part of the contract it is a principle of all companies to establish the minimum and maximum age below or beyond which they will not write policies. The lower limits vary from 15 to 21 years of age and the upper from 60 to 75. The object is to confine the premium-paying period to the productive years of life. The so-called investment policies are sold by some companies after age 60 of the applicant, and children's policies are sold by industrial companies.

Privileges in the Policy. — It must not be inferred that the privileges, or the liberal provisions, as they are called in present policies, were adopted wholly as a result of legislative compulsion. In fact, the liberalization of the policy is not due primarily to legislative enactment, but to the following causes: first, in the early days of insurance no data had been accumulated to determine conclusively that the proposed plans could be successfully applied. To guarantee solvency as completely as possible, absolute forfeiture was provided in many cases in order that the insurance fund might be augmented; extra premiums were required for a change of occupation and residence, even though the latter was in the same latitude; premiums paid in were forfeited in case of suicide, death at the hands of justice, or in the military or naval service, or if the statements made in the application were untrue in any respect. When experience disclosed that many of these restrictions were unnecessary and the decision of courts failed in some cases to recognize their validity, the companies gradually began to omit the harsher restrictions. Second, as insurance companies became more numerous, the competition thus brought into existence did more than all the legislation to liberalize the insurance contract. The beneficent effects of competition have clearly shown themselves in the case of the insurance business. Companies have so vied with each other in making the policy contract attractive to the purchaser that it may be increasingly true that one of the chief functions of state supervision will be to compel companies to keep their liberality within the bounds of safety. The above statement seeks in no manner to minimize the actual accomplishments of legislative enactments and state supervision, but the chief work in liberalizing the contract has been voluntarily done by the companies as a matter of business. The best work of the state has been in establishing standards of solvency and compelling, by continuous supervision, the companies to maintain these standards.

Effect of State Regulation. — Since Insurance is a subject for the regulation of each state and not of the federal government, the legislation of any one important state may force a company to adopt in conformity to such action a uniform practice in all the states in which it writes insurance. Suppose Ohio should require that a certain provision be printed in every life insurance contract issued or delivered to a citizen of that state. This means that all life insurance companies doing business in Ohio must have printed one set of policies for

Ohio and another set for other states, or it must include this provision in all its policies. If the requirement is one which, if not included in policies in other states, means a marked saving, the company may decide to pay the extra printing bill. If it is an important reform, it is likely to be adopted by other states, and the company will very probably incorporate it voluntarily in its policies. However, in the actual practice of insurance the policy requirements of less than a dozen states practically decide the terms of the printed contract. Competition of other companies from various states is also a powerful force in bringing about general uniformity in the terms of the printed policy.

The policy, after having been granted by the executive department of the company, does not, as a general rule, become binding on the company until it has been accepted by the insured in good health and the first premium has been paid by him. A receipt called " the binding receipt " may be issued by the agent for the premium which is paid at the time of soliciting the application. . This binds the company to pay the face of the policy as soon as it is issued.

Chief Provisions of the Policy. — Premiums are paid " in advance." Premiums are not in reality paid in advance, for the purchaser — the insured — secures possession of his commodity — protection — as soon as he receives and pays for the policy. So long as the insured has any surplus payment with the company available to continue the policy, any later neglect or refusal to pay the annual premiums due will not cause the protection to cease. The protection will be continued in the form of extended insurance to that future date which the payments that he has already made will purchase.

The title to the policy may rest either in the insured, his estate, or in the beneficiary, depending upon the conditions upon which the policy is written. The insured may make the policy payable to himself or his estate. He may later make some person or organization a beneficiary. The contract may also permit the insured to change the beneficiary at will, in which case the beneficiary has only a contingent interest in the policy.

The policy may also be assigned, but in this case there are definite restrictions. An insurance policy, as contrasted with most forms of personal property, cannot absolutely be transferred from person to person for the purpose of conferring a valid title upon these third parties. The policy is a personal contract between the insurer and the insured. It is a " chose in action," that is, a thing of which the owner has not the possession but which he has a right to recover by means of a suit or action at law. If a beneficiary is named in the policy, an assignment is not valid in most cases until the consent of the beneficiary is obtained. Likewise, the insurer may be an interested party in an assignment and must usually give consent; otherwise, policies might come into the possession of third parties who would be interested in hastening the time of their payment. The company, however, assumes no responsibility for the validity of the assignment. It pays to that one who is judged at the time of maturity the owner. Assignment always assumes some kind of a consideration. It may be for a loan granted, or in the case of marriage as a free gift for the consideration of love and affection. In the latter case, however, the more common form of procedure is to change the beneficiary, and the assignment is of present importance chiefly as a transfer for a pecuniary obligation incurred by the insured for a short period.

Insurable Interest. — The laws of the greater number of states do not make the proceeds of the insurance policy an asset for meeting the debts of the insured, unless it is made payable to his estate, or unless possibly the creditors can prove that an insolvent debtor took out the insurance after insolvency with fraudulent intent. In this connection the question of what constitutes an insurable interest arises. It may be stated that this interest exists in all cases when the proposed beneficiary is dependent upon the insured for support, or is his creditor, or would suffer a monetary loss by the death of the insured. Mere affection or mental anguish does not constitute a basis for an insurable interest. Nor does relationship in itself establish an insurable interest unless, as is often the case, the relationship involves legal claims. A brother may, for example, have an insurable interest in a brother if he has advanced money for his education. The underlying principle of the insurance contract is indemnity, that is to say, it is a compensation for a loss sustained. It therefore follows as a consequence that the idea of profit is excluded so far as the insured is concerned, and the idea of pecuniary interest included so far as the one having an insurable interest is concerned.

The amount of the insurance is ordinarily a matter to be decided by the company and the insured, but if the amount of the insurance taken out by a creditor on the life of his debtor is far in excess of the creditor's claims, the contract may be declared a wager by the courts and therefore be illegal.

Many companies for reasons described in a previous chapter limit the amount of insurance which they will write in a single policy on an individual life. This sum varies from $10,000 to $1,000,000 or more. In some companies when a large amount on a single life is granted, it is the practice to reinsure a part of it in other companies.

Beneficiary Right and Insurable Interest. — It must be understood that there is a difference between an insurable interest and the right, legal or otherwise, of the insured to select his beneficiary. The first has to do with the right of A to take out insurance on B in favor of himself or to have B insure himself in favor of A. The second has to do with the right of B to select his beneficiary. It is becoming increasingly the practice of companies and courts to permit the insured, if he pays his premiums from his personal income, to select whomever or whatever he pleases as his beneficiary, since ordinarily a person always has an insurable interest in his own life. This practice is but in harmony with the general principle that one has a right to do with his own as he chooses, so long as he does not injure others or himself in the disposition which he makes of it. However, neither the companies nor the courts could afford to encourage crime by permitting an individual to take out a policy on the life of another individual in the prolongation of whose life he would not be interested.

When the beneficiary is the wife or a child, the proceeds of the policy are protected by the laws of most states against the claims of the insured's creditors. This is on the theory that the policy creates a trust fund for the family of the policyholder. Where other than such beneficiaries are named, no vested interest resides in others than those who have an insurable interest, that is, hold a pecuniary obligation against the insured.

The disclosures which were made as a result of the investigations of the life insurance business in 1905 led to laws establishing a standard policy in New York, but this soon gave way to standard provisions in the policies. The requirement of standard provisions is now the general rule in most states, and what we have to state further about the policy contract will be included in our description of these standard provisions.

The Disability Clause. — The greater number of life insurance companies in the United States now incorporate in their policies the Disability Clause. This was begun by the Fidelity Mutual Life Insurance Company in 1896. The chief purpose of this clause is to relieve the insured from premium payments and to secure for him the benefits of the insurance when he has suffered an injury or accident or sickness which " disables him from earning a living." This provision resembles somewhat accident and health insurance, but the insertion of the disability clause in a life insurance contract makes this phase of the protection quite different from that granted by health and accident policies. Such last-named policies can be canceled at the close of a year at the option of the company if it gives notice to the insured of the intended termination, whereas in a life policy there is no possibility of such termination. It is argued that such disability insurance is a proper part of life insurance, since the waiving of the premium by the company may be considered an incident to the business of life insurance. That is, it is just as reasonable that premiums shall cease with the loss of earning power by the insured as that premiums shall cease after a stipulated number of years. The disability clause provides in brief that after one year's premium has been paid, and in the event that the insured shall become totally and permanently disabled by bodily injury or disease so that he is incapacitated for life and prevented from pursuing any gainful occupation, the company waives the payment by the insured of future premiums due. It further specifies in most clauses that the loss of both eyes, both hands or feet, or the loss of one hand and foot shall constitute total disability.

In the event of disability the insured may in most companies select one or two options. First, the policy becomes paid up for its face amount and is payable at death, or, second, the policy is paid in an equal number of installments, usually ten or twenty. Some limitation upon this disability benefit is necessary in old age, when it is often difficult, if not impossible to distinguish between permanent disability, due to the stated reasons, and that due to old age. It is therefore common to make the age limit before which the benefit can be claimed, age 60. The additional charge for such a disability benefit has varied from company to company, and in very few cases is it established upon scientific data. Twenty-five cents per $1000 of insurance was adopted by some of the first companies writing the disability clause. The New York Insurance Department has adopted standard disability rates. These rates may be indicated from the following examples. At age twenty for the waiver of ordinary life 3 per cent net premiums per $1000 of insurance in the event of disability before age sixty, the rate is 10 cents; for a twenty-payment net premium at age twenty the addition is 6 cents; at age forty it is 25 cents; and at age fifty-five it is $1.16. These are additions to the net premiums, that is, the premium which is established by the mortality table and assumed interest earning and does not include what is added to this net premium for expenses and other contingencies. Disability statistics show that at the younger ages disability more frequently results in death than at the older ages, when it is likely to be continuous. Unless this condition is guarded against, there will be an adverse selection against the company.

Advantages of the Disability Clause. — This disability clause has increased the attractiveness of life insurance policies and its general incorporation in policies is probably only a question of time. In some states special laws have been enacted to permit the incorporation of such a feature in life insurance policies, since it has been generally considered and so expressed in some laws that an insurance company is prohibited from writing in one policy two kinds of insurance. Some states refused to permit disability clauses to be written, on the ground that it is not a proper form of the life insurance contract.

The Loan Clause. — Another provision in present life insurance policies which has assumed great importance is the loan clause. This clause grants to the policyholder the right to borrow from the insurance company, usually at a specified maximum rate of interest, a certain percentage of the payments which he has made to it. The policyholder makes application to the company for the loan; he, as well as the beneficiary, signs a note and assigns the policy to the company as a security for the loan. Such an extensive use has been made of this benefit that the matter has become a serious one, both for companies and policyholders.

Loans on life insurance policies is a subject which is receiving the earnest attention of life insurance officials and state supervisors of insurance. The granting of loans on policies has had a marked effect already upon the practice of insurance, and it threatens to affect the theory of life insurance.

The present situation is due to legislation, to court decisions, and to the practice of some companies. The loan in its present form was devised by some of the enterprising companies primarily as a desirable selling feature of life insurance. Later the legislatures required by law the granting of the loan. The courts by their interpretation of the insurance contract encouraged the practice of granting loans. Early in the history of

N

life insurance, notes were accepted as a partial payment for the premium. This was done in the belief that future dividends would liquidate the debt, and, when later experience proved this belief false, these notes were consolidated into one note which was made as a loan against the reserve on the policy.

However, it was not until about 1880 that the practice of making loans against the policy was begun. These loans were not necessarily made for premiums due. They were granted on the theory that each policyholder had a basic right, in insurance theory, in law, and in morals, to use in whatever manner he chose, the cash value of his policy, which approximated its reserve value. It assumed that the reserve was divisible at any time into individual reserves, a contention which in strict insurance theory cannot be admitted. It was found that the loan feature in a policy proved an excellent selling device, and the insurance companies willingly or unwillingly adopted it. The Armstrong laws in New York required this feature in all policies sold in that state. Other states, when it was necessary, adopted a similar requirement. Thus, what had originated as a practice of some companies soon became legalized for all companies.

This legislation and company practice were also in harmony with the interpretations which the courts had increasingly placed upon the character of the insurance contract. From the earliest decisions of the courts in both England and the United States, the insurance contract has been held to be one from which the insured could in no manner profit. The underlying assumption of this principle is that the insurance contract is either one of indemnity, as in the case of property, or one primarily for the benefit of a second party, the beneficiary, as in life insurance.

Legal Aspects of the Contract. — The life insurance contract is in strict theory a trilateral contract with the insurer, the insured, and the beneficiary, as the parties to the contract, the rights or benefits of the contract being vested in the beneficiary. It is only by recognition of such a principle that the theory of insurance can be made to work in practice, whatever modifications of the real theory may be found in the present-day practice of insurance. Notwithstanding that the early and late court decisions uphold the theory that the insured should not benefit from the contract, another line of decision has grown up parallel with this which is essentially opposed to it.

That is, the courts have been disposed, especially in later years, to rule that the insurance contract is unilateral. This has been shown not only in interpreting laws requiring a loan to be made upon the policy, but also in permitting a free choice of a beneficiary and a change almost at will of the beneficiary. This is but applying a theory which has come to be more and more adopted by the courts — that insurance is but a species of property. If the contract of insurance thus establishes a property right in the insurance and if this property resides in the insured, he is permitted to do what he pleases with it, just as with any other of his property, so long as no public injury is inflicted thereby. Thus, by classifying insurance in the same category with other kinds of property, the courts have greatly aided in modifying the earlier and more correct idea of what insurance really is.

Therefore, the courts, the legislatures, and the practice of companies have all contributed to encourage loans on policies and to give to existing life insurance transactions many of the general characteristics of any modern business.

Insurance as an institution has come to perform many of the functions of banking and saving institutions. It is frequently asserted by the officials of insurance companies, especially when they are seeking exemption from tax laws or modifications of them, that insurance is not a commercial business; that it is not a business for profit.

The Reason of Loan Clause's Popularity. — The loan privilege, just as the development of the so-called investment policies and many other features of present-day operations, has undoubtedly furthered the sale of policies; but the incorporation of these many attributes has been at a sacrifice, to a greater or less degree, of the fundamental principles of insurance. Insurance is not primarily either a saving or an investment institution. It cannot hope to compete with financial institutions, especially as these institutions become better organized and the people become more intelligent in matters of insurance and investment. Insurance is primarily a means of assuming and distributing risks in order to grant protection. Whatever saving or investment features it may have, are but incidental to the main purpose.

Evidence is not wanting that there is a disposition to return to elementary principles. The present interest in the loan clause is a part of this evidence. The increasing interest in state insurance is another. The reorganization of the fraternal companies on a sound basis may prove a means of bringing insurance practice back to fundamental principles. But the laws of many states, the decision of many courts, and the practice of many companies will need to be revised, if life insurance is to return to first principles and perform its primary service of granting protection to third parties. That is, the normal insurance contract should be a trilateral contract with vested rights in the beneficiary.

How extensive loans on policies have become and the relation of policy loans to the reserve is shown by the following table:

STATISTICS OF COMPANIES REPORTING TO NEW YORK INSURANCE DEPARTMENT

YEAR	SUM OF POLICY LOANS AND PREMIUM NOTES	RATIO POLICY LOANS AND PREMIUM NOTES TO RESERVE PER CENT	YEAR	SUM OF POLICY LOANS AND PREMIUM NOTES	RATIO POLICY LOANS AND PREMIUM NOTES TO RESERVE PER CENT
1888	$18,804,810	3.32	1901	$108,438,671	6.85
1889	19,839,332	3.22	1902	127,927,668	7.36
1890	19,903,242	2.97	1903	158,567,609	8.27
1891	21,053,640	2.90	1904	189,738,779	9.03
1892	22,170,066	2.81	1905	255,568,149	9.83
1893	27,669,171	3.24	1906	265,902,863	10.76
1894	30,839,727	3.38	1907	348,458,980	13.15
1895	35,524,530	3.62	1908	413,265,207	14.61
1896	44,833,176	4.28	1909	446,276,468	14.74
1897	51,962,850	4.65	1910	495,099,854	15.34
1898	57,258,660	4.76	1911	541,789,999	15.71
1899	70,836,554	5.35	1912	587,704,733	16.03
1900	88,500,575	6.13	1913	614,451,877	16.47

There are no satisfactory data for determining the purpose for which loans are made, the time the loans remain outstanding, the expense of making the loans, the relation of loans to lapses, and the kind of policy upon which loans are most numerous. Statistics show that not over 10 per cent of the loans are ever paid.

Causes of Loans. — The number of loans is, as indicated by the preceding tables, responsive to the industrial conditions. This is true not only because the loans are easy to negotiate but also because in many companies the contracts guarantee that the loan will be granted at a rate of interest which is frequently lower than many policyholders could secure from other loaning institutions during a period of " tight money." The very fact that the loan can be secured by filing a request is an inducement for the policyholder to make the loan which he desires, either because he is hard-pressed for ready funds or desires money to take advantage of the low price of securities or the business embarrassment of others.

Objections to Loans. — The objections to the loan privilege are, therefore:

First, it reduces the insurance; that is, the beneficiary's protection is reduced by the amount of the loan. If insurance is primarily for protection, it logically follows that to the extent the loan defeats protection, it is opposed to insurance.

Second, the loan feature in its operation not only promises serious difficulties in the practical administration of insurance, but it is also opposed to the theory of insurance. By granting the loan privilege, the company is forced to keep either in cash or in liquid assets a large amount of its funds. This usually would mean a low interest earning on the funds unless a most extraordinary adjustment of inflow premiums to outflow loans and paid loans could be secured. The only other possible choice which the company has, is to be willing to market its long-time securities when a large volume of loans is demanded. Since this large demand is likely to come when industrial conditions are below normal, it means a sacrifice sale of securities. Thus the practical result is likely to be a reduced net interest earning on investments. Since the interest rate and the mortality rate constitute the foundation of the whole superstructure of insurance, the stability of the structure itself may be weakened.

Third, the loan privilege, as now practiced, denies another fundamental principle of insurance, namely, its mutuality. It assumes that insurance is primarily individualistic; that each one pays a certain sum which does not lose its identity in a general fund for the protection of all the members of the group; that each one may use at any time this personal fund for whatever purpose he pleases. In the reaction against the earlier practice of companies in refusing to give any surrender value when the policyholder failed to pay his due premium, an extreme application has been made of the policyholder's equity in the general fund. The correct reasoning which grants a surrender value is quite different from that which leads to a loan value. A surrender value is given when the individual ceases to continue a member of the group. He withdraws his equity.

He takes out from the whole protection, that protection which up to that date he has purchased. But in the case of a loan, he practically takes out that protection and still remains a member of the group whose existence is making possible the continued protection for all its members. It is individuality amidst mutuality. Insurance cannot concern itself primarily with individuals. It may, from one point of view, often be individually inequitable, but collectively it is always fair and equitable.

It may be urged that a loan is warranted in the case of an individual whose business is threatened with ruin; and that if such aid were not extended, the protection which the business gave to the dependent would be destroyed. Such cases, in which a loan would protect a policeholder's business, may occur; but if there is any one thing against which insurance does protect, it is the vicissitudes of modern business.

When a Loan is Justified. — The one reason most frequently assigned to justify a loan is, that it is needed for the payment of a premium due. Yet in such cases it reduces protection and, considering the actual and possible abuses of the loan, it is questionable if the loan granted for this purpose will in the end best serve insurance. The policy contract now provides for extended insurance in case a premium is not paid, and it might be better to compel the policyholder to take the extended insurance. If he is really interested in having that protection which insurance alone can supply, he will pay the premium past due and revive his insurance. If, however, a loan is secured to pay a due premium, sufficient additional insurance should be taken to protect the beneficiary while the loan is in force.

The loan privilege is a very desirable feature of an insurance policy, especially in increasing its selling value, but its abuse needs to be provided against if insurance is to fulfill its prime function of protecting the dependant. Many companies are making commendable effort to prevent the abuse of this privilege, but mere moral suasion is likely to prove ineffective, as is so often the case when a monetary value is placed in competition with it.

The Forfeiture Clause. — The forfeiture clause in the policy is one which provides that the insured, in case he defaults his premiums, shall not forfeit his insurance, but shall be entitled to receive either paid-up insurance or extended insurance or a cash sum. These sums must be equal at least to the reserve held on the policy and the dividends due on the policy less any indebtedness on it and less a sum not in excess of $2\frac{1}{2}$ per cent of the face of the policy.

The causes which have been responsible in most cases for a forfeiture are: (*a*) nonpayment of premium when it was due; (*b*) residence in an unhealthy climate, change of occupation, or suicide; (*c*) fraud in obtaining a policy; (*d*) the absence of an insurable interest. The last two causes have not been modified to any extent by the action of legislatures or by the companies, except, as we shall see later, a definite period is fixed within which actions at law must be instituted to determine whether fraudulent means have been used. The first and second reasons for forfeiture have been very materially modified, both by law and action of the companies. The Massachusetts legislature under the leadership of Elizur Wright, its noted insurance commissioner, led the way in requiring nonforfeiture provisions in a policy when it required all companies doing business in that state to grant a retiring policyholder extended insurance. This law was passed in 1861. The length of time the insurance was extended beyond the date of withdrawal was determined as a matter of course by the reserve value of the policy.

We shall remember that in level-premium insurance the policyholder pays more than the natural premium or cost of his insurance in the early years, and accumulates a reserve and pays perhaps less than the cost in the later years. Many of the companies at this time were paying either surrender or cash values, but the companies did not incorporate in the policy what some were doing in practice. A cash-surrender clause did not appear in any policies until 1869 and did not become a general practice, whether made a part of the policy or not, until very recent years. Both the cash-surrender value and the extended insurance, which, as its name implies, is extending to a future period the face of the policy after premiums are no longer paid, were feared by the company officials. They feared an unfavorable selection.

Forfeiture on account of a change in residence or occupation has tended to disappear on account of the better knowledge of regions, dangers of occupations, and better understanding of sanitary and hygienic principles. The companies now refuse to insure those who live in certain districts or those who are engaged in certain occupations. The few insured lives who do go to these unfavorable regions or engage in hazardous occupations do not appear to produce serious results on the mortality experience of the companies. An example may be given of what this nonforfeiture meant fifty years ago in comparison with policies now written by a reference to the policy provisions of one of the large life insurance companies' policies. The purchaser agreed fifty years ago that his policy became null and void if, without the company's consent, he passed beyond the settled limits of the United States or Canada or even visited those parts of the United States west of longitude 100°. Nor could he go south of Virginia and Kentucky in the summer time or live within ten miles of the Mississippi or Missouri rivers south of latitude 40°. All service on boats or trains was forbidden, as well as military service, except in time of peace. Death by suicide, dueling, and execution by the state voided the policy. At present all policies in this company are free from restrictions of residence, travel, occupation, and failure to pay the premium, after two full premiums have been paid, does not void the policy.

Cash-Surrender Clause. — It was a marked improvement in the policy contract when the policyholder was permitted to withdraw his share of the common insurance fund. At present, if one wishes to withdraw from a company, he may have a specified cash-surrender value at any age, usually after the second or third year, or he may secure a loan, or he may have his insurance extended to that future date, which his past payment will purchase. In addition the policyholder is granted certain days of grace, usually thirty, for the payment of the premium and in the event that he fails to pay the premium, there remains the reinstatement clause. This clause provides that the insured may revive his policy by paying the past premiums due, with interest, provided he is in insurable condition. Contrary to what is often accepted as a fact, insurance companies do not, as at present conducted, encourage or passively permit the lapse of policies. They expend large amounts of time and money in persuading policyholders not to permit their policies to lapse, and when they lapse the companies often endeavor to revive them.

Incontestability Clause.—The incontestability clause is one which provides that after a certain date, frequently two years, the company is estopped from contesting the payment of the policy for all causes, except the nonpayment of the premium, and in some cases the violation of specific provisions, such as military and naval service in time of war. Some companies have voluntarily made their policies incontestable after one year, under the policy contract. There has been much discussion of this clause, both as to its advisability and as to the extent to which it binds the company. It is a means of affording greater security to the older policyholders. Its adoption has manifestly led to the withdrawal of other restrictions, since if this clause is binding on the company, the latter is not free to resist any claims made upon it by a policyholder who has violated any one of the many earlier restrictions of the policy. It led to a withdrawal of many of these former restrictions. The question naturally arises, Should a company be thus prevented from resisting the payment on a policy which was obtained by fraud? Does public policy demand that the wit and ingenuity of the company officials should be pitted against that of the individual who seeks to obtain for himself or others money by fraudulent means? In actual practice it means that the company must discover, before issuing the policy or within a comparatively short part of the time that the contract runs, even if fraud has been used. It has been held (Reagon v. Insurance Company, 76 N. E. Reporter, 217) that a provision in a life policy which makes it incontestable for fraud from date of issue is invalid, but that such a provision, operative after a certain date, is valid. There is without doubt a danger from making the policies too liberal in this particular, not so much because the financial security of the company is seriously injured, but rather in thus permitting, if not encouraging, fraud. This clause indicates more forcibly than does any other, the reaction that has taken place against the harsh restrictions of the old policy contract. The companies have sought to make their policies more attractive by thus liberalizing them, and the modifications have resulted more from business competition than from legislative or judicial action.

Other Clauses. — Among other minor benefits and prohibitions in the standard provisions of policies, the following may be mentioned:

(a) The distribution of the surplus; that is, the payment of dividends must be made annually after the third year of the policy. In some states dividends may be paid quinquennially. The details of this provision are reserved for discussion in a succeeding chapter.

(b) Loans must be granted up to the reserve value of the policy, less a small deduction of not more than two and one half per cent of the face of the policy. A failure to pay the loan does not forfeit the policy unless the total indebtedness should exceed the reserve value of the policy; and then thirty days' notice must be given the insured before canceling the policy.

(c) The policy must contain a copy of the application, and the policy with the application must constitute the entire contract. All statements of the insured are to be considered as representations and not warranties.

(d) A table must be in the policy which shows extended insurance, cash and the loan values, and non-forfeiture values in case premiums are not paid.

(e) Death claims must be paid within at least sixty days after due proof of the death of the insured. A table must be in the policy which shows the amount of installments in which the proceeds of the policy may be payable.

(f) The policy must definitely set forth the options of settlement. The policy is matured either by death or by completion of the contract; as, for example, by the payment of all premiums in the case of a twenty-year endowment policy.

(g) The failure to pay a loan or the interest on it may not forfeit a policy if the total indebtedness is less than the loan value, and in no case can forfeiture for this failure take place before the policyholder has been notified at least one month previous to the forfeiture.

(*h*) No clause may be included by which the policy shall purport to be issued or to take effect before the original. application for the insurance was made, if thereby the insured would rate at a younger age than his actual age at the time at which application was made. This clause permits only the age at the nearest birthday to be taken and prevents " dating back " of policies, a method of rebating practiced by some agents.

(*i*) No provision is permitted for a settlement at maturity of less value than the amount insured on the face of the policy plus any dividend additions and less any indebtedness.

(*j*) No policy can be issued until the form has been filed and approved by the insurance commissioner. This prohibition is intended to prevent the numerous " frill " policies, designed to attract the impressionable purchaser, but which had little to commend them. Both the standard provisions and the standard prohibitions are now used in many states.

Suicide. — Suicide, which has been the cause of considerable contention between beneficiaries and insurance companies as well as frequently being a matter of adjudication by the courts, is now in many policies covered as a valid claim for the proceeds of the policy. In a number of policies it is provided that if death occurs within a certain time, frequently one or two years from the date of issue of the policy only the premiums paid will be given to the beneficiary. In other policies the face of the policy is paid in case of suicide occurring any time during the life of the policy.

Annuities. — In addition to life insurance policies of the character described in the preceding pages, insurance companies and other organizations, including some governments, sell annuities. An annuity contract is one which provides for a series of periodical payments by the company or organization granting it to the purchaser either annually throughout his life or for a specified term of life. The most common form of annuity is that under which for a single payment the company agrees to pay a fixed sum annually, semi-annually, or quarterly to the annuitant so long as he lives. This contract guarantees to the purchaser, therefore, a definite income whether he lives a few or many years. Its chief characteristic as regards payment is therefore the opposite of an insurance policy under which the purchaser annually pays small sums in order to secure at the close of the period the one large sum.

Annuities also arise in the case of levying inheritance taxes when a proper basis is sought for levying this tax by a calculation of the value of life estates, temporary estates, joint life estates, survivorship estates, and contingent estates. Since the basis upon which the annuities are calculated is much the same as that upon which insurance policies are calculated, that is, the mortality table and the compound interest principle, a brief description of the different kinds of annuities may be given.

The practice of granting annuities is very old, a Roman law of 40 B.C. having laid down the conditions under which annuities could be granted. Tables were drawn up from the very early experience of annuitants which have been made more exact from later experience just as in the case of the ordinary mortality table. The actual experience on annuitants varies from that on insured lives, due to the fact that no one will purchase an annuity unless he feels confident that his physical conditions give good promise of longevity. An annuity contract is issued to any one without a medical examination, for it is evident that the sooner the annuitant dies the greater the gain is to the company. In this respect an annuity is again the opposite of life insurance. The chief kinds of annuities are:

First, an annuity contingent, in which the beginning or continuance of the amount is contingent on the occurrence or non-occurrence of a particular event involving the duration of one or more lives.

Second, an annuity deferred, in which the payment begins only after a certain time, as, for example, when an annuity begins after a period of twenty years.

Third, an annuity due, which is a life annuity, the first payment of which is now due.

Fourth, a joint-life annuity, in which the annuity is payable to two or more persons, the payments ceasing upon the first death.

Fifth, a survivorship annuity, which is a life annuity in which the payments to one or more persons are contingent upon these persons surviving one or more persons. Such a contract may be purchased by a husband in favor of his wife for a comparatively small sum and is sometimes called a reversionary annuity.

An annuity certain is a payment of a certain sum of money annually for a given period of time. Some-

o

times an annuity certain is classed with annuities, but it is not correctly so classed, for the annuity certain does not depend fundamentally on the life of the recipient. It is a fixed sum to be paid for a fixed period of time and therefore involves only the interest principle and in no way the mortality table. In those states in which a life insurance company is prohibited from doing a banking business, a life insurance company could not issue an annuity certain, which is really a banking business. However, the holder of a life insurance policy may provide in his policy for the payment at his death of its proceeds in installments of a fixed number and amount, which is an annuity certain. It is always stipulated that if the beneficiary should not live to receive all the installments, the remaining installments — or their commuted value — will be paid to some other person.

Calculation of an Annuity. — The calculation of an annuity certain is simple, since it requires only the calculation of the present worth of definite sums to be paid in the future.

If, for example, it is desired to calculate the amount which a company must have on hand to pay a life annuity of $1.00 to each person alive at age 56 and each succeeding year according to the American Experience Table of Mortality, the following calculation is made. At age 56 there are alive according to this mortality table 63,364 persons, and since each is to receive $1.00 at the beginning of each year, there must be paid out at once $63,364. During the year 1260 of these persons die, leaving 62,104 persons to receive the $1.00 or $62,104 annuity at the beginning of the second year. The present worth of this sum at 3 per cent interest for one year is $60,295.15. At the beginning of the tenth year of the annuity payments, that is, at 65, there are alive 49,341 persons, and this will require a payment of $49,-341. The present worth of this sum at 3 per cent is $37,815.77. Likewise at the fortieth year, or at age ninety-five, there will be according to the mortality table three persons alive to receive the amount of $1.00, that is, $3.00 will have to be paid out at the beginning of this year. The present worth of this $3.00 invested for thirty-nine years at 3 per cent is $0.947. Calculating all the present worths of the intermediate sums to be paid and adding these sums will give the total sum which the company must have on hand at the beginning of this fifty-six year period in order to pay each member $1.00 at the beginning of each year that he is alive. This total sum amounts to $824,117.31, which 'divided by the 63,364 persons who wish to purchase the right to receive $1.00 at the beginning of each year that they are alive, that is, a life annuity of $1.00, gives $13.006, or the amount that each will have to pay at the beginning in order to receive the life annuity of $1.00.

If, therefore, v is taken to represent the present value of 1 due in one year, and d the discount on 1 due in one year, and the amount of 1 due in a year as $(1 + i)$, the sum which invested at the beginning of the year would produce 1 at the end would be $\dfrac{1}{1 + i}$. This is the present value of 1 due one year hence. The present value of 1 due in n years would be

$$\frac{1}{(1+i)^n}.$$ Therefore $v = \frac{1}{1+i}$ or $(1+i)^{-1}$

$$\text{and } v^n = \frac{1}{(1+i)^n}.$$

The present value of an annuity certain is represented by $a\overline{n|}$ and the formula for calculating its value is

$$a\overline{n|} = \frac{1-v^n}{i}.$$

The following table shows the number and amount of the different kinds of policies in force at the close of 1914 for the thirty-five leading life insurance companies:

	Number	Amount
Whole Life	4,908,922	$9,823,394,878
Endowment	2,297,816	3,277,860,013
All other	644,461	1,831,896,007
Total	7,851,199	$14,933,150,898
Average amount of policy $1902		

REFERENCES

Yale Readings in Insurance, Vol. I, Chaps. XI and XII.

Annals American Academy of Political Science, Vol. XXVI, pp. 229–242.

Business of Life Insurance. M. M. Dawson, Chaps. VI and XVIII.

Educational Leaflets. The Mutual Life Insurance Company.

Insurance Guide and Handbook, Fifth Edition, Chap. XII.

Notes on Life Insurance. Edward B. Fackler, Chap. XIII.

Life Insurance Primer. Henry Moir, Chaps. VIII and IX.

CHAPTER VII

The Premium Defined. — The premium is the sum that is paid by the insured to the insurer for the indemnity or benefits which the latter sells. The premium may be a single payment, a series of annual payments, or payments made weekly, monthly, quarterly, or semiannually. In case they are paid in periods less than a year, an addition to the fractional part of the annual premium is made because all premiums, so far as they are determined by the mortality table, are based on the annual death rate and not on the weekly or semiannual death rate. The company loses one half a year's interest on the premium which is paid semiannually.

Kinds of Premium. — There are various kinds of premiums, which must be distinguished. The following include the most important: The Single Premium, The Annual Uniform or Level Premium, and the Natural Premium. Each of these is subdivided into the Net or Pure Premium and the Gross or Office Premium. The Single Premium is the one payment made in a lump sum which secures the benefit of insurance either at the end of a stipulated period or at death, or in the event of some contingency. The amount of the premium varies according to the age and the character of the benefits granted. Its amount also depends upon the mortality table and the rate of interest, since the first shows the years which will be lived by a group, and the interest table, the amounts which will be earned by funds placed at accumulation during the period. The annual uniform or level premium is the stated sum which is necessary to be paid each year to secure the insurance benefits desired. It is the amount of an annuity, payable in advance either throughout life or for a specified period which the Single Premium will purchase. The Natural Premium is that premium which yearly in-

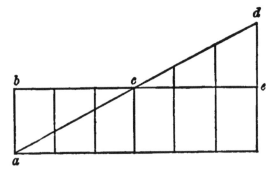 creases with age to correspond with the increasing rate of mortality shown by the mortality table. It is the term used to mean the annually increasing premium which is necessary to meet the annually increasing chance of death. In this sense it means that if the young man, aged 25, prefers to pay for his insurance year by year, as he obtains the protection, he must pay an annually increasing sum. In this sense it is contrasted with the level premium, which is the sum that neither increases nor decreases during the length of the contract, but which by its periodic payments secures the benefit guaranteed. The level premiums are the mathematical equivalent of the natural premiums. This can be expressed by the preceding figure in which the triangle represents the natural premium and the

rectangle the level premium. The perpendicular lines represent the annual payments under each premium plan. The area of the rectangle equals the area of the triangle, that is, the natural premiums are equivalent to the level premiums. The excess payments of the earlier years, namely, the triangle *abc*, balance the deficient payments of the later years, namely, the triangle *cde*. That is to say, the payments represented by the triangle *abc* constitute a reserve or a sinking fund thus accumulated out of premium payments for the purpose of meeting obligations as they fall due.

The Natural Premium is the one which has been used by the Assessment Companies and is still in use either in its pure or modified form by most of these organizations.

The Level Premium is the one used by the old-line, regular companies. While one premium, theoretically, is as scientific as the other, the practical difficulties of conducting insurance on the natural premium plan are insurmountable. It is for this reason that so many of the assessment societies have failed. As the members of the pure assessment society became older, the necessarily higher premiums became so burdensome to the surviving members that they often gave up their insurance, and new members are loath to enter a society when the rates are increasing. The theoretical plan, then, of paying for your insurance as you get it, has never been successful in practice. Insurance must be paid for during the productive years of life and not become an increasing burden with increasing age with its accompanying unproductive years.

The Natural Premium. — Year by year insurance involves such an increasing cost, as indicated by the table on page 209, that the cost becomes prohibitive for most individuals in old age.

Assessment companies transacting business on the natural premium basis are accustomed to point to the low death rate during the early years of their existence as a proof of their ability to meet all their claims without increasing their rates. This is utterly fallacious, since the organization when formed is usually composed of a large number of persons in young or middle life who as they approach older ages will cause the death rate to increase rapidly. The rates must necessarily increase if the organization is to provide for the claims which will fall due as a result of this increasing mortality. Assessment insurance at its best is only a temporary expedient to cover the liabilities of death during a short period. No one desiring permanent insurance, that is, life insurance, should be lured from the firm ground of level premium insurance to the quicksands of assessment insurance.

The Net Premium. — The Net Premium is simply that sum which provides for the amount of insurance desired, as determined by the Mortality Table and the Interest Table. Life insurance organizations like all businesses have expenses connected with their transaction, and these expenses must be paid by the policyholders of the company. These expenses include commissions to agents for soliciting the business, office expenses, rents, taxes, advertising, and such contingencies as unfortunate instruments. All these items when added to the net premium make up the Gross or Office Premium. In the preceding chapter the important kinds of life insurance policies have been classified as Whole Life, Term, Limited Payment Life, and Endowment. It is now necessary to explain how the premiums on each of these policies are calculated. The premium to be calculated is the Net Premium, since the Gross or Office Premium differs from company to company to some extent, owing to the kind of insurance written and in any case represents but an addition to this Net Premium which is determined by the Mortality Table and Interest Tables. In order to explain these premiums it is necessary to make the following calculations.

Methods of **Calculating Premiums.** — First, to calculate the net single premium, since the net annual level premiums are the equivalent of this net single premium.

Second, to calculate a life annuity due, that is, the sum necessary to be paid at a stated time in order to secure another stated sum at the beginning of each year that the individual is alive.

Third, to calculate the net annual premium which is derived from the first and second calculations.

Fourth, to calculate a temporary annuity due, that is, a sum which paid at a stated time will secure a certain payment at the beginning of each year for a given number of years, as, for example, twenty. From this calculation and the first, the net annual premium for a Limited-payment Life Policy is calculated.

Fifth, to calculate the Single Premium for a pure

endowment, that is, that sum which paid at once will secure certain sums to those living at the close of a given period.

From this can be calculated, first the net annual premium of a pure endowment policy by using the results of the first part of the fourth calculation and then, second, this result added to the result of the second part of the fourth calculation will give the net annual premium for an ordinary endowment policy. Any other premium on the majority of the policies now issued is some modification of these premiums.

Calculating a **Net Single Premium.** — First, to calculate the net single premium; assume that there are 1000 men who desire to buy the right to receive $1000 each from an insurance company, and assume further that they wish to pay for this right in one payment. Let us suppose that the limit of life for the group of 1000 purchasers at 50 years of age is 53 years and that 200 die the first year, 300 the second, and 500 the third. Since the company is to pay $1000 to each, the total sum to be paid out is $1,000,000, but since only a part of this, $200,000, will be paid out the first year, another part, $300,000, the second year, and still another part, $500,000, the third year, the company will not need to collect the total sum, $1,000,000, at the beginning, because only a part is to be demanded each year, and the sum paid in will increase by its interest earnings. Assume that 3 per cent interest can be earned. Now, since $200,000 is to be demanded at the close of the year, the question is, What sum bearing 3 per cent interest for one year will amount to $200,000? The present value of $1 for one year at 3 per cent is .970874 cents, and therefore the present value of the $200,000 is .970874 times the sum, or $194,174.80. Likewise the present value of $300,000, which is to be demanded only at the close of the second year and therefore has had two years to accumulate interest, is $282,778.80; that is, it is .942596, the present value of $1 to be paid in two years, times 300,000. In the same manner the present value of the $500,000, which is to be demanded the third year, is found to be $457,571. The total amount of the present value of these three sums is $834,524.60, and since there are 1000 persons who are to be insured, each should pay $834.52 in order that the company may be able to pay to each $1000 insurance.

It is assumed that the payments by the company are to be made at the close of the first, second, and third years, when all of the persons will have died. This single payment of $834.52 is, then, the net single premium necessary to secure $1000 insurance under the above assumptions. Since we have shown in a simple way how a single net premium might be calculated under an assumed mortality table, that is, one in which each of 1000 persons aged 50 would die by age 53, we may now apply the same method of calculation to an actual mortality table and determine the net single premium necessary to be collected in order that the company can pay $1000 upon the death of the insured.

The problem is to calculate the net single premium for a whole-life policy of $1000 for a person of age 50. By referring to the American Mortality Table, it will be found that of 100,000 persons aged 10 only 69,804

are living at age 50. It is also observed that 962 will
die within a year and therefore the company will be
compelled to pay out $962,000. But the present value
of this sum or the amount necessary to be collected at the
beginning of the year is $933,981, which with its interest
accumulations at 3 per cent amounts to the $962,000.
Likewise the company will not need to collect the
$1,001,000 for the 1001 who die in their fifty-first year,
but only the present value of this sum for two years at
3 per cent, which is $943,539. So, too, it will not need
to collect in the beginning the $3000 which will be
demanded according to the mortality table by the
death of the last three survivors in their ninety-fifth
year, but only the present value of $3000 for 46 years,
which is $770. Likewise the present value of the sums
to be demanded each year is calculated, and the amount
of all these present values is $38,756,240. This is the
sum necessary to be collected at the beginning of the
first year, viz. the fiftieth, in order that the company
can pay to each of the 69,804 the $1000 when they die.
Since each is to have the same kind of a contract and
no one knows when he will die, each should pay $555.22
or $38,756,240 divided by 69,804. This is the net single
premium for a whole life policy of $1000 at age 50.

The table on page 208 shows in detail the process of
calculating the net single premium for this period or for
any shorter period.

If we wish to calculate the net single premium for a
policy, which is not for life but for only a term of years,
say twenty, we add the present values for the first twenty
years and divide by the 69,804, which would give $317.60,

which is the net single premium at age 50 for a twenty-year term policy. This is less than the preceding net premium, because in this case we assume that the company obligated itself to pay $1000 only to those who died during the next twenty years. Those living beyond 70 would, under such an assumption, be paid nothing. However, for very obvious reasons few persons wish to pay for their insurance at one payment, although such a payment can be made for a policy to an insurance company. It is purchasing protection far distant in a future which the purchaser may not live to enjoy. He prefers to purchase protection as he lives, that is, by installments or in annual periods. That is, the ordinary buyer of insurance desires to pay annual premiums and not single premiums. It is, then, necessary to express the net single premium in net annual premiums.

As we proceed to calculate other forms of premiums, let the reader remember that they are equivalent in value to the single premium.

Calculating the Annual Premium. — As the first step in calculating the net annual premium for a whole-life policy, we must make our second calculation, that is, calculate a life annuity due. An annuity due is the payment of a stated sum at the beginning of the year to a person as long as he lives. It is thus the exact opposite of an ordinary life policy, since the latter is paid only in case of death. The value of the annuity due is the sum which the company must receive in order to make its annual payments at the beginning of the year to those living. Whereas the premium is ordinarily the small annual sum paid in order to receive the large sums at the close, the annuity calls for the large sum paid to the company at the beginning in order that it may pay the small annual sums at the beginning of each year.

The value of the annuity is calculated in the same manner as the single premium. Reverting to our first example of 1000 men at age 50, of whom 200 die the first year, 300 the second year, and 500 the third year, the problem is, How much should each of these 1000 men pay to a company in order that each shall receive $1 at the beginning of each year that he is alive? Manifestly $1000 is demanded now to pay the 1000 now living, hence there is no interest. But at the beginning of the second year only 800 are alive and at the beginning of the third year only 500 are alive. That is, the company will have to pay out a total of $2300. But the second and third payments have the benefit of interest for one and two years, respectively. Therefore, we calculate the present worths of $1000 due now, $800 due one year from now, and $500 due two years from now. These amount to $2248.0172, which is the sum that the company must collect in order to pay a $1 annuity to each now, and to each of the survivors at the beginning of each year that he lives. This sum divided by 1000 equals $2.248, which is the sum each annuitant must pay under the assumption, if he is to receive the $1 at the beginning of each year that he lives.

If now we substitute the American Mortality Table and follow the same process of calculation, we find that the value of a life annuity at age 50 is $15.27; that is, such a payment made by each of the 69,804 persons at age 50 will secure to each a payment of $1 now and a like payment to each survivor at the beginning of each year from 50 to 95 inclusive. If we desire, as in the former case, to determine the sum that should be paid by each of the 69,804 persons at age 50 in order to purchase a twenty-year annuity of $1, we simply calculate the present value of each of the sums demanded at the beginning of each of the years and divide it by 69,804. This is $12.92, a less sum than the former, because the annuity of $1 does not need to be paid by the company to each person surviving beyond the sixty-ninth year or twenty years beyond fifty.

The purpose in calculating an annuity was to use it as a means of changing the net single premium into a series of net annual premiums. We have seen that at age 50 the sum of $15.27 will purchase a life annuity of $1. That is, $1 can be paid to him now and at the beginning of each year to which the applicant survives. Therefore, $555.22, the net single premium, will purchase as many dollars of an annuity as $15.27 is contained in it, which is $36.36. That is, the $36.36 paid now and at the beginning of each year to which the person survives is the equivalent of $555.22 paid now and once for all time. Since this $555.22 was the net single premium for $1000 of insurance, so must its equivalent, the $36.36, purchase by these annual payments the right to receive $1000 insurance. This $36.36 is, then, the net annual premium for a $1000 policy on the whole-life plan at the stated age.

	AMERICAN EXPERIENCE TABLE OF MORTALITY		COMPUTATION OF NET SINGLE PREMIUM AT AGE 50			
1	2	3	4	5	6	7
Age at the beginning of the year.	Number living at the beginning of each year.	Number dying during the year.	Amount to be paid out for death claims at the end of each year indicated in column 5.		Present worth of $1 at 3 per cent compound discount payable at time stated in column 5. This decimal, multiplied by the number of dollars set out in column 4 for corresponding year, will give present worth as set out in column 7.	Present worth of amounts set out in col. 4; or the amounts to be collected at the beginning and invested at 3 per cent compound interest to produce sums necessary to pay death claims set out in col. 4 as they fall due at end of each year.
50	69,804	962	$ 962,000	End 1st year	$.970874	$ 933,981
51	68,842	1,001	1,001,000	" 2d "	.942596	943,539
52	67,841	1,044	1,044,000	" 3d "	.915142	955,409
53	66,797	1,091	1,091,000	" 4th "	.888487	969,339
54	65,706	1,143	1,143,000	" 5th "	.862609	685,962
55	64,563	1,199	1,199,000	" 6th "	.837484	1,004,143
56	63,364	1,260	1,260,000	" 7th "	.813092	1,024,495
57	62,104	1,325	1,325,000	" 8th "	.789409	1,045,967
58	60,779	1,394	1,394,000	" 9th "	.766417	1,068,386
59	59,385	1,468	1,468,000	" 10th "	.744094	1,092,330
60	57,917	1,546	1,546,000	" 11th "	.722421	1,116,863
61	56,371	1,628	1,628,000	" 12th "	.701380	1,141,842
62	54,743	1,713	1,713,000	" 13th "	.680951	1,166,471
63	53,030	1,800	1,800,000	" 14th "	.661118	1,190,012
64	51,230	1,889	1,889,000	" 15th "	.641862	1,212,477
65	49,341	1,980	1,980,000	" 16th "	.623167	1,233,869
66	47,361	2,070	2,070,000	" 17th "	.605016	1,252,383
67	45,291	2,158	2,158,000	" 18th "	.587395	1,267,598
68	43,133	2,243	2,243,000	" 19th "	.570286	1,279,151
69	40,890	2,321	2,321,000	" 20th "	.553676	1,285,083
70	38,569	2,391	2,391,000	" 21st "	.537549	1,285,281
71	36,178	2,448	2,448,000	" 22d "	.521893	1,277,593
72	33,730	2,487	2,487,000	" 23d "	.506692	1,260,145
73	31,243	2,505	2,505,000	" 24th "	.491934	1,232,295
74	28,738	2,501	2,501,000	" 25th "	.477606	1,194,493
75	26,237	2,476	2,476,000	" 26th "	.463695	1,148,108
76	23,761	2,431	2,431,000	" 27th "	.450189	1,094,409
77	21,330	2,369	2,369,000	" 28th "	.437077	1,035,436
78	18,961	2,291	2,291,000	" 29th "	.424346	972,176
79	16,670	2,196	2,196,000	" 30th "	.411987	904,723
80	14,474	2,091	2,091,000	" 31st "	.399987	836,372
81	12,383	1,964	1,964,000	" 32d "	.388337	762,693
82	10,419	1,816	1,816,000	" 33d "	.377026	684,679
83	8,603	1,648	1,648,000	" 34th "	.366045	603,242
84	6,955	1,470	1,470,000	" 35th "	.355383	522,413
85	5,485	1,292	1,292,000	" 36th "	.345032	445,781
86	4,193	1,114	1,114,000	" 37th "	.334983	373,171
87	3,079	933	933,000	" 38th "	.325226	303,436
88	2,146	744	744,000	" 39th "	.315754	234,921
89	1,402	555	555,000	" 40th "	.306557	170,140
90	847	385	385,000	" 41st "	.297628	114,587
91	462	246	246,000	" 42d "	.288959	71,084
92	216	137	137,000	" 43d "	.280543	38,434
93	79	58	58,000	" 44th "	.272372	15,798
94	21	18	18,000	" 45th "	.264439	4,760
95	3	3	3,000	" 46th "	.256737	770
	Totals . . .	69,804	$69,804,000			$38,756,240

The following table shows the result of receiving an annual net premium from each of a group of 81,822 individuals. The table is based upon the American Experience Mortality with three per cent interest earning and with net annual premiums of $21.08236 to age 86, $21.081 from age 87 to 92, and $21.08 from age 93 to the end.

It also shows the importance of the interest accumulations in level premium insurance and the amounts which any such company must have at the close of each year in order to mature its contracts. This sum is known as the reserve, and this table will have added importance in connection with the succeeding discussion of reserves and surplus.

TABLE SHOWING THE NET PREMIUMS PAID, THE INTEREST RECEIVED, THE DEATH CLAIMS PAID, AND THE RESERVE FUND ON HAND AT THE END OF EACH YEAR, FOR 81,822 PERSONS INSURING FOR $1000 EACH AT AGE 35 — ACCORDING TO THE AMERICAN TABLE OF MORTALITY WITH INTEREST AT THREE PER CENT PER ANNUM.

Net Annual Premium used, — $21.08236 to age 86, $21.081 age 87 to 92, $21.08 age 93 to end.

AGE	NUMBER SURVIVING	NUMBER OF DEATHS	PREMIUMS	INTEREST	TOTAL INCOME	DEATH CLAIMS	RESERVE FUND END OF EACH YEAR	RESERVE PER $100 OF INSURANCE
35	81,822	732	$1,724,908.89	$51,747.27	$1,776,656.16	$732,000	$1,044,656.16	$12.88
36	81,090	737	1,709,477.43	82,624.01	1,792,101.44	737,000	2,099,757.60	26.13
37	80,353	742	1,693,940.56	113,810.94	1,807,751.50	742,000	3,165,509.10	39.76
38	79,611	749	1,678,298.28	145,314.22	1,823,612.50	749,000	4,240,121.60	53.77
39	78,862	756	1,662,508.43	177,078.90	1,839,587.33	756,000	5,323,708.93	68.16
40	78,106	765	1,646,571.02	209,108.40	1,855,679.42	765,000	6,414,388.35	82.94
41	77,341	774	1,630,443.87	241,344.97	1,871,788.84	774,000	7,512,177.19	98.11
42	76,567	785	1,614,127.00	273,789.13	1,887,916.13	785,000	8,615,093.32	113.68
43	75,782	797	1,597,578.23	306,380.15	1,903,958.38	797,000	9,722,051.70	129.65
44	74,985	812	1,580,776.48	339,084.85	1,919,861.33	812,000	10,829,913.03	146.01

Age	Number Surviving	Number of Deaths	Premiums	Interest	Total Income	Death Claims	Reserve Fund End of Each Year	Reserve per $1000 of Insurance
45	74,173	828	1,563,658.52	371,807.15	1,935,465.67	828,000	11,937,378.70	162.76
46	73,345	848	1,546,203.25	404,507.46	1,950,710.71	848,000	13,040,089.41	179.87
47	72,497	870	1,528,326.37	437,052.47	1,965,378.84	870,000	14,135,468.25	197.35
48	71,627	896	1,509,985.69	469,363.62	1,979,349.31	896,000	15,218,817.56	215.16
49	70,731	927	1,491,096.90	501,297.43	1,992,394.33	927,000	16,284,211.89	233.28
50	69,804	962	1,471,554.60	532,672.99	2,004,227.59	962,000	17,326,439.48	251.68
51	68,842	1,001	1,451,274.45	563,331.42	2,014,605.87	1,001,000	18,340.045.35	270.34
52	67,841	1,044	1,430,172.13	593,106.52	2,023,278.65	1,044,000	19,319,324.00	289.22
53	66,797	1,091	1,408,163.32	621,824.62	2,029,987.94	1,091,000	20,258,311.94	308.32
54	65,706	1,143	1,385,163.69	649,304.27	2,034,467.96	1,143,000	21,149,779.90	327.58
55	64,563	1,199	1,361,067.84	675,325.43	2,036,393.27	1,199,000	21,987,173.17	347.00
56	63,364	1,260	1,335,791.44	699,688.94	2,035,480.38	1,260,000	22,762,653.55	366.52
57	62,104	1,325	1,309,229.08	722,156.48	2,031,385.56	1,325,000	23,469,039.11	386.14
58	60,779	1,394	1,281,296.44	742,510.07	2,023,806.51	1,394,000	24,098,845.62	405.81
59	59,385	1,468	1,251,909.20	760,522.64	2,012,431.84	1,468,000	24,643,277.46	425.49
60	57,917	1,546	1,220,961.95	775,927.18	1,996,889.13	1,546,000	25,094,166.59	445.16
61	56,371	1,628	1,188,370.35	788,476.11	1,976,846.46	1,628,000	25,443,013.05	464.77
62	54,743	1,713	1,154,050.10	797,911.89	1,951,961.99	1,713,000	25,681,975.04	484.29
63	53,030	1,800	1,117,937.95	803,997.39	1,921,935.34	1,800,000	25,803,910.38	503.69
64	51,230	1,889	1,079,991.72	806,517.06	1,886,508.78	1,889,000	25,801,419.16	522.92
65	49,341	1,980	1,040,169.27	805,247.65	1,845,416.92	1,980,000	25,666,836.08	541.94
66	47,361	2,070	998,428.42	799,957.94	1,798,386.36	2,070,000	25,395,222.44	560.71
67	45,291	2,158	954,790.26	790,500.38	1,745,290.64	2,158,000	24,982,513.08	579.20
68	43,133	2,243	909,296.95	776,754.30	1,686,051.25	2,243,000	24,425,564.33	597.35
69	40,890	2,321	862,011.74	758,627.28	1,620,639.02	2,321,000	23,725,203.35	615.14
70	38,569	2,391	813,082.19	736,148.57	1,549,230.76	2,391,000	22,883,434.11	632.52
71	36,178	2,448	762,676.96	709,383.33	1,472,060.29	2,448,000	21,907,494.40	649.50
72	33,730	2,487	711,070.09	678,556.93	1,389,627.02	2,487,000	20,810,121.42	666.07
73	31,243	2,505	658,641.06	644,062.87	1,302,703.93	2,505,000	19,607,825.35	682.30
74	28,738	2,501	605,832.56	606,409.74	1,212,242.30	2,501,000	18,319,067.65	698.21
75	26,237	2,476	553,108.39	566,165.28	1,119,273.67	2,476,000	16,962,341.32	713.87
76	23,761	2,431	500,911.25	523,897.58	1,024,808.83	2,431,000	15,556,150.15	729.31
77	21,330	2,369	449,662.76	480,174.39	929,837.15	2,369,000	14,116,987.30	744.53
78	18,961	2,291	399,721.32	435,501.26	835,222.58	2,291,000	12,661,209.88	759.52
79	16,670	2,196	351,424.20	390,379.02	741,803.22	2,196,000	11,207,013.10	774.29
80	14,474	2,091	305,129.81	345,364.29	650,494.10	2,091,000	9,766,507.20	788.70
81	12,383	1,964	261,048.95	300,826.68	561,875.63	1,964,000	8,364,382.83	802.80
82	10,419	1,816	219,645.40	257,520.85	477,166.25	1,816,000	7,025,549.08	816.64
83	8,603	1,648	181,361.87	216,207.33	397,569.20	1,648,000	5,775,118.28	830.35
84	6,955	1,470	146,620.01	177,652.15	324,272.16	1,470,000	4,629,390.44	844.01
85	5,485	1,292	115,630.58	142,350.63	257,981.21	1,292,000	3,595,371.65	857.47
86	4,193	1,114	88,392.48	110,512.92	198,905.40	1,114,000	2,680,277.05	870.50
87	3,079	933	64,908.40	82,355.56	147,263.96	933,000	1,894,541.01	882.82
88	2,146	744	45,239.83	58,193.43	103,433.26	744,000	1,253,974.27	894.42
89	1,402	555	29,555.56	38,505.90	68,061.46	555,000	767,035.73	905.59
90	847	385	17,855.61	23,546.74	41,402.35	385,000	423,438.08	916.53
91	462	246	9,739.42	12,995.33	22,734.75	246,000	200,172.83	926.73
92	216	137	4,553.50	6,141.79	10,695.29	137,000	73,868.12	935.04
93	79	58	1,665.32	2,266.00	3,931.32	58,000	19,799.44	942.83
94	21	18	442.68	607.26	1,049.94	18,000	2,849.38	949.79
95	3	3	63.24	87.38	150.62	3,000	00.00	1,000.00

Calculating the Limited-payment Premium. — It must be evident that the method of calculating the payments for the purchaser who neither wishes to pay a single premium nor annual premiums throughout his life is simple. Suppose he wishes to pay for his $1000 life policy in five annual payments. We must in this case calculate the equivalent of $555.22 — the single premium — in terms of a five-year annuity. By the previous method we calculate the present values of the sums due at the beginning of each of the five years, and find that $4.59 is the value of an annuity temporary for five years. Dividing this into the single premium, we have $121.08, the net annual premium for a five-payment life policy of $1000 at age 50.

In a limited-payment life policy, as for example a twenty-payment life policy, the policy insures for the whole period of life and is therefore not necessarily payable in twenty years, but matures whenever death occurs. Its maturity may well be beyond a twenty-year period. That is, the policy is one for the whole period of life, but it is paid for within the period of twenty years. The present values of the net premiums to be received must therefore be the same as those received under a whole-life policy. In one case the insured pays a smaller annual sum for a greater number of years if he lives his normal lifetime, while in the other case of the limited-payment life policy he pays a larger annual sum for a shorter number of years.

If it is desired, then, to calculate the net annual premium for a twenty-payment life policy of $1000, the same method is used. That is, we calculate the value of

an annuity temporary for twenty years, the first payment
due immediately, assuming as has been the case in all
the illustrations that age 50 is selected and the American
Mortality Table with 3 per cent interest accumulations.
The value of this annuity is $12.92. We then divide
this into the net single premium for a whole-life policy,
a sum previously calculated to be $555.22, and get as a
quotient $42.95. This is the net annual premium for a
twenty-payment life policy of $1000 at age 50.

Calculating the Endowment Premium. — There remains, then, only one other of the important premiums
to be calculated, namely, the endowment policy premium. An endowment policy premium is composed of
a pure endowment premium and a term policy premium.
A pure endowment is that form of a policy which guarantees the payment of a stated sum on condition that an
individual lives to a certain date. In case of death
previous to this time the sum named is not paid. Such
policies are not frequently written and the words "endowment policy" now mean a pure endowment policy
combined with a term policy, that is, a policy the face of
which is paid either at death during the premium-paying period or at the close of this period. It is thus both
a life and a death insurance policy. It is the only
form of an insurance policy under which the insured
may live to receive the proceeds of his policy.

To calculate the premium on such a policy we must,
therefore, calculate the premium on a pure endowment
and the premium on a term policy. The sums of these
will be the premium of the endowment policy. The
problem is: Calculate the net annual premium for a

twenty-year endowment policy at age 50. We first determine the net single premium for a twenty-year pure endowment policy at age 50. That is, for what sum can a company agree to pay $1000 to each of the persons living at age 70? By reference to the mortality table we learn that of the 69,804 persons living at age 50 only 38,569 will be living at age 70, and hence the assumed company will be called on to pay out $38,569,000 at the end of twenty years. But the company can earn for twenty years 3 per cent interest on the single premium to be paid now. Hence the present value of the above sum is $21,354,729, and this is the sum to be collected at once from the 69,804 persons. Therefore the net single premium would be $305.92. But again few will care to pay single premiums, preferring to pay annual premiums. We therefore calculate the value of a $1 annuity temporary due now and at the beginning of each of the succeeding 19 years. This we previously found to be $12,926. Dividing the single premium $305.92 by 12,926 we have $23.67, the net annual premium for a $1000 pure endowment policy at age 50. Adding to this the net annual premium for a twenty-year term policy, $24.57, which is found by dividing $12.92 into $317.44 — the single premium for a twenty-year term policy — we have $48.24 as the net annual premium for the commonly sold twenty-year endowment policy which in this case was at age 50. The premium for the twenty-year term policy is calculated by the same method that the five-year term premium was previously calculated.

It must be evident that while we have selected age 50

for our calculations, any other age could have been selected, and exactly the same methods would be used.
The student should familiarize himself with the methods
by calculating for the different ages the net single, the
net annual premiums on whole-life policies, and the net
annual premiums for limited-payment and endowment
policies.

Summarizing the preceding discussion it is shown:
First, that the mortality table determines with the
interest table the amounts which must be collected from
each individual at each age in order to secure for him or
his beneficiaries at death or at the close of a period a
stated sum.

Second, that the cost increases from year to year with
the increased mortality, but that this annually increasing
cost can be equated into a fixed level cost for each
year by making the present value of such payments
equal to the present value of the insurance. Such annual
level payments will in the early years of the insurance
be in excess of the cost of the insurance as determined
by the mortality table and in the later years less than
this mortality cost. The excess payments of the early
years accumulate at compound interest and thus make
up for the deficient payments of the later years, becoming at the close of the period equal to the insurance sum
granted.

It must also be evident that the net premiums of
companies which use the same mortality table and the
same rate of interest will be the same for the same kind
of policy. But this net premium is not the one which
appears in the rate book of companies nor the premium

which is quoted by the agent as the price of a particular policy. It is the gross premium which is usually meant when the word " premium " is used.

Gross Premiums. — The preceding calculations have had reference solely to net premiums and not to gross or office premiums. The amounts added to the net premium to cover expenses and contingencies is called the loading. The gross premiums which are charged on the basis of $1000 of insurance are directly proportional to the amount, that is, the premium for $2000 of insurance is twice that for $1000 and therefore the loading varies directly with the amount of insurance. Since the loading is for the purpose of covering expenses and contingencies, and since the expenses are largest during the first year of the policy because in that year come the heavy expenses of paying the agent's commission and the medical examination fee, it might seem reasonable in theory to reduce the loading after these first-year acquisition expenses. Providing for the first year's expense has occasioned considerable discussion as to the best methods.

The Preliminary Term Plan. — One of the methods used, is writing policies on the preliminary term plan. That is, the first year of the insurance is written on the one-year term plan, and this is followed by the regular policy plan. If the contract is a twenty-payment life policy it would be written as a one-year term policy, followed by a nineteen-payment life policy. This does not mean that there are two contracts, but that the first year is considered term insurance. The premium collected is usually the same for the first year as for the succeeding years, but since the first premium is considered as purchasing only one year's insurance, it does not need to make any contribution to the reserve. There is, therefore, a wide margin between the net premium for the one-year term insurance and the actual premium collected. This difference is used to meet the large expenses of the first year. For example, the net one-year term premium for $1000 insurance at age 30 under the American Mortality Table at 3 per cent is $8.18, while the quoted premium for a twenty-payment policy at this age from the rate book of a company writing insurance on the preliminary term plan is $31.72. The difference is the sum taken for the first year's expenses. This preliminary term plan of writing insurance is widely used both in America and Europe. Several other devices are in use to provide for the large expenses incident to the first year of insurance, such, for example, as the modified preliminary term plan, the select and ultimate plan, but each has the same purpose in view.

Basis of Loading. — Another aspect of loading in connection with first year's expenses is seen in connection with small and large policies. If X purchases a $10,000 policy and Y a $1000 policy, the loading in the former policy as compared with the latter is directly proportional to the amount of the insurance, whereas the expenses, especially the first year's expenses, are in no such direct proportion. It is true that the agent's expenses are greater, since he is paid on a commission basis, and it may be that the medical fee is larger. However, it is not necessarily true that either the agent or the medical examiner has in connection with the $10,000 policy expended more time and energy than in the case of the $1000 policy. In the actual practice of insurance the determination of the amount to which each particular premium is to be loaded has often not been decided by matters of principle but by practical considerations and legal requirements. It must also be remembered that insurance does not concern itself so much with individuals as with groups of individuals, and that in its actual operation tests of individual equity cannot be applied. In no mutual coöperative organizations can every individual expect to secure a good personal bargain as determined by the consideration of the market.

The Loading on Non-participating Policies. — The amount of the loading is very materially affected by the fact whether the policy is participating, that is, shares in the surplus earnings, or whether it does not receive any of this surplus, that is, non-participating. In the first case the premiums are deliberately made larger than is absolutely necessary, with the idea that the company will return to the policyholder in the form of " dividends " any surplus or overcharge which experience shows it is not necessary to keep. The policyholder is not guaranteed any such returns. The return depends upon the opinion of the officials of the company, but in actual practice the competition of other participating and non-participating companies compels such a return of these overcharges.

Under a non-participating policy the loading is less, for the policyholder does not expect any return. The loading or the gross premium may in non-participating insurance approach the net premium by whatever amount the company considers will take care of expenses and contingencies in addition to whatever source of surplus earnings the company may have, such, for example, as surplus interest earnings and a lower mortality cost than the calculated. The difference in the participating and non-participating company, so far as loading is concerned, consists in the fact that the stockholders of the latter company assume the risk of expenses and losses for the privilege of securing any surplus earnings from the business.

Assessing the Expense. — It is not an easy matter in any business to separate and properly assess the expenses of the business, and in the insurance business the problem is particularly difficult. There are joint, fixed, and variable expenses, almost defying any scientific analysis. For example, the expense of rent is largely fixed. An office force of a hundred persons is required to transact a certain amount of business, but probably an addition of fifty persons could transact twice as much business.

A common classification of expenses of an insurance company is as follows: (a) new business; (b) collections; (c) investments; (d) settlements; (e) general. Even assuming that proper provision has been made for the first year's expenses, the problem remains of determining the distribution of expenses other than those due to new business. In other words, how and how much should the regular net premium be loaded? So far as the expenses can be definitely fixed and determined, a certain percentage of the net premium may be added to it. But there yet remain other expenses, such as the general expenses, which are varying, and for which it is difficult to secure a satisfactory basis on which to calculate this part of the loading.

Percentage and Flat Loading for Expense. — If to take care of these expenses a flat or constant sum is added to the net premium, the loading on a short-term policy would be much heavier at the younger ages than on a high-premium policy such as the endowment at the same age. For example, the net premium on a Five-year Term Policy at age 20 for $1000 of insurance is $7.64 and for a Twenty-year Endowment Policy at that age $38.90. If, therefore, $5 be added as the loading to make the Gross or Office Premium in each case, this loading is 39 per cent of the first premium and only 11 per cent of the second. In this case a percentage has real significance, since the former policy is contributing to a much greater extent to the expenses of the company than the latter without incurring by its character any such added expense.

If, however, instead of a flat sum being added to the net premium for loading, a percentage of this premium is added, the result is equally undesirable. Those entering the company at the older ages and those purchasing the higher-price policies would be paying an unduly large sum in the loading on their policies.

For example, suppose the loading is 20 per cent of the net premium. In the preceding case the person having the Five-year Term Policy would pay each year as loading $1.52, while the other person with the Twenty-year Endowment Policy would pay $7.78. The expenses, as has been shown, are in most cases of a joint character and are not capable of being individualized. The method of loading most common is to add a fixed percentage to the net premium for a whole-life policy at the age of the insured, and in the case of Limited-payment and Endowment Policies to add in addition a certain percentage of the net premium for the particular policy. The percentage addition to the whole-life net premium thus becomes a constant sum or addition and the other a percentage addition. The percentage addition thus becomes an increasing sum with the increase of the net premium at older ages and for large amounts of insurance, while the constant addition takes care of those expenses, administrative and otherwise, which are in the nature fixed and constant during the life of the policy, and in general do not vary with the amount of the insurance. Special classes of policies may have their loading determined otherwise than by this simple method.

Net Cost as a Basis for Loading. — It has been suggested that the net cost of insurance is a proper basis upon which to add these general expenses. At age 56 the amount at risk during the first year on a $1000 whole-life policy is $970.10, that is to say, it is the face of the policy less the reserve at the end of the first year, which is set aside for future mortality. The amount of risk is sometimes wrongly called self-insurance. In our hypothetical company of the 63,364 persons surviving to age 56, 1260 will die during the following year. If, therefore, the company had insured 63,364 persons at age 56, the expected net loss would be 1260 times $970.10 or $1,222,326. This is the cost of insurance for the first year, and the sum divided by the 63,364 persons living at the beginning of the year makes the annual per capita cost of insurance for a $1000 whole-life policy at this age $19.29. This sum, it is argued, supplies a fair basis upon which to determine the loading for general expenses. Yet this is a somewhat arbitrarily selected basis, since some of the general expenses bear no necessary relation to it.

It has been suggested in view of the heavy taxes levied on insurance in some of the states that the premiums on policies sold in the offending state should have their normal loading increased: but this is practically impossible, whatever might be its theoretical justification. It is argued that this would serve as an object lesson in the incidence of insurance taxes. The subject of taxation is, however, reserved for later consideration.

In the table at the close of the chapter are given the net, the gross participating, and the gross non-participating premiums on policies at different ages and on different types of policies from which the loading in each case can be secured by taking the difference between the net and the gross premium.

The Premium on Industrial Policies. — The premium of the industrial policies determines the amount of insurance, whereas in the ordinary insurance company the amount of the insurance determines the premium. The calculations of the premiums for industrial insurance are made in much the same manner as the premiums in ordinary companies, although the industrial companies are basing their premiums more and more on their own mortality experience. They are, however, level premiums. The loading in industrial insurance premiums is, however, much greater than in the ordinary life insurance company's premiums, due chiefly to the higher cost of transacting the business.

The Premium on Assessment Policies. — The practice of assessment and fraternal companies has been sufficiently described for the reader to understand that it is impossible to give such an explanation of the premium calculations as in the regular and industrial companies. In some of these companies the premium is simply the pro ratio mortality cost of the year, no reserve being accumulated; in others a mortality table, such as The National Fraternal Congress Table of Mortality, is used. In this case the premiums are determined as in the ordinary company, a reserve being collected. Some of the fraternal organizations use the ordinary mortality tables, and the premiums are calculated in the same manner as in the regular companies; some claim to use their own mortality experience as a basis of calculating the premiums. For the other organizations operating on unscientific plans, no logical explanation of their premium calculations can be given.

NET, GROSS NON-PARTICIPATING, AND GROSS PARTICIPATING PREMIUMS

AMERICAN TABLE, 3½ % $1000 INSURANCE

AGE	WHOLE LIFE			20-PAYMENT LIFE			20-YEAR ENDOWMENT		
	Net $	Gross N.P. $[1]	Gross P. $[1]	Net $	Gross N.P. $[1]	Gross P. $[1]	Net $	Gross N.P. $[1]	Gross P. $[1]
25	15.10	16.46	19.63	22.53	24.11	28.55	39.14	41.22	48.48
35	19.91	21.70	25.88	27.40	29.32	34.87	40.12	42.52	50.14
45	28.35	30.91	36.86	35.07	37.53	44.92	43.08	46.07	54.53
55	44.13	46.60	57.37	48.70	51.01	62.85	52.21	54.86	67.07

REFERENCES

Dawson, Miles M.   The Business of Life Insurance, Chaps. X, XI, XII, XX, XXIV, XXVI.

Graham, W. J.   The Romances of Life Insurance, Chap. IV.

Yale Readings, Vol. I, Chaps. XV, XVI, XVII, XX.

Report of the New York Joint Committee of the Senate and Assembly on Life Insurance, 1906, pp. 415-416, 435-437.

Alexander, William.   The Life Insurance Company, Part I.

Walford, Cornelius.   Cyclopedia of Insurance.

Wolfe, S. H.   Inheritance Tax Calculations.

Transactions of the Faculty of Actuaries, Vol. III, pp. 1-30.

[1] The premiums quoted are from the rate books of representative non-participating and participating companies.

CHAPTER VIII

THE RESERVE AND VALUATION OF POLICIES

The Reserve. — We have seen in the previous chapter that the net annual premium collected by the insurance companies operating on the level premium plan is in excess of the actual cost of the insurance during the early years of the contract, but below the cost in the latter years. This excess of the earlier years is accumulated into a sinking fund or a reserve to meet the deficiencies of the later years. The reserve is the difference between the present value of the benefits promised in the policies and the present value of the net annual premiums to be collected in the future. Therefore the reserve is sometimes called the unearned premium income. This assumes that all the net annual premiums at a given date have been paid and that the future experience will be in harmony with the calculated experience. This fund together with the later annual premiums received and the interest accumulations will pay for that protection which is promised at the later date when the net premiums are less than the annual costs. Recalling our illustration of the rectangle and the triangle and thinking of a single life insured on the level premium plan, the reserve originates from the excess collections in the early years, which are used to balance the deficient collections in the later years.

If each of the members of the theoretical insurance company, starting with 100,000 members and insuring no new lives, would pay his single net premium, this would constitute a fund which with its interest accumulations would be sufficient to pay all the future death claims.

The reserve includes all the funds in the possession of the company set aside for the payment of policy claims. It might, therefore, be more properly called the mortality fund. From one point of view the reserve is also called the reinsurance fund, that is to say, it is such a collected fund that the original company or any other company could meet all its obligations by the proper care of this fund, augmented by future collections from policyholders. It is on account of the accumulation of this sinking fund that old line level premium companies are able to close up their business by selling or reinsuring their business in another company. This assumes that the lives have been properly selected. If this is not the case, or if the company and its investment have not been properly managed, another company might not be willing to assume these obligations on the basis of the reinsurance reserve held for these risks.

Source of the Reserve. — The source, therefore, of the reserve is the excess payments in early life, made to provide for the increasing mortality charge of late life. With increasing age the value of these payments by the insured — the premiums — grows less to the company, since as the insured sum or policy approaches maturity the company must have on hand funds to pay the claim. This fund is gradually accumulated during the term of

Q

the policy by the current payments and their interest earnings and hence the source of the large amount of funds which all insurance companies writing policies on the level premium plan have. The amount of the reserve at any one time depends upon the character of the business on the books of the company. If the company has, for example, a large number of its policies on the endowment plan, it will have, all other things being equal, a larger reserve than another company with a smaller percentage of such policies. Likewise the age of the company affects the amount of its reserve. To argue, as is sometimes done, that a high ratio of Accumulated Reserves to Mean Insurance in Force is indicative of the strength of a company is not justified by the facts and proves nothing regarding the excellence of a company.

Methods of Increasing Reserve. — The chief methods open to a company to strengthen its reserves are as follows. First, it may use a Mortality Table, if the law permits, to value its policies, which shows a higher standard than that experienced. It has been shown that mortality tables differ in their standards, such tables as the H^m and the National Fraternal Congress Table having higher standards than the Actuaries or the American Table.

Second, it can adopt, in valuing its policy obligations, a lower rate of interest than the normal one. That is, it can assume that it will earn only $2\frac{1}{2}$ per cent interest on its invested funds when, as a matter of fact, it earns 3 per cent.

Third, it may value its funds invested in bonds and

stocks at less than their actual market value. It is, however, a general legal requirement in the various states to establish by law the mortality tables and the interest rates upon which the policy obligations must be computed. This will be discussed in detail under the subject of Valuation.

Calculating Reserves. — In order to understand the method of determining the reserve, let us take for an example the company of 100,000 persons insured under the American Mortality Table on a 3 per cent interest basis. At age 50 only 69,804 are living, and the company promises to pay to each $1000 at death. It has been shown that the single premium for such a policy at this age is $555.22. The total collections by the company must, then, be sufficient with the annual interest additions to mature all of its obligations. The company will, therefore, collect at the beginning of the fiftieth year a total of $38,756,576.88, which will draw a 3 per cent interest, making the total sum at the close of the year $39,919,274.18. From this sum the death claims of $962,000 must be paid, leaving $38,957,274.18.

Terminal and Individual Reserve. — This last sum may be called the terminal reserve, which divided by the number now living, 68,842, gives $565.89, which is the individual reserve at the close of the fifty-first year of age. In a like manner this sum will accumulate, and payments will be made from it on account of death claims until, under our assumptions, there will be in the ninety-fifth year of age just enough, with the interest accumulations of that year, to pay the final claims of the three expiring policyholders. It can be seen from the above example that the aggregate reserve or the reserve held for all policies in this assumed company is a continually decreasing sum, but that the individual reserve is annually increasing. It must also be evident that the individual reserve at the close of any year of age is the single premium for $1000 of insurance on the ordinary life plan at the attained age. For example, the individual reserve at the close of the fifty-fifth year of age is $621.18, and this is also the net single premium for any person at age 56 who wishes to become a member of the company. Those who have become members earlier have provided for their insurance by paying once for all a sum which, on account of its longer interest accumulations, is smaller than this sum, although the entrant is of the same age as the other members. It is necessary for him to do this in order to equalize the difference in length of membership or in other words to balance the effect of the interest accumulations. We have seen, however, that few persons care to pay the single premium, but prefer to pay annual premiums, which it has been shown must be collectively the mathematical equivalent of the single premium. Likewise it may be shown that the reserve accumulated from annual premiums will be as effective as that accumulated from the single premiums.

We have found that the annual premium at 50 years of age for a whole-life $1000 policy under the American Mortality Table at 3 per cent is $36.36. If each of the 69,804 members now living pay this sum, the amount at the close of the year with its 3 per cent interest accumulations will be $2,615,215.64. From this sum the

$962,000 death claims will be paid, leaving $1,653,215.64 as the terminal reserve at the close of the first year of the policy, which divided by 68,842 then living at age 51 gives $24 as the individual reserve at the close of the first policy year. But we have just shown that the individual reserve in the case of the single premium was far greater than the sum just calculated. Again the net annual premium for a person at age 51 is not $24, the individual reserve of the last calculation. Can the company be said to be equally as solvent as in the first case? If so, how shall we reconcile these apparent discrepancies?

The explanation is to be found in the difference in the terms of the contract. In the first case, that of a single premium, the company agreed to pay to each policyholder at his death $1000, because each paid the large sum, the single premium, once and for all time. In the latter case, the insured agreed to pay the $36.36 at the beginning of each year during life. If he lives throughout the year and does not pay his second premium, the company is not under obligations thereafter to pay the $1000 at his death. It is true, since it is a net annual level premium and not a net annual natural premium, that he has more than paid for his protection and therefore a sum may be returned to him as a cash surrender value which is based upon the difference of these two premiums; but the company is then freed from any future obligations to him. Let us notice further how the discrepancy is removed. If the company has the promise of each to pay annually these net premiums, it may take credit for their present value as an offset to the present value of its promised benefits. At age 50 there were living 68,842 persons, each of whom agreed to pay $36.36 annually as long as he lived. The question then is, What is the present value of these future payments? The value at age 51 of an annuity of $1 paid at the beginning of the year and at the beginning of each subsequent year is on 3 per cent interest accumulation $14.9045. Therefore, the value of $36.36 would be 14.9045 times this sum or $541.9286 for each of the 68,842 persons, and for all of them $37,307,448.68. This sum added to the aggregate terminal reserve at the close of the first policy year under the net annual premium paying plan beginning at age 50 equals $38,960,664.32, the aggregate terminal reserve at age 51 under the net single premium paying plan. The small difference would disappear if decimals had been used in the calculation. Thus the small reserve on the annual premium policy is just as effective as the large reserve on the single premium policy. Again, the present value of the $36.36 premium is $541.92 (36.36 times $14.9045), and this sum subtracted from $565.89, the individual reserve under the net single premium plan, leaves $23.97, or practically $24, the individual reserve under the net annual premium plan.

The table on pages 232–233 illustrates how the reserve accumulates under an ordinary life policy.

The net premium and not the gross premium is the basis of the reserve calculations. Column five represents the initial reserve which after the first year is made up of net premiums and the terminal reserve at the close of the year just preceding. The year's interest on this sum is added to it, death claims are paid, and the remainder makes up the terminal reserve which divided by the number of policies gives the individual reserve, or reserve on each policy. This table can also be used to prove the adequacy of the net premium. It also shows that an insurance company transacting business on the level premium basis could at any time discontinue writing business and assuming that its mortality and interest experience would be in harmony with that calculated, it would be able to pay all its obligations. The net premiums which have been collected are with their interest accumulations used to pay the mortality claims owed in the ninety fifth year, the three net premiums with the initial reserve of that year and the interest earned being sufficient to pay the three death claims of $3000. The reserve is thus constantly being drawn upon for the payment of death claims and if in an actual company as compared with the hypothetical company, taken in the table, the reserve is an increasing fund, it is because the company is increasing the number of policies on its books.

The table also proves the adequacy of the ordinary life net premium. Since the limited-payment life premium has been shown to be the equivalent of the whole-life premium at the same age, the table is equally a proof of the adequacy of the limited-payment life premiums. A similar calculation would show the sufficiency of the endowment net premium, since the endowment policy is composed of a term policy and a pure endowment. Expressed otherwise, a whole-life policy may be considered an endowment policy to the

VERIFICATION TABLE

Ordinary Life, $1,000.   Age 56.   Net Yearly Premium $47.760895.   American Experience 3 Per Cent.

1 Age	2 Members Living	3 Deaths	4 Net Premium Income	5 Initial Reserve	6 Add One Year's Interest	7 Deduct Death Claims	8 Balance, Terminal Reserve	9 Reserve on each Policy	10 End of
56	63,364	1,260	$3,026,321.35	$3,026,321.35	$90,789.64	$1,260,000	$1,857,110.99	$29.90	1 yr.
57	62,104	1,325	2,966,142.62	4,823,253.61	144,697.61	1,325,000	3,642,951.22	59.94	2 yr.
58	60,779	1,394	2,902,859.44	6,545,810.66	96,374.32	1,394,000	5,348,184.98	90.06	3 "
59	59,385	1,468	2,836,280.75	8,184,465.73	245,533.97	1,468,000	6,961,999.70	120.21	4 "
60	57,917	1,546	2,766,167.76	9,728,167.46	291,845.02	1,546,000	8,474,012.48	150.33	5 "
61	56,371	1,628	2,692,329.41	11,166,341.89	334,990.26	1,628,000	9,873,332.15	180.36	6 "
62	54,743	1,713	2,614,574.67	12,487,906.82	374,637.20	1,713,000	11,149,544.02	210.25	7 "
63	53,030	1,800	2,532,760.26	13,682,304.28	410,469.13	1,800,000	12,292,773.41	239.95	8 "
64	51,230	1,889	2,446,790.65	14,739,564.06	442,186.92	1,889,000	13,292,750.98	269.41	9 "
65	49,341	1,980	2,356,570.32	15,649,321.30	469,479.64	1,980,000	14,138,800.94	298.53	10 "
66	47,361	2,070	2,262,003.75	16,400,804.69	492,024.14	2,070,000	14,822,828.83	327.28	11 "
67	45,291	2,158	2,163,138.70	16,985,967.53	509,579.03	2,158,000	15,337,546.56	355.59	12 "
68	43,133	2,243	2,060,070.68	17,397,617.24	521,928.52	2,243,000	15,676,545.76	383.38	13 "
69	40,890	2,321	1,952,943.00	17,629,488.76	528,884.66	2,321,000	15,837,373.42	410.62	14 "
70	38,569	2,391	1,842,089.96	17,679,463.38	530,383.90	2,391,000	15,818,847.28	437.25	15 "

80	14,474	2,091	691,291.19	10,162,261.32	304,867.84	2,091,000	8,376,129.16	676.42	25 "
81	12,383	1,964	591,423.16	8,967,552.32	269,026.57	1,964,000	7,272,578.89	698.01	26 "
82	10,419	1,816	97,620.77	7,770,199.66	33,105.99	1,816,000	67,305.65	719.20	27 "
83	8,603	1,648	410,886.98	6,598,192.63	97,945.78	1,648,000	5,148,138.41	740.21	28 "
84	6,955	1,470	32,177.02	5,480,315.43	64,409.46	1,470,000	4,174,724.89	761.12	29 "
85	5,485	1,292	61,968.51	4,436,693.40	33,90.80	1,292,000	3,277, 94.20	781.73	30 "
86	4,193	1,114	20,261.43	3,478,055.63	04, 41.67	1,114,000	2,468, 97.30	801.69	31 "
87	3,079	93	47,055.80	2,615,453.10	78,463.59	93, 00	1,760,916.69	820.56	32 "
88	2,146	44	102,494.88	1,863,411.57	55, 92.35	744,000	1,175,313.92	838.31	33 "
89	32	55	66,960.77	1,242,274.69	37, 68.24	, 90	724, 42.93	855.42	34 "
90	47	85	40,453.48	764,996.41	22, 99.89	, 90	402,946.30	872.18	35 "
91	42	46	22,065.53	425,011.83	12, 30.36	, 90	191,762.19	887.79	36 "
92	26	137	10,316.35	202,078.54	6,062.36	137, 00	71,140.90	900.52	37 "
93	79	58	3,773.11	74,914.01	2, 47.42	, 90	61.43	912.45	38 "
94	21	18	1,002.98	20,164.41	64.93	, 90	2,769.34	923.11	39 "
95	3	3	143.28	2,912.62	87.38	, 90			40 "

NOTE — A larger number of decimals than those given in the above table were retained in the actual calculation.

end of life, since the reserve becomes equal to the face of the policy at the close of life in the table, that is, at age 96.

It will thus be seen that there is nothing mysterious about the reserve. It is not to be compared, as was done by the early supporters of assessmentism, to a fifth wheel of a wagon. It is the indispensable requisite of scientific insurance on the level premium plan, and as it has been previously shown that the natural premium plan is in practice impossible, the reserve becomes the *sine qua non* of all insurance. It is not the result of legislative enactments, but is the cause of most laws which have reference to it. It is a deposit and a convenience for the policyholder and not a source of profit for the company. The reserve is not an asset but a liability by which the annual premium is kept from increasing in face of the increasing risk against which it protects the policyholder.

Reserve not Individualistic. — While the term "individual reserve" or "reserve on each policy" is used, it must not be understood as that sum which in all cases determines the equity of the particular policyholder. In the case of a policyholder withdrawing from the company, it has individual importance in determining the cash which will be granted to him. It is not, however, strictly considered an individual sum, as may be indicated when a policyholder dies after having paid only a few premiums on a policy. He receives, for example, $1000, the face of his policy, and not the amount, for example, $30, which he has paid to the company. Thus again is emphasized the fact that insurance is primarily concerned with the group and not with the individual; that is, insurance is a mutual association for purposes of individual protection with little question as to the amounts paid in and the amounts received by any one person. Insurance funds are held for the protection of all members.

The Reserve in Insurance and in a Bank. — The reserve of an insurance company cannot be accurately compared with the reserve of a bank. The purpose in mind of the collection is different in the two cases. If any element of comparison can be made, it exists between the reserve of an insurance company and the deposits of a bank, since in each case these are the amounts received from the persons with whom the bank and the insurance company are doing business. They are respectively the debits to the patrons of the two companies. The reserve of a bank is only a small part of its obligations to the depositors. Nor does the percentage existing between the reserve and deposits of a bank and the reserve and the face value of the policies in an insurance company bear any definite relation. The bank has obligated itself to pay to its depositors all their deposits, but an insurance company obligates itself to pay the face of the policies only in the event that the policyholders continue to pay the specified annual premiums. In an effort to understand the insurance business, attempts are often made to compare its funds with those of a bank, but such comparisons usually result in greater confusion.

Valuation. — An insurance company desires to know from time to time for its own protection the status of its business in respect to its assets and liabilities. The state also is interested in protecting those of its citizens who are insured, and it therefore has by legal enactment laid down rules regarding the time and methods of determining the relation of the insurance company's obligations to the funds set aside for meeting them. This process of calculating what corresponds in a general way to the " trial balance " in business is in the case of insurance companies called Valuation. The insurance laws of most states in the United States require that every regular insurance company have in its possession either cash or securities equal to the net value of each policy contract which it has written. This net value refers to the reserve on the policy and, as has been shown, is equal to the difference between the present worth of the net premiums to be paid under the policy and the present worth of the monetary benefits granted by the contract. These monetary benefits include death claims, surrender, cash and loan values, and any other forms which the benefit may take. The valuation is the process of calculating these amounts. The statutes usually establish only a minimum legal standard of valuation which the companies must have. For their own purposes they may and do make other calculations of values. But it is this minimum legal standard of valuation by the state which is the basis of the frequent assertion that a life insurance policy in a regular company on the level premium plan is absolutely safe. It is safe because the state compels each company to maintain this cash or equivalent value for each policy. The life insurance policy is therefore as safe and secure a possession as anything human can be.

It has been shown how the company bases its premium calculations on the death rates of a mortality table, derived from carefully collected data and by mathematically exact formulas. It carefully chooses the lives to be insured in order that the mortality may be in harmony with that shown by this table. It also assumes that it will be able to loan at a certain rate of interest the surplus funds which are intrusted to it by those paying for their insurance in part in advance under the level premium plan. This rate of interest is based upon the knowledge of what interest has in the past actually been earned, together with a study of the present and prospective factors determining rates of interest. Just as it has been shown that the actual mortality experienced is kept within the expected or calculated, so the interest which the company assumes it can earn is taken at a rate which it expects to exceed in its actual earnings. When a company has been in existence for a great number of years, this interest-earning basis has changed, so that it will have a part of its business, for example, on a 4 per cent and another part on a 3 per cent basis. As is well known, the rate of interest fluctuates over long periods of time, and the insurance company adjusts the rate at which it assumes it can invest the funds, always endeavoring to realize in its actual results something above this assumed rate. In the statutes enacted to establish methods of valuation, the interest rate established is generally $3\frac{1}{2}$ per cent, 4 per cent, or $4\frac{1}{2}$ per cent. The valuation, then, of the policies, that is, the obligations incurred under them, is based upon the element of mortality and interest. It is not necessary to explain why it is based on the net premium and not on the gross premium.

Methods of Valuation. — There are three chief methods which may be used in the valuation of policies: the Preliminary-term, the Modified Preliminary Term, and the Select and Ultimate Method.

The Preliminary-term Method is that one in which the policy contract is written as a one-year term contract with the regular life insurance contract beginning the second year. That is, the company grants the insurance for one year and continues the policy thereafter for the whole life or a limited number of years, according as it is either a whole-life or a limited-payment life policy. There is no change in the premium. Since the net premium for a one-year term policy, that is, the mortality cost, is much less than the net premium for a whole life or limited-payment life policy, this leaves a large margin of the first year's premium for expenses. It has been shown that the loading on an insurance premium is often not large enough to cover the first year's expenses. Under this preliminary-term method, therefore, all the first year's premium, except what is necessary for the actual mortality cost, can be used as expenses. That is, the real loading on the first year's premium under this method is a very large part of it. For example, the gross premium in a representative company for an ordinary life policy for $1000 at age 56 at 3 per cent is $63.68; the net premium is $47.76. This leaves a loading for expense of $15.92, but if the policy is written under the preliminary-term method, the net premium or the mortality cost for the year is only $19.31. This sum subtracted from \$63.68 leaves \$44.37 to be used as a loading or expense as compared with the above, \$15.92. In the valuation of policies written under this plan, the company is not charged with any reserve for the first year on such policies. After this date, the charge for the reserve is the same as if the policy had not been written on such a plan, and the loading continues the same, that is, in the above example, \$15.92. The advantage of this method is easily recognized to exist in providing for the cost of acquiring new business. This is especially an advantage for new companies, particularly those which are organized as mutual companies. Such companies have no funds to establish the organization and secure business except as it is advanced by the incorporators of the company. There are no stockholders as in a stock company to advance money and run the risk of securing its returns from the later business of the company. It has been shown, however, that in the case of mutual companies it is frequently the practice for the incorporators to have a minimum amount of stock, either because the law requires it or because they use the proceeds of its sale for initial expenses. This stock, as has been described, is frequently retired. The important point is, however, in this connection that every insurance company must have on hand the reserve for all its policies written in the first year and at the same time provide for the expenses of organization and writing these first-year policies.

Preliminary-term Method. — When the pure preliminary-term method is applied to limited-payment and endowment policies, the loading of the first years becomes quite significant, as shown by the following table:

POLICY AGE 56, AMERICAN TABLE, THREE PER CENT

	Gross Premium	Net Natural Cost	Loading
Ordinary Life	63.68	19.31	44.37
Twenty-payment Life . .	69.26	19.31	49.95
Ten-payment Life	99.33	19.31	80.02
Twenty-year Endowment .	72.66	19.31	53.35
Ten-year Endowment . .	121.06	19.31	101.75

The Modified Preliminary-term Method of Valuation is a method originated to reduce the heavy loading of limited-payment and endowment policies under the pure preliminary-term method. Under this second method, the loading is limited to the amount which the ordinary life policy would have at that age under the pure preliminary-term method. This would leave a part of the premium to be used as a reserve during the first year, and in effect reduce the loading of the subsequent years. It should be stated that a number of modifications have been made of this Modified Preliminary-term Method.

Select and Ultimate Method. — The third method is the Select and Ultimate Method of Valuation. The chief difference between it and the other methods is that it affects the calculations of the reserves only for the first five years, while the other methods affect the reserves throughout the premium-paying period. It will be recalled that in the chapter on Selection of Lives the influence of the benefit of selection was described.

It was there shown that in the early years of insured lives the mortality experience was very favorable, that is, it was far below that indicated by the figures in the Mortality Table. This Select and Ultimate Method of Valuation assumes that this benefit of selection lasts for five years. The American Table of Mortality being assumed to be an Ultimate Table, that is, one showing the final mortality results, there is a margin in it during these early years.

The essence of this Select and Ultimate Method of Valuation is, that the mortality of the first policy year after the medical examination is calculated to be fifty per cent of that shown by the American Experience Table; in the second year, sixty-five per cent; in the third, seventy-five per cent; in the fourth, eighty-five per cent; and in the fifth, ninety-five per cent. In the subsequent years the mortality is assumed to be one hundred per cent of that indicated in the table. By this method, therefore, there is, as under the Preliminary-term Method of Valuation, funds available for expenses during the first years of policies, since the terminal reserves for the first four years will need to be less than that indicated by the American Table. The company collects the full premium during these five years, but because of the smaller reserves required, the margin can be used and anticipated for the expenses of securing new business. This method of valuing policies was first required by the New York Law in 1906. It will be understood that it also fixes a limitation on expense. Reference to the table on page 266 will illustrate the financial status at the close of the first year on the

R

three chief kinds of policies as given by a representative company.

It is the valuation which not only determines the financial status of the company's business, but also determines the paid up, the cash surrender and the loan values, the surplus, and the dividends. The cash surrender value, the paid up, and the loan values may be discussed at this point, reserving the surplus and the dividend for more extended discussion in the succeeding chapter.

Cash-surrender Value. — The cash-surrender value is that sum which the policyholder may withdraw from the company in the event that he wishes to discontinue his policy. In the early days of insurance no such privilege was a part of the contract, but it is now found in all policies. This has been due in part to legal enactment and in part to the competition of companies, which as insurance science and practice developed found that they could grant such a privilege without jeopardizing either their contracts or their dividends. The cash-surrender and loan values are ordinarily the same and are based upon the amount of the reserve held by the company for each $1000 of insurance at the end of each year of insurance. It does not follow, however, that these values will be the same in all companies on a particular policy at a stated age. The particular amount depends upon the method of valuation used, the legal requirements of a particular state, the practice of other companies, and the judgment or wishes of the officials of a particular company. Surrender and cash values are usually not granted until the policy has been in force two years, and in all states a surrender charge is permitted. This charge is often established by law, such as 2½ per cent or 3 per cent of the insurance; in other cases it is 20 per cent of the reserve on the policy. The reason for establishing a surrender charge is that the insured has contracted with the company, that is, with the other members of the group, to remain in the organization until the close of the period of this contract, that is, for life or for a given number of years. The company has been at considerable expense in taking the insured into the group. He has been solicited to join; he has been examined by a physician, and the granting of the policy occasions extra expense and, as has been shown, his first premium leaves practically nothing after these initial expenses are paid. Life insurance is a coöperative arrangement to protect against contingencies which occur over a long series of years. If absolute freedom of withdrawal were permitted it might well happen that many risks would often withdraw. A penalty on withdrawal is thus established by the surrender charge, which is assumed to cover, in part at least, the expense of securing a new member to take the place of the withdrawing member.

Paid-up Insurance. — The Paid-up Insurance Value is the amount of insurance which the cash surrender value will as a single premium purchase at the attained age of the insured. Since the cash surrender value depends upon the reserve, so the paid-up insurance also depends upon it. This results from the fact that the insured sometimes neglects or is unable to pay his premiums, although he may not voluntarily withdraw from the company. Paid-up insurance may also be granted at the close of the period of an endowment policy, but it then also depends upon the cash value which is in turn dependent upon the accumulated reserve. The paid-up insurance is manifestly a larger sum than the cash or surrender values, since the latter sum is to remain with the company to draw interest to provide for the amount of insurance granted.

Extended insurance is also another result of the valuation policies. Extended insurance is that number of years and months beyond the date when the policyholder lapses his policy during which the policy as a whole still remains in force. If it is later matured by death, the company pays the sum assured minus any past debts with interest due to the company. The time of the extension depends upon the cash value of the policy at the time of the lapse, and results from the fact that the policyholder under the level premium plan has been paying premiums in excess of the cost of the insurance which has been accumulating with their interest as a reserve.

REFERENCES

Dawson, Miles M. The Business of Life Insurance, Chaps. V, XIX.

Smith, G. W. Notes on Life Insurance, Chaps III, VII.

Yale Readings, Vol. I, Chap. XIII.

Report of Joint Committee of Senate and Assembly of New York, pp. 378–388, 418–429.

Insurance Guide and Handbook, Fifth Edition, Chaps. XIII, XIV.

Practical Lessons in Actuarial Science, Miles M. Dawson, Vol. II. pp. 122–204; Vol. I, pp. 204–250.

CHAPTER IX

THE SURPLUS AND DIVIDENDS

THE methods of valuation discussed in the preceding chapter determine the legal solvency of an insurance company. But the test thus applied, if just met by an insurance company, is not a safe basis for operating the company. Any marked increase in the mortality. or the expense or a depreciation of the investments would bring the company into bankruptcy. It is the practice, therefore, of all insurance companies to maintain a sum in excess of this minimum legal requirement. This excess is called a " surplus," " the undivided surplus," " the contingency reserve," or " unassigned funds."

The Surplus. — The term " surplus " is used in two leading senses when applied to the insurance business: first, that sum which remains at the close of any calendar year after death claims and the current expenses of conducting the company have been paid; second, the sum remaining after current expenses, annual death claims, and the reserve are deducted. It does violence to the ordinary meaning of the word " surplus " to apply the first definition. A somewhat parallel example would be for a person to borrow $32,000 to engage in a business. Suppose he pays $30,000 for the business, $2000 for equipment, and at the close of the year finds

that he has $3000 as a result of his operation.   He would
not be justified in claiming that he has a surplus of
$1000 because he has $1000 remaining after he pays for
his equipment.   Nor would $500 be his surplus, if he
allowed $500 for his services, for he owes $32,000 for
the business with the interest thereon.   Just so the
life insurance company cannot call a surplus all that
sum which remains after the current year's expenses
and death claims are paid.   A sum equal to the aggregate reserve on all policy obligations must be set aside.

Origin of the Surplus. — Let us again consider the
net premium in order that we may understand the composition and origin of the surplus.   It will be recalled
that a company assumed that a certain rate of interest
could be earned and also assumed from the mortality
tables that a certain number of claims would fall due.   It
was able then to calculate the sum which it would need
to collect.   To this sum, the net premium, it made
certain additions, called loading, for the purpose of
covering expenses and contingencies.   There would
thus be three main sources from which a surplus might
be secured, namely, interest, mortality, and loading.
That is to say, a saving might be effected from any one
or all of these sources.

A fourth source of the surplus may be from the excess
of the policy reserve over the surrender values on such
policies when they are discontinued.

Surplus Interest. — The rate of the interest which
the insurance companies assume that they can earn on
their assets has always been conservative, and in actual
practice they have been able to earn more than the

assumed rate. The rates now most generally assumed are 3 per cent and 3½ per cent. The expenses incurred in investing the assets are charges against the interest income. Since these investment expenses may amount at least to one half of 1 per cent on the assets, it is necessary to earn sufficient to cover the investment expenses in addition to the interest at the assumed rate before there is any surplus from interest. Many of the old policies now in force on the books of insurance companies were issued on a 4 per cent interest assumption, and on the reserve of such policies, 4 per cent interest must be earned in addition to the investment expenses before there is any surplus for these policies from interest.

In the later years of a policy when the reserves are large, the gain or saving from interest become important.

Mortality Savings. — The company has assumed a certain death loss, and if the actual mortality is below the expected, a saving will be effected. The importance of this saving may, however, be easily overemphasized. If the company had based its premiums on a mortality table of the general population, the mortality saving might constitute a permanent addition to the surplus, provided it had used care in selecting the persons for insurance. But the tables of mortality now in use are based on the experience of insured lives after the benefit of selection has disappeared. The actual results are therefore likely to approach through a long series of years the calculated results, although by a careful selection of new insurants the actual experience may be kept below the assumed. If, however, a very favorable

mortality is experienced for a series of years, this suspended mortality as it is called may become actual
mortality later.   The important point in this connection
is to understand that these claims must be paid, and
whatever of gain there is to come to the company results, not from writing off the face of the claims, but
simply from the added number of premiums the company collects and larger interest accumulations on the
sums which continue to draw interest after the time at
which it was calculated they would fall due by death
claims.   Therefore, it would not seem wise, for a mutual
company at least, to consider the total sum as an addition to the surplus for the purpose of distributing it
as annual dividends.   It is evident that the mortality
experience of one year is no criterion by which a company can be guided.   The mortality may fluctuate
from year to year, and hence a part of a large saving in
mortality in one year may wisely be retained from the
dividends of that year in order to balance a smaller
saving in mortality in a later year and so prevent marked
decreases in dividends.   An examination of the annual
mortality experience of most insurance companies will
disclose the fact that the actual mortality is less than
the calculated.

The saving in mortality will for reasons previously
discussed be greatest in the early years of a policy's
duration.   This is true notwithstanding that the actual
death rate of the company may continue below the calculated normal rate.   This results because the saving is
measured by the amount at risk and not by the face
amount of the claim.   This saving is, however, offset

in part by the higher expenses of the early years, as well as the lower interest earnings or savings on the small reserves of the early years.

Saving in Loading. — The third source of the surplus is from loading. If, for example, the net premium has had an addition of 25 per cent made to it for expenses and contingencies, which is 20 per cent of the gross premium and only 12 per cent of the gross premium is used, there is a margin of 8 per cent left to accumulate from each year's premiums at compound interest. The word "contingencies" used in connection with expense has a rather indefinite meaning, but so far as it means an abnormal death rate due, for example, to a plague, it has little importance. It has little more importance so far as it refers to continually unfavorable investments, for as we shall see later the investments are so widely distributed in respect to regions and kinds of loans, that abnormal returns on the funds as a whole are not likely to be experienced for any considerable number of years.

The Character of Expense in Insurance. — The discussion of saving from loading is therefore taken as referring to expense. This is a subject of very great importance in the business of life insurance, for in no other business are the evil effects of excessive expense so vital. The desire for new business on the part of strongly competing old companies, as well as on the part of the newly formed company, seeking to establish itself, has been so great that many states have considered it necessary to lay down the limit of expense for new business. In no other commercial enterprise are the evil effects of unregulated competition more clearly shown. The evil effects of abnormal expense do not show themselves immediately after the expenditure, as in most kinds of business, and hence the greater fortitude required to resist the temptation to increase rapidly the business of a new company. The new company in the early years will have collected sums far in excess of the death claims, both on account of the excess premiums of those years and the low mortality. No purchaser of insurance, however, should be deluded into thinking a new or an old company excellent because it has written a large volume of new business, for the amount of new business is in itself no proof of present wisdom or future prosperity. The initial expense of insuring new members is necessarily very large. This expense together with the mortality cost and the required statutory reserve is greater than the premium income for the first year in full reserve companies and frequently is equal and sometimes in excess of the first year's premium even in preliminary-term companies.

Significance of New Business. — If sufficient insurance, both as to number of policyholders and amount of insurance, has been obtained so that average results are secured, the policyholders might be satisfied to insure only sufficient lives thereafter to meet the canceled policies. If it is a company selling participating policies only, and average results are being received, there may be no gain by increasing absolutely its membership, because the larger membership means that the profits are distributed among a greater number. This may be illustrated by an example from the business world. Suppose A places $100,000 in a business and secures $5000 profit but later takes in a partner, B, with $100,000 capital. At the close of the second year suppose there is $10,000 profit but A has gained nothing by the partnership. It is true he has given B an opportunity to engage in business, but this is worth nothing to him in a financial sense. Just so an insurance company may take in new members, but this does not necessarily mean that the net cost of the insurance to the old policyholder is less.

This point is stated with emphasis for the reason that it has been the subject of much erroneous discussion in these later days of big companies and new companies. We do not overlook the fact that the insurance business is one which in certain respects is subject to the law of decreasing cost. Having an office force, the business can often be increased many per cent without any very great increase in this part of the expense. It is manifestly impossible to lay down hard and fast rules to determine the amount of new business which a company should write. It may be necessary to write sufficient new business to secure average results in the old company whose policies are being continually matured by death or otherwise. Quality rather than quantity of new business will, however, be the rule of all good companies.

However, the frequently assumed need of large size in order to secure these average results is not justified by the facts for there has been no clear case where a well-managed company has suffered from excessive death losses. On the other hand, no indictment can be drawn against a company because it is large. Its size may have been a result of long age, or of aggressive, able, and ,economical management. Large yearly increases may result from reckless management. Small yearly increases in business may result from incompetent management or it may be due to economical management with great liberality to its policyholders.

Certainly no obligation rests upon an insurance company to extend its business because it is a means of encouraging thrift, for however important to society the inculcation of thrift is, the insurance company is not primarily a philanthropic organization for the purpose of teaching social morals. It is a business corporation organized chiefly for the profit of its members. The company is to be judged, then, not by the volume of its business, but by the ratio of the expense to the premiums on the new business acquired, the ratio of actual to expected mortality, the average interest earned, and other criteria previously discussed.

Lapses. — The subject of lapses in relation to the surplus may be considered at this point chiefly on account of its significance in the past when lapsing policyholders were treated with much less liberality than at present. In the earlier days of insurance the policyholder who discontinued the payment of premiums often received no return from the company, regardless of the length of time that he had been paying premiums. In the case of some individuals who lapsed, their last payments produced an addition to the surplus, but the additions from this source were often much less than was commonly believed, and this for two reasons:

First, because the better lives were more likely to lapse, and hence an increased or unfavorable mortality experience resulted. Notwithstanding that the surrender value allowed is often less than the reserve value on the policy, this may be in part offset by the selection against the company. The lapsing of the better risks is more likely to be true when there is dissatisfaction with the company, its rates, or loss of confidence in its management. Later investigations seem to show that when lapses are normal, those withdrawing are, as a class, little if at all inferior to those remaining in the company. However, lapses are not a matter of indifference to any company. There is the additional expense of securing a new risk to take the place of the old one, which at the beginning of the contract had the proportionate share of the expense assessed against its premium. Even if the new risk was as good as the lapsed one, the insurance fund would not be the same because two subtractions have been made from it to secure a policyholder. At the present time profits from lapses are small, owing to the liberal surrender values, whether granted voluntarily to the policyholder in his policy by the company or made compulsory by statute. It is understood from the previous discussions that the first year's expenses are necessarily large. The law now requires that a cash sum, based on the reserve value of the policy, be paid to the lapsed member, usually after the third policy year, although some companies voluntarily grant such a cash surrender value earlier. Provision has been made, either by the preliminary-term plan or some modification of it, for the large expense of the first policy year. This was not the case in the earlier years of insurance, and hence the gain from lapsed members, numerous as they sometimes were, often was exaggerated in the popular mind.

The surplus, then, arises chiefly from the savings in mortality, the savings in interest, and the savings in expense or loading.

The Surplus and Legal Expenses. — The amount of this surplus, at least the minimum amount, is determined by the laws that have been passed by the legislatures. These specify the methods of valuing policies and the sums which may be spent as expenses. These statutes differ in detail from state to state, but the New York law may be taken as an example, both because it has been adopted by some other states and because of the large number of important life insurance companies chartered in New York. This New York law, as regards the amounts which may be used as expenses, makes a distinction between first year and succeeding years' expenses. The first year's expenses must not exceed: (1) the loading upon the first year's premium and (2) the present values of the assumed mortality savings for the first five years of policies in force at the end of the calendar year as valued by the select and ultimate method, and (3) the gross premium on policies issued and terminated during the year less the net cost of the insurance in force under them. These three sums make up the amount which may be used as first year's expenses.

Total expenses are limited to: (1) the total loading on premiums received; (2) the assumed mortality gains;

(3) an amount for investment expenses not exceeding one fourth of 1 per cent on mean invested assets; (4) real estate taxes and other outlays made exclusively on real estate. The amount paid as renewal commissions, that is, commissions on other than the first year's premium, is also limited. On endowment policies of less than twenty annual payments it is 5 per cent for fourteen years. On other policies it is 7½ per cent for nine years and 5 per cent for the next five years. On all policies after the first fifteen years, a collection fee of 3 per cent is permitted.

In the case of the mortality, the New York law requires the Insurance Superintendent to make annual valuations on the net premium basis as follows. The minimum standard for all policies written prior to January 1, 1901, is the Actuaries Table of Mortality with interest at 4 per cent per annum; and for policies issued after this date the American Experience Table of Mortality with interest at 3½ per cent is used, provided that the legal minimum valuation of all policies issued on or after January 1, 1907, shall be on the basis of the select and ultimate method. It should be observed that the law permits " any life insurance company to voluntarily value its policies or any class thereof according to the American Experience Table at a lower rate of interest than that prescribed, but not lower than 3 per cent with or without reference to the select and ultimate method." But any such excess valuation must be reported to the Insurance Superintendent.

As a result of the New York insurance investigations

in 1905, that state and some others enacted a law which limited the amount of surplus which a company could hold. It varies from 20 per cent to 5 per cent of the reserve liabilities, the former being the percentage in the case of smaller companies and the latter referring to companies whose reserve liabilities are over seventy-five millions of dollars. This was done on the ground that a large surplus was a continual temptation for misappropriation or misuse by the officials of the company, and also because it was thought that no large surplus need be held for such contingencies as excessive mortality or deficient interest earnings. It was argued that the surplus, being the property of the policyholders, should be returned to them either in the form of dividends or lower premiums. This assumes that a large surplus is not an indication of conservative management in the life insurance business. There is not, it is argued, anything in the life insurance business to correspond to a conflagration in the fire insurance business. The only parallel that could be found would be a plague or possibly continued and widespread unprofitable investments, each of which is considered by the lawmakers a too remote possibility to deserve important consideration.

Disposition of the Surplus. — The surplus having been determined, the question of its disposal arises. The officials may decide to set aside a part of it for contingencies which may arise from unusual fluctuations in interest earnings, or for an unusual death rate, or hold it temporarily and use it to equalize the dividends, which are made to policyholders over a series of years.

One company, for example, sets aside a part of these surplus accumulations and calls it a surplus mortality fund. Another company may hold such a fund for the general effect it has in suggesting security and strength of the company. Others simply call it a contingency reserve. In all such cases it constitutes an undivided or undistributed surplus. This remainder therefore makes up a divisible surplus which is granted to the policyholders as dividends. It must be understood that no question of a dividend arises when a policyholder has purchased a non-participating policy, since he has purchased the policy at a lower gross premium, and for this consideration he foregoes any right to obtain dividends.

Before a participating policy is entitled to share in this divisible surplus, the following charges are assessed against it: (*a*) its share of the death losses; (*b*) its share of the expense of the company; (*c*) its legal reserve at the close of the year; (*d*) such contribution to the contingency reserve as the officials of the company may think should be assessed against it.

Dividends. — The dividends are therefore that part of the overcharges which the officials of the company decide may safely be returned to the policyholders. This fund is sometimes called the profit or interest fund, but it will contribute to a better understanding of insurance if a more careful use of the word is preserved. Profit is the chance element in production and could be properly applied to the life insurance business in two cases. First, in the early days of insurance when, on account of the high rate of lapses and the terms of

s

the contract, considerable sums were forfeited to the company; second, when a pure stock company sells non-participating policies and by unusually good investments is able to sell insurance at a low net cost and still has a fund to divide among the stockholders.

Profits constitute a fund out of which real dividends are paid. Nor should interest be confused with dividends. Interest is the sum paid by the borrower to the lender for the use of capital. It is a guaranteed return, as in the case of bonds, mortgages, collateral loans, or personal security. The policyholder is neither guaranteed an interest nor promised a dividend. He agrees to purchase an article — indemnity — the cost of which cannot be exactly determined at the time of purchase on' the condition that any excess payment in the case of a participating policy will be returned to him. In the case of a non-participating policy, the possible excess cost is discounted in the form of a lower premium.

The Determination of Dividends. — The only sources of income for an insurance company are the present and future premiums from its policyholders and the returns from the investments of the assets which have been accumulated from past premiums. If this income is in excess of the needs of the company, the practical question arises, How shall the overcharges be returned to the policyholders? In other words, How shall the company determine the amount of the so-called dividend which shall be paid to each policyholder? A question now arises which is not easily decided and one upon which there is much difference of opinion.

The Percentage Plan. — In the earlier days of insurance it was the practice to distribute the surplus earnings on the basis of a percentage of the premium without regard to the kind of policy or length of time that the policy had been in force. The chief error in this plan was that a policy in its later years received no more than in its earlier years when, as a matter of fact, its large reserve accumulation was contributing annually from its interest earnings a greater sum to the surplus which was being divided. This percentage plan had little to recommend it other than its simplicity, and it was generally superseded by the contribution plan.

The Contribution Plan. — This plan is, as its name implies, the method by which it is sought to return to each policy that share of the surplus which it has contributed. It takes into consideration the kind of policy, its duration, and the age of the insured. A policy is credited for any given year with the terminal reserve of the preceding year, the annual premium of the current year, and the interest earned therefrom during the year. It is debited with the proportionate share of the expense of the year which this policy should bear, the mortality cost of the insurance for the year, and the reserve for the end of the year. The difference constitutes the accumulations on this policy. If the total of the amounts so calculated for each policy should exceed the amount which has been set aside for distribution, a pro ratio reduction is made. If the policy has been debited with an $8 contribution to the annual mortality and the actual mortality is only 75 per cent of the calculated, there is then only $6 to be paid and the $2 is that part of the entire surplus contributed by this policy, so far as mortality surplus is concerned. Likewise if 3 per cent is the interest assumed and 5 per cent net is earned, the 2 per cent is a surplus; and if the initial reserve for the year is $100, this policy will secure $2 from this source. Similarly, if the loading is $7 and the actual expense charged to this policy is only $5, the remaining $2 will be the surplus from this source. Adding these amounts the policyholder would secure a dividend of $6.

This method would appear from the description equally as simple as the earlier percentage method and theoretically there seems to be little to criticize in it. However, difficulties are experienced in applying this plan and many modifications of it are made in practice. The chief difficulty centers in attempting to apportion to each policy for each year of its duration its proper share of the expenses. We have already seen how complex the expenses of an insurance company are, not only because the individual policy expenses vary at different times, being very high when issued and later decreasing, but also because there are so many joint expenses. The idea at the basis of the contribution plan is that no member or class of members should have assessed upon him or them the expense due to any other insured individuals or groups of insured individuals, assuming that such sufficient numbers and amounts of insurance have been obtained as will secure average results.

Analyzing the Expense. — It is true that many of the expenses can be identified. The expenses of investments can be discovered and assessed with a reasonable degree of accuracy. The same is true of the medical examination, the agency fees, rent, and supplies. The salary of officials, clerks, and office expenses, also, have some relation to the amount of business done. But assuming these last-named expenses at a given amount when a given volume of business has been transacted, it does not follow that a business of double this volume would require a doubling of these expenses. Nor do such expenses as advertising and postage bear any necessary relation to the business transacted. The expenses due to settlement of policies often vary greatly. The same is true of taxes, which vary greatly in different taxing districts. If one state levies a tax of $2\frac{1}{2}$ per cent and another state a tax of 1 per cent on the premiums collected in the state, should the policyholders in the latter state help to pay the tax in the former state? Theoretically they should not, but practically it is impossible to assess the tax on the policyholder in the former state in the form of a higher premium.

The difficulty, then, of determining accurately individual policy expenses is apparent and in practice the companies are forced to group some of these expenses and assess them upon the premium or upon the death cost. Mr. Daniel H. Wells, the actuary of the Connecticut Mutual Insurance Company, advanced the following plan for assessing expenses: (a) assess the investment expense upon the investment income; (b) assess upon the premiums such expenses as are determined by the premium; (c) assess upon the death cost or technically the cost of insurance all other expenses. The plan has the merit of definiteness, but it does not guarantee that the various expenses will be properly identified and assigned to the proper place. This plan would imply that the expense of securing new business would be borne *in toto* by the new members, which could be done only on a preliminary term plan or its equivalent. The old line companies which would set aside a full reserve from the start would be forced to borrow from the surplus to pay initial expenses.

The public often has become supersensitive and unfair in its criticisms of the conduct of the insurance business within recent years because the management of such business has not upon demand come forth with hard and fast rules for determining each element in the expense of conducting the business. If the same demand had been made of the management of most private enterprises, the reply would have been almost equally unsatisfactory. None the less it is important in the business of such a quasi public character as the insurance business that plans as definite as possible for determining expense be devised and followed. Absolute definiteness cannot be secured, since the best devised principles for assessing insurance expense will meet many difficulties when the attempt is made to apply them.

Methods of Distributing Dividends. — Dividends under most policies are now required to be calculated and distributed annually, although there are yet in force many contracts which were written under the deferred dividend plan. That is, the dividends were distributed at the close of five-year or longer periods.

The semitontine idea applied to dividends divides policyholders into classes based upon the date of entry and the length of the distribution period. All gains from lapsing members of the group and savings on the insured lives continuing are at the close of the period for distribution divided among the members living. The pure tontine method which was a plan of insurance rather than a method of distributing dividends was that under which a lapsing policyholder forfeited all rights to a surrender value on his policy and this sum was also divided among the surviving members of the group. This plan of insurance is illegal in most states, and the semitontine method of distributing dividends as well as the deferred method is rapidly decreasing in importance.

The deferred dividend plan was extensively used previous to the legislation which followed the insurance investigations of 1905. This plan provided that no dividend would be paid until the close of certain periods, usually 5, 10, 15, or 20 years. Such policies were often called accumulation, distribution, or semitontine policies. The theory underlying this plan was that it tended to security, since an interval of this length would be a safer basis on which to determine the real gains than would a year; and second, that the persisting policyholder was more entitled to whatever gain resulted rather than the policyholder who lapsed, but who under an annual dividend plan enjoyed a reduction in his insurance cost by receiving the annual dividend. It is evident that under the deferred dividend plan the company holds large sums, and this condition theoretically not only insures a greater guarantee of solvency, but also by its compound interest accumulations and wise investments returns to the surviving policyholder a large amount of so-called dividends. In practice, however, these expected greater results were not always obtained. It was found that these large funds were a continual temptation for extravagant expenditures by the management of some companies. No accounting to the policyholders for this sum was necessary until the close of the period and in the strong competition for business the management of some companies depleted this fund. Then, too, the agents of the companies often made extravagant statements and promises to prospective purchasers of policies regarding the amount which they might expect these deferred dividends to be. The policy contract did not guarantee any specified dividend, and when the time for distribution came, many policyholders were disappointed because their dividends were much smaller than they had been led to believe they would be. Some companies issued estimates of dividends, but these were not always accepted by the public as estimates. Doubtless many officials and agents were sincere in thinking that the company would be able to pay the sums indicated in the estimates, but they made the mistake of assuming that the interest rate would continue as high in the future as it had been in the past, and the further mistake of assuming a heavier lapse rate than actually occurred. Many policyholders consequently believed that they had been intentionally deceived, as doubtless some were, and they expressed their demand to the state legislatures, which enacted the annual distribution laws.

How Dividends Are Used. — Annual dividends are now the rule. These dividends may be used by the policyholder in any one of several ways:

First, they may be taken in cash.

Second, they may be applied to the reduction or payment of any premium.

Third, they may be used to purchase participating paid-up-additions to the policy.

Fourth, they may be left with the company to accumulate at compound interest at a specified rate of interest and be paid upon the maturity of the policy. Such accumulations can be withdrawn on any anniversary of the policy.

The first and second option is practically the same except in those rare cases where the insured has paid all his premiums, as, for example, when he takes out the policy and pays all his premiums in one sum, or when he has paid all his premiums before the maturity of his policy, as in the case of a limited-payment policy. If no choice is made by the insured as to the method of using his dividend, the company usually applies it to the purchase of paid-up insurance.

The annual dividend plan affords a method of securing the insurance at an immediate and continually lower cost, and since insurance is primarily a protection and not an investment, the plan will probably prove more and more popular as the purchasers of insurance come to understand better this plan of paying dividends. This statement does not imply that, for the same policy at the same age, the annual dividend plan has resulted in a lower net payment for the insurance than on the deferred dividend plan, since the company might have been able to keep what has been paid in annual dividends so invested that it would have earned a larger sum in their possession than when it was invested by the policyholder. Indeed, when considered individually, the chances of securing a better investment of this dividend sum by the company are decidedly more favorable than when it is invested by the average policyholder.

As an example of the items which enter into dividend calculations and also as an illustration of the reasons why an insurance company cannot pay dividends on first-year policies, the following table[1] is given:

ORDINARY LIFE POLICY

Premium received		$28.11
Acquisition expenses [2]	$15.58	
General expenses 7.81 % of premium	2.20	
Total expenses		17.78
Balance		$10.33
Add interest at 4.238 %		.44
Total		$10.77
Deduct net cost of insurance [3]		4.45
Balance		$6.32
Select and ultimate reserve		6.19
Surplus		$0.13

[1] Hudnut, p. 56, Studies in Practical Life Insurance. This table and its items apply only to the particular case of the New York Life Insurance Company.

[2] The legal expense margins are: loading $7.03, assumed mortality gains $10.75, total $17.78, of which 87.61 per cent is $15.58.

[3] The net amount at risk is $1000 less the reserve on hand at the end of the year. The cost is found by multiplying the net insurance $994 by the risk of death .004473, which is 50 per cent of the table rate.

TWENTY-PAYMENT LIFE POLICY

Premium received $38.34
Acquisition expenses [1] $16.65
General expenses 7.81 % [2] 2.59
    Total expenses 19.24
    Balance $19.10
Add interest at 4.238 % 81
    Total $19.91
Deduct net cost of insurance [3] 4.40
Balance $15.51
Select and ultimate reserve 15.50
Surplus $0.01

TWENTY-YEAR ENDOWMENT POLICY

Premium received $51.91
Acquisition expense [4] $17.65
General expense 7.81 % [5] 3.12
    Total expense 20.77
Balance $31.14
Add interest at 4.238 % 1.32
    Total $32.46
Deduct net cost of insurance 4.35
Balance $28.11
Select and ultimate reserve 28.35
Deficit $0.24

Buying Insurance. — The subject of buying insurance may now be discussed, since the intelligent purchase of insurance must be based upon an understanding

---

[1] The legal expense margins are: loading $8.49, assumed mortality gains $10.52, total $19.01, of which 87.61 % is $16.65.

[2] Calculated on the adjusted premium $\frac{28 + 38.34}{2} = 33.22$.

[3] The net insurance, $1000 − $15.50 = $984.50.

[4] The legal expense margins are: loading $9.94, assumed mortality gains $10.21, total $20.15, of which 87.61 per cent is $17.65.

[5] Calculated on the adjusted premium $\frac{28.11 + 51.91}{2} = 40.01$.

of the different kinds of companies, policies, and premium, the significance of dividends, and the reserve as well as the character of insurance investments.

The prospective purchaser must realize in the first place that insurance is not and cannot be made primarily an investment in the sense in which this word is ordinarily used. It cannot be considered an investment in the same sense as the purchase of a farm or a bond. If an allowance is made for the protection afforded, some policies may be considered as an investment, but not as a true competitor with the ordinary investment. They afford an opportunity for systematized saving, and thus whatever of the character of an investment they have is indirect rather than direct in its returns. The purchaser must decide, first the kind of a company from which he will purchase his insurance; that is, he must decide between an old line legal reserve company, a fraternal, and an assessment company. His decision will depend very largely upon whether he appreciates the importance of the reserve in the insurance business. If he does understand its character, he will purchase his insurance either from one of the ordinary legal reserve companies or from a fraternal order which operates on the reserve plan.

Selecting the Policy. — In selecting the kind of policy, whether whole life, limited-payment life, endowment, or term, the purchaser will be governed by many considerations, among which may be mentioned the extent of his obligations, the amount and character of his present and prospective income, and his age. The man with a family of six children needs more insurance than the man with three children, and the man with an income of $5000 a year can purchase either more insurance or the more expensive policies than a man with an income of $2000 a year.

It must be recognized that there is no such a thing as an absolutely best policy, no more so than there is an absolutely best company. It must also be understood that what is the best policy for the buyer at the time of the purchase may not be the best twenty years later, when his family position is different. The change in the relations of a man to his obligations and the difference in his ability at later periods to meet them, make it absolutely impossible to select a policy that is certain to be throughout its length the absolutely best for him. For this reason those policies which permit change in the beneficiary and the terms of settlement commend themselves to many buyers.

Advantages of the Ordinary Life Policy. — The ordinary life policy is not held in great favor and most of the insurance now in force is on the limited-payment life and endowment plans. This lack of appreciation of the ordinary life policy is unfortunate, but the insurance officials and not the public are largely responsible for this condition. In the early days of insurance, when this policy was the one usually purchased, the companies were led, as we have seen, to make promises of large dividends, which were never realized. Many policyholders were forced to lapse their policies. In the second place, the plan of paying commissions on the percentage plan, especially since the larger commissions were given for other forms of policies, caused the life policies to be neglected.   In the third place, the absence of savings banks and other saving institutions in many localities caused the purchasers of insurance to select the endowment and limited-payment policy with higher premiums than the whole-life policy because they served as a method of saving.

The ordinary life policy on account of its low premium recommends itself to at least two fairly well defined classes: (a) those receiving relatively small incomes; (b) those who receive moderate but certain incomes during the productive years of their lives and who have large family obligations. They are able on account of the low premium to carry a large amount of insurance during the period of dependency of the children and beyond this period the premiums may either be paid in part by the children or the policies surrendered or changed to paid-up insurance, assuming that the policyholder is not financially able to keep up the payments. The ordinary life policy of a present-day insurance company has so many privileges in the contract and is so excellent as to its general character that it is a great misfortune, both to the public and the insurance business, that it is not more frequently sold. There is some evidence, however, that this policy will become more popular, as the public and the insurance officials become divorced from the idea that insurance is an investment.

Advantages of the Limited-payment Policies. — The limited-payment life policies commend themselves to those individuals who desire their premium payment period to be confined well within their productive years.

This policy will appeal to the young man who is uncertain of an income after a given period or who does not
wish insurance to be a part of his annual expense after
middle life. Out of the relatively large and certain
income of his early productive years, he pays for his
insurance. He has the satisfaction of realizing that he
has purchased and paid for the protection which his
family has a right to expect from him. This policy
is often also selected by the man of middle age who has
previously neglected to purchase protection, but who
wishes then to buy it and pay for it while he is yet a
producer. The ordinary life policy premium may cause
an undue pressure on the decreasing income of his de-
clining productivity. The length of the premium paying
period, that is, whether a 10, 15, 20, or 30 year life
payment policy is selected, will be determined by the
prospect of his years of productivity. The man of 45
years of age can purchase a ten-payment policy and thus
complete his payments well within his productive years.
The average man of 25 years of age, receiving a salary
which will probably decrease rapidly after 45, can purchase a twenty-payment policy at a rate not greatly in
excess of the ordinary life policy premium and complete
his payments before his salary decreases.

Advantages of the Endowment Policy. — The endowment policies commend themselves to those who desire
to have in addition to the protection a material incentive to save. The premiums are considerably higher
than those in the other policies for the reasons discussed
in a previous chapter. They not only afford a means of
saving for the young man or woman, but they also ma-

ture at a time when the individual, as a result of his larger business experience, is often better able to make profitable investments of large funds. If past investments have been wisely made from other savings and the individual does not need the face of the policy for current use, he may purchase a considerable amount of paid-up insurance, because his insurance premiums have been large. Again this policy has larger loan values than any other policy, and this sometimes becomes an advantage for the young person. The argument that the individual could secure a better return if he would invest his savings in a savings institution, organized for that purpose, is more interesting than true, for the average individual will not save regularly unless under pressure. No one compels him to go to the savings bank to make his deposits and no one prevents him from withdrawing them at his pleasure.

The term policy can be recommended only as a temporary expedient. It is no cheaper than any other form of insurance, but since the immediate outlay is small, it commends itself to those who incur temporary obligations or to the man with the family whose present financial condition will not permit of larger outlays for insurance, but whose financial condition in the near future will permit a transfer to one of the other kinds of policies.

Selecting the Company. — After deciding the kind of a policy which he needs, the prospective purchaser must select a company, and this is a selection which is doubtless made with the least intelligence because the average person does not know how to compare companies, and the average insurance agent does not make a practice of advertising the good points of companies, other than the one whose policies he sells. The prospective purchaser should examine the annual reports of the companies, the annual statements made to his state insurance department and the gain and loss exhibit, if the latter is available. From these sources he will secure information on the following subjects: (a) the character of the investments, that is, in what manner the insurance funds are secured and what they are earning; (b) the liabilities of the company and the relation of the assets to it; (c) the expenses, that is, how much money is being spent to maintain the company a going concern and how much money is spent to secure new business; (d) the ratio of actual to calculated mortality; (e) the number of lapses; (f) the amount of the surplus and the manner of its divisions, that is, how much is retained, how much is paid to policyholders as dividends, and how much to' stockholders, if it is a stock company.

It will also be advisable for the intending purchaser to ask the companies in which he is interested or the agents to supply him with a statement of the dividends paid on policies of the kind which he desires. This statement should show the dividends paid for the past several years, for manifestly one year's dividends are not sufficient to determine a fair judgment. He will not lay too much stress on dividends as a criterion for comparing companies, because a good policy has many other important characteristics besides good dividends. If the purchaser is seeking to compare participating and non-participating policies, he will need to be careful, lest he make false conclusions in regard to apparent cheapness. The dividend scale on the particular policy of the participating company will aid in comparison. That is, he can deduct it from the premium and compare the result with the premium of the non-participating company. However, this is not conclusive proof. He must ask himself what returns he could secure for himself on these small annual sums which represent dividends paid to him by the participating company or not collected from him by the non-participating company. He must understand that the non-participating premium includes a loading, but not the same degree of loading as does the participating premium. Possibly some participating company can secure for him accumulations which in the end will make his participating policy quite as cheap as his non-participating policy. It is not sought in these statements to make any claims of advantages for either one or the other kind of policy, but rather to encourage the purchaser to make a careful investigation in order that he may secure that policy which is best suited to his needs.

After the prospective purchaser has informed himself on these points, he will then make a comparison of the terms of the contract of different companies. This problem has been solved in part for him by the enactment of the standard provision laws which require all policies to contain certain provisions, which have been discussed in a previous chapter. There remains, however, some points of difference in the policies of different companies.

He will examine the options in settlement, both upon maturing and lapsing the policy; the restrictions of the policies; the terms of conditions of loans; the freedom with which he may change to other forms of policies and change the beneficiary. He will also examine the guaranteed values, if any, on the different policies. He may also give some weight to the character of the representatives of the companies who solicit his insurance, for a good insurance company will not knowingly keep in its employment a dishonest representative. After he has made all these examinations and comparisons, the purchaser of insurance should complete the task by acquainting himself thoroughly with the terms of his contract. Every sentence deserves careful study, and he owes it to himself, his family, and society to make himself an intelligent possessor of insurance in order that he may fulfill his part of the contract, secure the protection for his family, and become an interpreter to and missionary for the uninsured.

REFERENCES

Surplus and Dividends

Fackler, Edward B.   Notes on Life Insurance, Chap. XIV.

Yale Readings, Chap. XIX.

Insurance Guide and Handbook, Fifth Edition, Chap. XIV.

Journal of Insurance Institute, Vol. VIII, p. 317.

Zartman, Lester.   The Investments of Life Insurance Companies.

Annals American Academy of Political Science, Vol. XXVI, pp. 256–268.

Dawson, Miles M.   The Business of Life Insurance, Chap. XXVII.

Graham, W. J.   The Romance of Life Insurance, Chap. XI.

CHAPTER X

The Importance of Investments. — One of the most difficult problems in the practical operation of a life insurance company is the management and investment of insurance funds. The importance of this subject is due chiefly to the fact that these funds are advance collections from the policyholders to aid in the payment of claims which will not fall due for many years. The contract made by the company is with one person, but the benefit is usually paid to another person. It is this reserve fund which guarantees the payment at maturity of these long-time contracts in which several parties are interested and whose payment means so much to the beneficiaries. The calamity which would result if all the insurance companies should default their contracts is beyond imagination. From the previous discussions, it will be understood that the assets must be at all times so invested as to equal at least the reserve value of the policies, for this is not only a requirement of the statutes, but, as we have seen, is also absolutely necessary under the level premium plan in order to mature the contracts. In addition, those companies which pay dividends expect to secure from their investments a part of the surplus from which dividends are paid. So large in amount have these funds become and such great financial ability is required for their wise management, that this problem may well be considered one of the most difficult in the insurance business. The subject of investments will be discussed under the following heads: (*a*) the character of the investments in the past and present; (*b*) the rate of interest secured on the different kinds of investments at different periods. The topic of the legal requirements in regard to investments is reserved for a detailed discussion in a later chapter.

The Character of the Investments. — An investigation of the investments of life insurance companies in the past shows that in 1851 the Connecticut Mutual Life Insurance Company and the Mutual Benefit Life Insurance Company of New Jersey, which are two of the oldest and may be taken as representative companies, had 56 per cent of their assets invested in premium notes, that is, notes given by the insured for premiums due. Of the other assets derived from cash payments held at that date 26 per cent was in real estate, about 9 per cent of the remainder was in city bonds and bank stocks, and about 9 per cent was held as cash. A very marked decrease in premium notes then followed, so that in 1858 only 21 per cent of the assets of the four largest companies was in the form of premium notes. Of the remaining 79 per cent of the assets about 67 per cent was in mortgage notes.

The Cash Item. — The cash item as a relative percentage did not, among companies as a whole, show any marked tendency to decrease preceding 1900. Cash held in the office has constituted a temptation which the management of some companies has not been able to resist, as the insurance investigations begun in 1905 disclosed. The cash item in theory should consist of money held to pay matured policy claims falling due, whether these be death claims, endowment claims, annuity claims, or cash surrender values; money held for current expenses, loans, and cash awaiting investments. Insurance officials are not always able to find immediate investments of a desirable character. There has been a tendency in some cases to hold an unduly large amount of cash which went to the call loan market. As it is well known, the interest rate on these loans is often very high, but the risk is also often great. Security should be the first criterion of judging the excellence of an insurance investment rather than the high rate of return secured. It is desirable, of course, to secure high interest returns, since this may result in greater dividends and lower premiums to the policyholder, but the fundamental question is to decide how high a rate of interest can be secured, consistent with the security of the investment. It was shown in the investigations of 1905 that as high as 20 per cent of the funds of some companies was deposited in banks and trust companies. This situation would seem a very natural condition of affairs when it is recalled that the insurance company has large funds to loan and that the bank and trust companies are institutions for making loans. This dual relationship, however, often placed the insurance official in a positon in which there was a conflict of interests. As an insurance official, he should desire to secure as much interest as possible for the insurance fund. As a bank or trust company official, he would be interested in having the insurance company keep as much cash as possible in the bank or trust company without it bearing interest. Then, too, we shall see that the field of desirable loans for insurance funds is much more restricted than in the case of these other two financial institutions. There is, therefore, a constant temptation to make loans of the less suitable kind.

Premium Notes and Loans. — In 1860 a large part of the assets of life insurance companies was in notes, given for premiums. In 1870, of the seventy-one companies doing business in Massachusetts, there were twenty-three which did not hold interest-bearing securities equal to the reserve value of the outstanding policies. When the panic of 1873 occurred, many of these companies failed, partly because these premium notes became worthless and partly on account of the high and strict reserve valuations required by some of the state laws. Others reduced the number of premium notes. It is now the practice to collect the premiums, then loan a sum on policyholders' notes based upon the reserve value of the policy. A very common method of paying a premium due, is for the policyholder to borrow from the company on his policy. This is debited against the policy, and since the loan is based on the reserve value of the policy, there is no such danger as in the earlier plan of premium notes. Loans, of course, are secured on the policy for other purposes than paying the premium. Premium notes are valuable as assets only to the extent that they are covered by the reserve value of the policy, since the company is relieved to this extent of its obligation to the policyholder.

Dangers of the Cash Loan. — The other questions which arise in connection with loans are; (*a*) to what extent loans on policies are conducive to lapses, and (*b*) the effect that they have in requiring the company to keep on hand a larger amount of cash than would otherwise be necessary, thereby preventing an interest accumulation from these uninvested funds. It is true that in the seventies a large number of policyholders who had given premium notes lapsed, but evidence is not conclusive that the plan of loans now followed is conducive to lapses. It is not so much that they cause lapses, but rather that they often go far to defeat the purpose of insurance and therefore the ultimate effect is much the same as if the policyholder had lapsed. The ease with which a loan is secured on a policy is often a great temptation to many policyholders, with the result that the insurance loan is devoted to speculative enterprises. The wife or children or other dependants for whose benefit the insurance is carried sometimes know nothing about these loans, and as a consequence they find in case of the death of the insured, that they have less protection than they expected. The companies may or may not make efforts to secure the payment of the loan, but too often the policyholder has not the will to pay it even when he is able to do so. There is no one to compel him to pay it, as is the case with the ordinary loan. The policy loan provision is largely an outgrowth of the strong competition among companies for business, and this provision was written into the contract as an inducement for the prospective purchaser to buy insurance.

As to the second point, viz. that the loan feature requires companies to keep a large amount of cash. It may be stated that these loans may place a strain on the company at certain times. That is to say, the demand for loans is greatest in times of industrial depression and in periods of speculation. If the increased demand occurs in the first period, the company is likely to be receiving less in cash payments for premiums due. If, therefore, it is forced to sell some of its securities, it will not receive a good price for them, or if it is forced to borrow funds to accommodate its policyholders under the terms of the contract, the rate of interest which it will be forced to pay is high. If the increased demand comes at times of speculative activity, there is great danger that the investment made by the policyholder from the loan on his policy will be unfortunate and he will therefore be less able to repay the loan as well as the future premiums. During the financial depression of 1907 many policyholders took advantage of the loan benefit in their policy and borrowed very large sums in the aggregate from the companies. While the companies met these demands with commendable promptness, yet to some of the companies it became a troublesome question. On account of their experience at this time, some of the companies seek to protect themselves by requiring that a notice shall be given to the company when a loan is desired in much the same manner as is done in the case of depositors in Savings Banks. This restriction will doubtless do much to protect the company, but it is not an absolute protection against the loan question becoming a serious one. When the loan is made to pay premiums, it is in its least objectionable form. It may be stated as a superficial reply to the whole question of loans that the reserve is the policyholder's property and that he ought to be allowed to use it as he pleases. A moment's consideration will, however, disclose the fallacy of such statement, since, carried to its logical conclusions, it would mean that there would be no such person as a beneficiary. It is above all for such a person or persons that the institution of insurance was devised. The insurer cannot, from one point of view, benefit by his insurance. The significance of the subject may be inferred from the fact that in 1914 the loans made to policyholders by the Life Insurance Companies in the United States aggregated about 15 per cent of the total admitted assets.

Mortgage Loans. — In 1860 loans on mortgages made up 59 per cent of the assets, but this proportion had decreased to 44 per cent in 1870. During the Civil War the United States bonds could be purchased so as to yield a high rate of interest, and insurance companies very largely followed the practice of investing all their available funds in these bonds. It must be recalled that corporation securities which were later available in such desirable quantities were not to be had to any large extent until in the last quarter of the nineteenth century. When the premium on gold began to decrease, and the interest on the United States bonds declined, the insurance companies began to seek mort-

gage loans. The Middle West during the third quarter
of the century sought large amounts of capital for the
construction of its railways and the general development of the region. Interest rates were high and large
amounts of insurance funds were invested in the West.
Mortgage loans increased rapidly from about 1865 to
1875 and then decreased until about 1885. The panic
of 1873 forced the insurance companies to foreclose many
of their mortgages, with the result that they found
themselves in possession of considerable real estate.
This was a species of property not suitable for possession by an insurance company, since the expenses of
management are not only excessive, but these assets are
not easily convertible.

Real Estate. — The real estate investments of an
insurance company are usually limited by law to office
buildings in which to transact its business. Usually
the law requires that the property obtained by fore-
closure must be sold within two years. We have shown
why the company does not want to retain, unless necessary, the second kind of real estate. All companies do
not own their office buildings. Many rent office space.
However, there was a very marked tendency as the
companies grew in size to construct their own office
buildings. This policy, it was argued, would be a good
advertisement for the company, and as a result many
of the companies spent profusely for the construction
of office buildings. Nor was the policy confined to the
large companies. Later investigation showed that in
many cases no adequate financial return was secured
on these office buildings, and in some cases misappro-

priation of funds was disclosed by permitting allied trust companies to use parts of the buildings at a nominal rent. Since 1905 the office buildings are showing better returns, and in several cases the branch offices of the larger companies have been sold.

Public Bonds. — Foreign bonds have been purchased only by those companies writing business in foreign countries in which the law requires such an investment. The early insurance companies invested considerable funds in the bonds of the different states during the period from 1835 to 1855. Many of the states were undertaking vast schemes of internal development, such as the construction of canals, railways, and roads. On account of the demands of the rapidly growing states of the Middle West and South, state bonds were very numerous. However, some of the states repudiated their debts, and considerable sentiment favored the same policy in other states. This caused the state bonds to become unfavorable securities. Since 1865 state bonds have not been numerous. City expenditures began to increase very rapidly after the Civil War, for the rapidly increasing urban population demanded many improvements in the cities. In 1880 about 15 per cent of the insurance companies' assets were invested in city bonds. Some cities attempted to repudiate their debts, and in some cases great difficulty was experienced with these investments in city bonds. As a result the insurance companies did not, for some time, seek these investments. State legislatures either of their own volition or as a result of a request from the cities were continually legislating on the subject of the city tax rate and the power of the city to contract debts. There is a tendency in later years, however, for the companies to seek again this form of a loan, for the security of city bonds has improved.

Private Corporation Securities. — A very great increase in the investments in corporation securities occurred in the last quarter of the nineteenth century, and especially since 1890. Both stock and bonds were purchased, although the investigations of the insurance business in 1905 resulted in the passage of laws by various states which either wholly prohibited or limited insurance investments in stock. The objections to investments in stocks are twofold: (a) A stockholder is a participant in the management of the corporation whose stock he holds, and manifestly such a function is not desirable for an insurance company. The insurance company thus becomes more than what the theory underlying its organization assumes that it is. That is to say, it becomes more than a trustee. It becomes a manager or a partner in a private business. (b) In the second place, stocks fluctuate greatly in value, thus causing the question of the solvency of the insurance company or its ability to pay dividends to arise continually with every change in the success of the commercial enterprises in which the funds are invested. The two most fundamental words in the insurance business, the two most pregnant with the purpose and theory of insurance, are certainty and stability.

In 1908 the statistics of the ordinary life insurance companies showed that they owned over one billion dollars of bonds and almost one billion of loans and mortgages. The amount of stock held was only $133,000,000. The New York law required, as a result of the investigations, that the companies dispose of their stocks. This was done on the theory that the holding of stocks would be a continual temptation to the insurance officials to organize and finance new companies from which they as individuals would gain. It was not desirable, so it was argued, for insurance officials to loan money to themselves as officials of other commercial corporations. This meant that the insurance funds were to be considered as trust funds, and as such were to be protected by every possible safeguard in order to insure that the funds should be kept intact even if only a low rate of interest was earned. It is quite true that the net return on stocks is often higher than on bonds, since the interest paid on bonds is subject to the fluctuating purchasing power of money and the loss falls on the bondholder, while in the case of stocks the loss may be recouped by an increase in the selling value of the stock. The following table taken from that valuable source of insurance statistics, the Year Book of the Spectator Company, is given to indicate the present character of the insurance investments. It will be understood that in the case of individual companies the characteristics of the investments differ very widely. For example, one of the older companies of the Middle West has had throughout its history a very large part of its assests invested in mortgages on real estate and has been able to receive throughout this time excellent results on this class of investments.

ASSETS OF THE THIRTY-FOUR LIFE INSURANCE COM-
PANIES REPORTING TO NEW YORK INSURANCE
DEPARTMENT AS OF JAN. 1, 1914.

Real Estate	$147,078,103 3 %
Bonds and Mortgages	1,454,001,586 33 %
U. S. Stocks and Securities	1,000,000
Other Stocks and Bonds	1,946,659,614 44
Collateral Loans	14,317,215
Premium Notes and Loans	614,451,877 14
Cash in Offices and Books	55,404,218 1
Deferred and Unpaid Premiums	55,588,896 1
All Other Assets	62,541,075 1
Total Assets	4,351,042,584

Rate of Interest Earned. — Let us now examine the
rate of interest which the companies assumed they
would earn and then investigate the actual rates of
interest earned. In the earlier practice of insurance,
the ordinary life policy was most generally written and
the average rate of interest earned was not so important,
as when endowment and limited payment policies came
to be written, because these early policies had no provisions for cash surrender and loan values or annual
dividends, and a failure to pay premiums usually forfeited the policy. There were considerable gains from
lapses. When state supervision began in the fifties,
some rate of interest earnings had to be assumed in
order to value the policies. Elizur Wright, the insurance
commissioner of Massachusetts, secured the passage of
a law in that state in 1857 which required the companies
to assume a 4 per cent interest earning as a basis of com-
puting their liabilities. Georgia established the same
basis in 1859, but no other state adopted a basis until
after the Civil War. The action of these states had,

however, caused most of the companies to adopt the
4 per cent basis of valuation. In 1862 eleven of the
seventeen companies doing a level premium business
were on a 4 per cent basis, three on a 5 per cent basis,
and one on a 6 per cent basis. The high interest rates
of the Civil War period caused New York in 1866 to
pass a law requiring a 5 per cent basis, but this was
lowered to $4\frac{1}{2}$ per cent two years later. In 1873 Maine,
New Hampshire, Connecticut, and Illinois required a
4 per cent basis and fifteen other states required a $4\frac{1}{2}$
per cent basis. The hard times of this period caused
a decided tendency to assume a 4 per cent basis, but
very few insurance officials thought that a lower rate
would be necessary for some years. The Connecticut Mutual Company announced, to the surprise of
the insurance world, that beginning with 1882 its
new business would be written on a $3\frac{1}{2}$ per cent basis,
but no state required a $3\frac{1}{2}$ per cent basis before
January 1, 1901. At the present time practically all
business is written either on a $3\frac{1}{2}$ per cent or 3 per
cent basis.

Such has been the history of the different rates of
interest earning assumed. What has been the history
of the actual interest rate earned? In 1859 seven level
premium companies were earning from 5.4 per cent to
6.4 per cent. In 1861 eleven companies earned a rate
below 6 per cent, but on account of the high interest
rates of the Civil War period the decade from 1860 to
1870 shows the highest rate of earning of any decade in
the history of insurance. Eleven companies earned
about 10 per cent, seventeen earned between 9 per cent

and 10 per cent, twenty-four between 8 per cent and 9 per cent, thirty-seven between 7 per cent and 8 per cent, and forty between 6 per cent and 7 per cent. On account of the hard times, the large number of premium notes, and other minor contributing causes, many companies failed in the decade 1870 to 1880, although the average earning of all companies was above 6½ per cent. This resulted, however, from the very high earnings of a few companies. After 1880 the decline in average earnings began and no company maintained a level earning of 6 per cent. During the decade 1890 to 1900 the average rate of earnings for most companies was below 6 per cent. Only two companies maintained a level rate of 5 per cent. During the years 1899 to 1908 inclusive, the average rate of interest earned by the twenty-five leading companies was 4.68 per cent, and from 1909 to 1913 inclusive, the average rate earned was 4.79 per cent.

Earnings on Particular Classes of Securities. — The earnings on particular classes of investments may be briefly described. The earnings on real estate were fair during the sixties but decreased during the next decade. In the decade from 1890 to 1900 the earnings on real estate were on an average below 3 per cent in many of the companies. During the latter part of the decade from 1900 to 1910 the earnings on real estate had greatly improved as a result of the great increase in real estate values. The laws of most states do not permit insurance companies to hold real estate except for office building purposes. During the years from 1860 to 1880 the earnings on mortgage loans were in

U

general very satisfactory, but during the next two decades the earnings on loans of this character were much less. A few companies have been able to secure almost continuously satisfactory results from mortgage loans. We have previously described why the investment in government bonds brought high returns during Civil War times, and why the insurance companies tended to reduce their investments in these securities. In the last quarter of the nineteenth century very large investments were made in the stocks of railroad and industrial corporations, but for the reasons already stated, the investments in stock have been so reduced that in 1908 only 4.61 per cent of the total assets of the one hundred and fifty-seven life companies was invested in stocks.

RATE OF INTEREST EARNED ON MEAN INVESTED FUNDS OF TWENTY-NINE LIFE INSURANCE COMPANIES

1900	4.67
1901	4.61
1902	4.58
1903	4.61
1904	4.63
1905	4.68
1906	4.67
1907	4.80
1908	4.77
1909	4.79
1910	4.78
1911	4.79
1912	4.79
1913	4.84
1894–1898	4.91
1899–1903	4.69
1903–1908	4.74
1909–1913	4.79
1894–1913	4.76

Regulation of Investments. — The laws of the states restrict the kinds of investments open to insurance companies. No specific rules can be laid down for the investment of insurance funds, which will be applicable to all companies or even to a single company at all times. It is a matter which must be adjusted to suit the changing conditions of the investment market. Those in charge of the finances of insurance companies must regard not only the interest of present policyholders, but must also anticipate the interest of the policyholders of the future. Subject to certain special conditions the following principles may be stated as applying to the investment of insurance funds : (*a*) The funds should be so invested that they will be subject to the least possible fluctuations in their value. Stable results for obvious reasons must be secured. (*b*) Subject to the above limitation the investments should be such as will bring the highest possible returns, for this means lower cost of insurance to the policyholder from whom the funds have been collected. (*c*) The larger proportion of the funds should be invested in long time securities, since this not only reduces the expense of investments, but also is likely to produce better returns over long periods, because the supply of capital seeking such investments is somewhat limited. That is to say, the competition for such investments is not great, and this tends to produce a higher interest rate. (*d*) The funds should be invested in sufficiently different classes of securities to prevent any marked decrease in earning due to unfavorable conditions which may affect a certain business from time to time. Deficiencies in one class of investments will then tend to be equalized by excesses on other classes of investments. (e) Investment in securities of corporations or in kinds of business, the earnings on which may be decidedly affected by a change in the policy of the management or by the death of a partner, should generally be avoided. (f) While mortgage investments have often been successful, yet great care needs to be exercised in making them in order to keep the loan on the property well within the fluctuating values of the property. Investigations must also be made as to the title of the property, the rate of taxation, and the character of the possession, that is, whether it is absolute ownership or a life estate. It is not surprising, therefore, to find that the expense rates of investments of this character are sometimes high. (g) From the viewpoint of the company a certain amount loaned on policies may be desirable, since they are absolutely safe loans, and return the normal rate of interest. They also make the company's policies more popular and aid in securing new policies. From the viewpoint of the borrower such loans are not to be commended except in cases of extreme necessity.

Those in charge of the investments of insurance funds must always remember that they are acting in the capacity of trustees; that while they need to be aggressive in their search for investments returning a high rate of interest, yet that the maintenance of stable results by obtaining secure investments is the most important consideration.

The following analysis of the source of income and expenditure of a dollar by a large mutual company is representative, although the particular items would differ from company to company.

SHOWING IN CENTS AND MILLS THE DISPOSITION OF EACH DOLLAR OF INCOME DURING 1915

INCOME

From premiums	$ .753
From interest, rents, etc.	.247
Total received	$1.00

DISBURSEMENTS

Paid for death claims	.207
Paid on endowments	.067
Dividend paid policyholders	.198
Surrender values and annuities	.171
Total paid policyholders	.643
First year commissions to agents	.031
Renewal commissions	.042
Other agency expenses	.001
Home office salaries	.014
Insurance taxes, licenses, fees	.017
Medical examinations, printing, and all other disbursements	.035
Total other than to policyholders	.140
Total disbursements	.783
Added to assets to meet future obligations and contingencies	.217
Total which is the original dollar fully accounted for	$1.00

REFERENCES

INVESTMENTS AND INTEREST

Zartman, Lester W. The Investment of Life Insurance Companies, Chaps. II, III, IV.

Journal of the Insurance Institute, Vol. I, pp. 305–335, Vol. VIII, pp. 312–332; Vol. VII, p. 343; Vol. V, p. 217.

Report of the Legislative Insurance Investigating Committee of New York, 10 Volumes.

Insurance Guide and Handbook, Fifth Edition, Chap. IX.

Transactions of Insurance and Actuarial Society of Glasgow, Fifth Series, pp. 167–184.

CHAPTER XI

Insurance for Wage Earners. — The chief kinds of insurance for wage earners are Industrial Insurance, Employers' Liability Insurance, and Workmen's Compensation Insurance. Our chief purpose is to describe the principal means employed to secure protection for the wage-earning class. In addition to the above enumerated plans, it must be understood that such protection is carried by local relief societies of many descriptions, by fraternal societies, and by trade-unions. These methods are usually so simple and well known that they do not demand a detailed discussion. It is also true that ordinary life insurance is carried by many of the wage-earning class. The term "wage-earning class" may be a somewhat indefinite one, but the phrases "laboring class" and "industrial insurance" have to most minds definite significance, and in the business of insurance there have been developed particular forms of insurance to serve the wage-earning class.

Industrial insurance may be supplied in the following ways: (*a*) By private stock companies organized for profit. (*b*) By private mutual companies. The business of private companies may be a direct result of legislative and judicial action in fixing responsibility for loss upon the employer, that is, it may be either voluntary or compulsory insurance. (c) The state itself may supply the protection.

Origin of Industrial Insurance. — Before discussing each of these methods, it is important to understand how the evolution of industrial society has caused the need of, and the demand for, insurance for the wage earners to arise.   In ancient and medieval times the social and industrial organizations precluded the existence of insurance for the wage earner.   Indeed, there was no such class as wage earners as we now know them.   During the existence of slavery a large part of the work was done by this class, and as the slave was considered a species of property, nothing was owed to him by his employer or owner.   He cared for him, not so much as a duty, but because it was to his economic interest to do so.   The comparatively simple industrial life of the early times gave little value to the life of an individual as such.   During medieval times, the feudal system prevailed and the masses of people, although having in many cases comparatively few rights, enjoyed protection from their lords.   The hierarchal form of social organization gave a definite status to each member of the social group.   Later, when the trade and labor classes had freed themselves from their dependence, guilds and fraternities arose.   One of the most important purposes of these organizations was to care for their members in times of sickness and for the deceased member's family in case of death.   The first classes to secure independence were the commercial and trade classes of the free cities, and as capital developed they assumed gradually a position of greater independence and importance.

Capital was being accumulated from the activities of the trading and commercial classes. The discovery of gold and silver in the new world supplied a stock of metals upon which a money economy could be established. The age of discovery opened up new lands for exploitation and brought into existence new commodities and new markets. The whole industrial world was on the eve of a revolution as a result of the accumulated capital, the stock of metals, and the new markets. This so-called industrial revolution is usually said to date from 1785 to 1825, but this period marks only the dates between which the transfer to a new industrial system was most rapid in England. The changes were so very marked that the word revolution may be applied to this period in England, but in other European countries and in the United States no such rapid changes occurred. It will be more accurate to call the change an evolution rather than a revolution and fix the dates to include the seventeenth, eighteenth, and the first half of the nineteenth centuries because during this period the capitalistic system was fully established in the European and American countries. The feudal system had disappeared, the household or domestic system of industry had largely given way to the factory system, which the previous accumulation of capital made possible and the new markets made desirable. But most important for our purpose the status of the laborer was radically changed.

The laborer lost his tool and gained the machine, which, on account of its high cost, was beyond his power of private possession. He lost his personal master, and gained the impersonal corporation. The conditions of labor were now to be determined, not by two persons, the laborer and his master, but by one person and a thing. The laborer gave up the workshop of the home and went into the factory. He worked for a money wage under a wage contract. He was no longer a capitalist and a laborer, but simply a laborer selling his only possession — time. In the unprecedented demand for goods, it is not surprising that the capitalistic class were often unmindful of the duties which they owed to the laborer as a man.

We need not rehearse how the humanitarian ideas slowly developed and how they gradually became expressed in various measures designed to protect the wage-earning class; nor what efforts were made by the wage earners themselves through the formation of friendly societies and trade-unions to protect themselves; nor how there came to be a labor question and why the neglect of the labor class during this period of the industrial evolution has caused the problem to become so acute in the present; nor how England, because she was the farthest developed industrially, began to enact laws for the protection of the labor class early in the nineteenth century and how other nations have followed her example. For our purpose it is sufficient to understand that the character of the industrial organization of the present demands institutions designed particularly for the industrial classes.

Purpose of Industrial Insurance. — The purposes of industrial insurance may be classified as follows: (*a*) to protect against the losses, resulting from death; (*b*) to protect against injuries; (*c*) to protect against old age; (*d*) to protect against sickness; (*e*) to protect against unemployment.

We have seen that the industrial insurance which is sold by the private companies, such as the Prudential and Metropolitan companies in the United States, provides for the insurance of every member of the family from ages 1 to 70. The premiums are paid weekly and are five cents or multiples thereof, depending on the age and the amount of insurance carried. For persons under 10 the average policy is about $30 and for those over 10 about $150. The premiums are collected weekly by the agents of the company, and this is the most important element in making the cost of the insurance high to the policyholder. This kind of insurance was first written in England in 1854 by the English Prudential Insurance Company and in America by the American Prudential Insurance Company in 1875. By this time there had developed in both countries a large number of wage earners and in both countries this kind of insurance soon proved popular. At present there are about thirty million industrial policies of this description in force in the United States. The amount of business in force in 1913 was about four billion dollars on thirty million policies, or an average of $133 per policy. The proceeds of these policies are intended and used in most cases to pay the expenses of burial.

The premiums are based on mortality tables which

the experience of such companies has shown are fully adequate to meet all obligations. Indeed, within the last decade some of the industrial companies have voluntarily distributed to their policyholders millions of dollars in dividends or in premium reductions or in additions to the insurance. The contract does not differ in a great many particulars from the ordinary life insurance company's contract except that it is a life contract, that is, it is death insurance. The lapse ratio is for obvious reasons much higher than in the ordinary company. The agency department is necessarily one of the most important departments, and in several of the large companies it has become a marvel of efficiency. The agent is paid on a commission contract, the terms of which make it to his interest to prevent lapses, as well as to secure new business. Some of the more important direct and indirect benefits claimed for industrial insurance are:

Advantages of Industrial Insurance. — First. It directly encourages thrift and saving on the part of the wage earner. He acquires the habit of saving and is often able to save funds out of his earnings in addition to his insurance premium. It is very questionable, however, if the saving habit is relatively increasing. The industrial conditions are probably making saving more and more difficult and at the same time making the incentive to save less and less. The standard of living has been rising so rapidly that there is a continual pressure on the workingman to spend his income for necessities, conveniences, and luxuries. There is less and less opportunity for the wage earner to purchase small amounts of property which, by its very material existence, would afford a powerful incentive to save because it would be a tangible expression of an intangible effort. It is probably true that few wage earners under the present industrial and social system can look forward to owning their homes.

Second. It doubtless does much to preserve self-respect and family affection by providing a burial fund, instead of receiving from the public, funds for this purpose. However, in many cases, human vanity is sacrificed to family needs in providing an extravagant funeral.

Third. It not only provides sufficient funds for burial and the expenses incident to the illness, but in many cases something is left for the support of the widow and children for such a time until adequate means of support can be found.

Fourth. It also in an indirect way supplies large accumulations of capital for the demands of modern industrial activity. The insurance sold by these private companies has far from solved the problem of securing adequate insurance for the industrial classes, for, as we have seen, it provides for a fund only in case of death, and the greater part of the fund is used for burial expenses.

Voluntary Associations for Industrial Insurance. — There are many voluntary organizations of the working class which supplement both the activity of private companies and also the compulsory insurance required by the state. Among the most important of these organizations are fraternal orders, trade-unions, local relief societies, and the organizations formed by corporations and their employees.

The fraternal societies are composed of a national organization and subordinate lodges, governed in all affairs of general importance by the charter issued to them by the grand or central lodge. Funds are collected by the central lodge from the local lodge in the form of assessments and out of these funds are paid the death benefits. Benefits are usually paid by the local lodge in case of illness of a member and very frequently "out of work" benefits are paid. Some few of them have attempted to found an old age pension fund. In addition to the insurance feature, the social and ceremonial aspects of the organization appeal to many. Not all the membership would admit of classification in the wage-earning class, but the greater number could be so classified. We have already seen that the greatest weakness of such orders is that the collections are not based on any scientific plan. Many of them do not even use the National Fraternal Congress Table of Mortality, whose rates of mortality are considerably lower than any of the commonly used mortality tables of the regular insurance companies. The state has done little in detailed supervision of these orders, and the beginning of state supervision now promised will undoubtedly do much to preserve and extend the benefits of these organizations which have been based on laudable motives and honestly conducted in most cases, although too often on unscientific plans.

Trade-union Insurance. — Trade-unions among their other activities have paid out large sums for the insurance of their members. They have as yet done little in the case of accidents and old age pensions, since they

have depended largely on the employer's liability laws
to secure awards for accidents. It is at the time of
sickness and death that the chief benefits are paid.
These benefits are sometimes paid out by the local union,
but there is a marked tendency towards the practice of
having these funds collected by the national union.
The ordinary plan is for each member to pay a certain
sum each week or month into a sick and death benefit
fund. The death benefits do not, however, usually
consist in the payment of a sum in excess of the expense
of burial and the illness connected with it. The premiums necessary for the payments of these benefits
manifestly vary from union to union. They are determined by the character of the organization or of similar
organizations. This activity of the unions has done
much to popularize them with the wage earners. The
members feel that they are providing for themselves,
and the management of these activities has usually
reflected much credit on the labor union. It is suggested
that as the state works out a suitable plan of insurance
for the industrial classes, it may find it advisable to use
the trade-union as an agency for distributing state funds.
That is to say, the state would subsidize the union by
transferring to it funds which have been collected by
taxation. This would not be giving these funds in any
sense of a charity. It would be a legitimate cost of
production which society ought to bear and which is
returned to those who are now unfairly bearing a high
cost of production. It is sometimes replied that this
deficient wage should be given to the industrial worker
at the time he earns it, that is, in an increased daily

wage, but the actual method of making the wage contract precludes any likelihood that this will be done.

Local Relief Societies. — The local relief societies which secure protection for the industrial classes are very numerous. They are purely voluntary organizations and have no central organization. They are most commonly formed by the employees of a large firm or corporation. The employers may or may not contribute funds to the employees' organization. A common bond of union and sympathy exists among the employees of any large business concern. In the more loosely formed organizations of this description no adjustment of the contribution on the basis of the wage received is attempted. Each pays what he pleases with the result that the contribution is not always equitable. In the better organizations adjustment of payments to wage is made. Membership in all cases is voluntary. Sick and death benefits are paid, but the amount differs widely from organization to organization. The greatest weakness in such organizations is that the plans on which they are conducted are usually unscientific and that each confines its activities to the particular plan, thereby depriving itself of the benefits of the general experience of such organizations. The retiring member receives no return for his past payments. Those in charge of the funds sometimes defraud and often no recovery against them is possible.

The relief societies formed by some of the large corporations, such as the United States Steel Corporation and the railways, differ from the above in that the former are organized, managed by, and composed of the employees, while in the latter organizations the employers have a part. In most cases the employer originated the plan. He contributes largely to the benefit fund and assists in its management. The amount — if any — paid by the employee is adjusted to his wage, but no employee is required to become or to continue as a member. Sick and death benefits are paid, the amounts differing in different relief societies. In many of them benefits are paid in case of accidents, and in case of death, benefits are often paid to some one dependent upon the employee. The dues of the members are usually deducted from their wages. In many cases pensions are paid after a specified period of service with the company.

The organization and management of this class of relief societies is usually very efficient and in marked contrast to that of the employees' organizations. There is a security and certainty about the contributions and payments. The cost of the pensions now paid by several of the railway companies is wholly borne by the company, but there are very definite limits under which the employee is entitled to receive the old age pension.

It is often argued that the activity of the state legislatures and courts in enacting and interpreting the employer's liability laws has had much to do in causing employers to organize such relief societies; that it is a deceptive generosity; that in effect there is a pressure felt by the employee to become and continue a member of such societies; that relief is thus sought from liability under the law for accidents and injuries to employees by thus making the employee less willing to institute a suit for damages. Even though a contract was made which by its terms freed the employer from liability because the employee received the specified benefits, the right of action for damages would in most cases still exist. Some states have enacted laws which specifically provide that an employee cannot thus contract away a common law right.

However, it must be recognized in fairness to the parties concerned in such industrial insurance that there has been a wonderful advance in the recognition of the obligation which employers owe to employees and a commendable willingness on the part of many employers to assume the legal as well as the moral obligation. It is true that we have only made a beginning, but the spirit now prevalent argues much for the better solution of the problem. In some cases firms and corporations pay the premium for accident insurance of the employees in private insurance companies.

Employer's Liability Insurance. — We have now to consider another form of insurance for the industrial classes, viz. liability or employer's liability insurance. The terms " liability insurance " and " casualty insurance " are often used interchangeably by the uninformed, but, properly considered, the former is included in the latter. Casualty insurance is insurance paid in case of bodily injury or death or for losses or damages to property, excluding losses by fire, which have been caused by accidents or contingencies not ordinarily contemplated. Its chief kinds are personal, accident, liability, steam boiler, plate glass, and elevator insurance. We are here concerned with only one form of liability insurance and first with the liability insurance sold by private companies to employers.

The rise of this form of insurance was a direct outgrowth of the action of legislatures and courts in either establishing new principles in regard to the obligations of the employer to indemnify his injured employee or by the enactment into statute law the common law principle of the employer's liability. It is therefore to be distinguished from other forms of insurance in that it is the result of the activity of the state either by its courts applying the common law or by the legislature enacting into law the principle of employer's liability.

Early Status of the Laborer. — We have seen that the relation of laborers to the employers in ancient and medieval times was quite different from what it has come to be in modern industrial times. The factory system was not in existence, and the bond of relation between the laborer and the employer was closer. The personal relation was more definite. In most cases the number of employees of one person was limited. The laborers worked for a person, not for a corporation. Out of this relationship of early times there grew up a common law principle of liability of the employer to his employees, which, although it did not secure full protection to the laborers, yet was thought sufficient until late in the nineteenth century, when the common law principle became expressed in statute law. No greater proof of the helplessness or disadvantage at which the laborer bargains with the capitalist for his wage is to be found than in the fact that it was over a century after the establishment of the factory system before an employer's liability law was enacted. Dependence was placed in the operation of the common law principle which had grown up from early times.

Early Theory of the Employer's Liability. — The principle of liability of the employer found some expression in Roman law, although the principle as stated in this country in its present form received its chief early development from the decisions of the English courts. In the early years, however, the master was not only responsible to the servant for any injury suffered by the latter when not due to the employee's carelessness, but the master was also subject to liability for an injury suffered by a third party as a result of the actions of the servant when in the employment of the master. It is important to understand, however, that the liability did not rest upon the master in the following cases: First, if the person injured was a fellow servant. This is known as the fellow-servant doctrine. Second, if the employee knew or had means of knowing the danger incident to the employment and voluntarily accepted the employment. This is known as the assumed risk doctrine. Third, if the injury resulted from the combined negligence of employer and employee, that is, the latter contributed to the negligence which resulted in his injury. This is known as the contributory negligence doctrine.

It is important to understand these limitations or exceptions, because practically all the legislation and all the court decisions from an early date, so far as they have given greater protection to the employees, have done so by modifying or doing away with these limitations. This is the goal from which we have started, and the goal to which we go is to assess upon society in some manner the total costs of production; to secure for the laborer, not only an adequate daily wage, but also a protection against accident however caused, against sickness, unemployment, invalidity, and old age. Not until then will many agree that an equitable system of distribution has been devised, for the burden now resting on the shoulders of the laborer is not all his own.

Without tracing the changes in the conditions of work and the changes which occurred in the industrial organization of the establishment of the factory system, we may at once state that as a result of these changes England passed an employer's liability law in 1880. England was the most advanced industrial nation, and this fact, together with the character of its people and government, accounts for this law. The most surprising fact about the law is that its enactment was so long delayed both in Europe and America. A few years later (1887), Alabama and Massachusetts passed a similar law. Other states have slowly followed, and we shall again have the very great difficulty of attempting a description of a form of insurance, the characteristics of which are determined by the action of the legislatures of various states.

Common Law and Statutory Law on Liability. — It must be remembered, however, that the common law principle of the employer's liability was in force in all the states, and in many states this common law had been expressed in statute law. In many cases the old common law principle was enlarged at the time of adopting it in the form of statute law, and the effect of the changes made by the states since then has been to enlarge the principle. The personal relation of the employer and employees has been more distant with the integration and concentration of industry, with the result that the state has felt it necessary to aid the employees in securing that protection which they could not of themselves secure. So much for the conditions which give rise to employer's liability insurance. It now remains for us to describe how this insurance is conducted.

The object of employer's liability insurance is to indemnify the employer for losses which he suffers as a result of the enforcement of legal claims made by his employees. These claims arise when injuries or death result to the employees while in the service of the employer or to third parties when about the premises or property of the employer. This protection is purchased by manufacturers, by contractors, by transportation companies, by mine owners, by owners of hotels and theaters, or by any other large employer of laborers. The indemnity may cover, not only employees, but any one who suffers an injury from the activity of employees and ownership of property. That is to say, it may be general liability, covering all liability for damages to third parties. The employer or owner purchases from a company this protection, and when an injury is suffered by a person, for which he may be liable for damages, the company settles the claim or defends it in the courts. The employer or owner has nothing to do with it. He has purchased this protection and freedom. The insured gives notice to the company, and the company disposes of the claim.

The premium is based, in the case of employers of labor, upon the wages paid and the character of the industry. The premium is a certain per cent of the total wages paid. It may or may not include salaries of the higher officials or employees. The calculation of the premium is not as simple a matter as it would seem. First, the number of employees and amount of yearly wage varies. There is therefore provision for a return of a surplus premium at the close of the year or for the payment of a deficient premium by the employer on the basis of the actual wages paid. When individuals leave the employment, this relieves the company of liability and hence affects the premium which should be collected. Second, in many occupations the degree of hazard varies widely in the different parts of the business, and equity would demand that the part with little risk should not be burdened by the part with the great risk. Third, the laws of the different states differ in the degree to which they make an employer liable. Some fix a maximum amount of damages which may be collected, while others do not, and juries differ very greatly in their idea of what constitutes fair damages. Again, frequent changes are being made in the laws, and these require a readjustment of rates. The adequacy of the premium was a matter for experience to disclose, and evidently no such accuracy as in the case of the life insurance premium has been or probably can be secured.

Coöperation among liability companies has been difficult to secure for continued periods. Competition has been so active, and new companies have been so frequently organized, that any central organization with standard rates and other uniform requirements has been disrupted by some one or more companies violating the general terms of the agreement.

Notwithstanding this difficulty, valuable results have been secured by compiling the experience of different companies. In no other kinds of insurance is coöperation needed so much as in casualty insurance, for its rates are the least scientifically determined, and even with the best coöperation certain elements in the cost cannot be determined.

The company writing liability insurance has inspectors whose duty it is to inspect plants or buildings upon which insurance against claims by workmen or users is desired. The character of the industry or building may preclude any company writing such insurance for the employer or owner, and it is the duty of these inspectors to inspect, not only proposed risks, but actual risks. They advise the employer and owner of methods by which accidents may be avoided. The owner is usually disposed to accept the advice, since it may favorably affect his premium.

Employer's liability insurance has developed since 1880, and in 1913 the premium collected on such insurance by the private companies was about $41,000,000 and the loss payments for the year about $29,000,000. The expense of conducting such insurance is large, for in addition to the ordinary expenses of an insurance company, such as soliciting the insurance and office expenditures, the expenses of inspection and settlement are very much larger than in an ordinary company. The very numerous changes which are being made by legislatures and courts in reference to the relation of employer and employee are producing very great changes in this form of insurance. Policies are being changed to comply with the new conditions.

Weakness of Liability Insurance. — There are many objections to the compensation of workmen under the law of negligence, but the most important objection is that in the actual working of the principle, the workmen receive a small part of the sum paid by the employer for such purpose. The New York Employer's Liability Commission states in its report of 1910 that the statistics collected from nine insurance companies which keep separate employer's liability records show that on an average only 36.34 per cent of what the employer pays in premiums for liability insurance goes to the injured workmen. That is, for every $100 paid by the employer for protection, less than $37 is paid to his injured workman. The $63 is paid to attorneys, claim agents, and for the cost of soliciting the business and for administration.

It must be understood that this contract of insurance covers only the legal liability of the employer to his employee and not the moral obligation which either the employer or society owes to the workingman. Then, too, as we have seen, this form of insurance has not been applied to some plants and scarcely at all to some industries, such as the agricultural industry. It must be evident, therefore, that great numbers of the industrial classes were not protected from the risks inevitably associated with their employment and which they must accept because they must sell their product — labor; and in contrast with all other products the seller — the workman — must deliver himself with his product.

Compensation Legislation. — Owing to the unsatisfactory results of the actual working of the old liability laws, the increased influence of the laboring class and the development of humanitarian ideas, there has been since 1910 an extensive adoption of the principle of workmen's compensation. The following named states enacted Workmen's Compensation Acts during the stated years: New York in 1910, Ohio, Washington, Massachusetts, New Jersey, Wisconsin, California, Kansas, Illinois, Nevada, and New Hampshire in 1911, Rhode Island, Arizona, Maryland, Michigan in 1912, Connecticut, Iowa, Minnesota, Nebraska, Oregon, West Virginia, and Texas in 1913, Kentucky in 1914; and other states are preparing to enact such a law. Many of these original acts have been amended.

Theory of Compensation Insurance. — The theory of the compensation acts is, that industry should bear the cost or loss of life or injury which is occasioned by production of the goods in the same manner as it bears the cost of replacing broken or worn-out machinery; that every worker or those dependent upon him should be compensated for death or accident, incurred directly in the service of the employer and indirectly in the service of producing goods for consumption of society. This principle disregards any question of fault of the employer or employee, since in the complicated business of modern production, the assignment of fault and negligence is often impossible. This theory therefore involves a practical abandonment of the older theory of employer's liability under the common law. This principle of entitling the workman to receive compensation for death and injuries received during the course of his employment was thought, and so held in some cases, to violate state and federal constitutions and in several states, notably in New York, California, and Ohio, amendments were made to the constitutions to authorize the enactment of such laws. The chief constitutional question raised was the depriving of a trial by jury, since the laws in some cases created a liability without fault and compelled the employer to pay compensation, thus taking, as the New York Court of Appeals said of the first New York law, " the property of A and giving it to B."

This led to the adoption of the " elective acts," under which the employer and employee were not governed by the legislation unless by some particular act, or, as provided in some of the laws, by a failure to act. The employer is offered in most such laws inducements " to elect to operate under the law," as, for example, by the removal of one or more or all the common law defenses if he fails to so elect. That is, he is estopped from setting up the common law defenses in the event he has not elected to operate under the Workmen's Compensation Act.

The Federal Government passed a Compensation Act in 1908, providing that certain of its employees should receive from the United States Treasury compensation in case of death and injury. This act has by amendments been extended, until now it includes practically all its employees which can be protected by such a law.

Plans of Compensation. — Compensation Laws may be classified as to their methods of administration into two divisions:

(*a*) The Direct Payment Plan. Under this plan the law fixes the amount which is to be paid for particular injuries, but leaves the fact of injury and the extent of disability to be settled by the employer and employee or by the court or by an administrative board of the state. Under this plan the compensation provided is either purchased from a private insurance company writing policies, granting the protection required by the Act, or by a mutual association of employers who protect each other in the payment of these claims. In either case the total cost is borne by the employer.

(*b*) The State Insurance Plan. Under this plan a fund is created by payments, made either by the employer or by the employer and employees and in some cases by certain contributions by the State. Under this plan there is also a State Board which collects these payments, establishes rates by classifying the hazard of different occupations, hears claims, and makes settlement.

Administration of Compensation Insurance. — The State Insurance Board for the Administration of the Compensation Law becomes under the circumstances practically an insurance organization, competing with the private companies for the privilege of insuring employers against the claims of their employees or dependants in case of death or injury.

In some states the law has made it practically compulsory, as, for example, in Ohio, for the employer to insure in the state fund. This has practically legislated out of existence the private companies so far as they attempt to write this particular kind of insurance. It is not to be understood that these Compensation Acts apply to all employers and include protection for all workers. The act frequently applies only to " employers having five or more employees," and excludes certain industries, as, for example, agriculture.

The acts, however, do apply to public employees; that is, to cities, counties, school boards; and these political organizations must either provide for such insurance through the state fund or from private companies. This is, however, kept separate from that insurance granted in the case of a state fund to ordinary employers. In fact, each of the classes of employment is kept separate, as well as the record of each employer in the class. On the basis of these classifications, premiums or contributions to the funds are adjusted according as the actual experience in one occupation or of one employer shows the charge is too high or too low. An inducement is thus given to each employer to install safety devices and adopt any method which will reduce his death or accident experience. This is of course the plan under which private companies writing employer's liability or compensation insurance operate.

There has been considerable discussion of the policy whether a state should make compulsory this insurance with the state in a state fund; that is, practically make compensation insurance a state monopoly. This practice is at present the exception, Ohio being probably the best exception. In most cases when the state has organized a board for the purposes of granting such insurance it competes with the private companies for the business.

The purpose of the changes which have been made in the older practice of Employer's Liability and are now being made in Workmen's Compensation Laws is to increase the protection to the working class, and the final result will probably be to lay down a broad policy of workingman's compensation under which the worker will be protected for all occupational injuries; or, if carried still farther, the working classes will be protected against unemployment, sickness, and infirmity. In any case liability insurance in the broad sense of the term will have a wonderful development. It may be secured from private companies organized for this purpose. This is the chief method now in use. In this event the cost of the greater protection will be shifted ultimately to society by the employer in an increased price for the goods.

This protection may be supplied directly by the state. In this event the funds for this purpose would be collected by taxation, and society would also bear the cost. No general agreement can be secured as to which of these methods would be most economical and most advantageous from a social standpoint. It must be realized that the cost of industrial accidents, unemployment, and dependent old age is now being borne

by society in the form of charity and various means of
relief and assistance.   The important points to realize
are, first, that those who suffer from these industrial
accidents are often not well enough cared for to maintain themselves as efficient and social workers, and
second, that in the present methods of relief there is great
danger of pauperizing them by creating the idea that
the relief is given to them as a matter of sympathy and
not as a matter of justice.

The costs of progress are always present.   A part of
these costs is a social cost and should be paid for by
society.   Another part may well be considered an individual cost, and it is too much to expect that the state
in some mysterious manner is to be able to prevent
misfortune from occurring to any of its members, or,
if it does occur, to indemnify him for the loss sustained
on account of his own ignorance, lack of thrift, and
industry.   Society must see to it that the individual is
given a chance to do and an incentive to do, but no more
fatal check to progress could be established than a
system which would encourage the individual member
of society to look to his fellow members to do his share
of the world's work, to reimburse him for all his personal
misfortunes, and to rectify all his mistakes.

Government Pensions. — Governments also directly
aid employees by a system of pensions.   The federal
system of pensions for those who have served the state
in time of war is too well known to need description.
This has been also applied to the life-saving service and
to the army nurses.   It has been proposed to apply it
to all civil service employees, as in the case of most

countries, but the proposal has never been accepted in the United States. The Southern states also provide a pension-system for those who served the confederacy during the Civil War. It is true that this form of insurance as well as that of the cities applies to a particular class of workers, but no account of industrial insurance would be adequate without reference to these systems.

City Pensions. — A number of cities in different states provide a pension fund for the firemen, policemen, and teachers. In the case of the first and second class the funds are derived from various sources. Sometimes the proceeds or parts of the proceeds of special taxes are set aside for this purpose. The subject has caused considerable discussion and the laws providing for such pensions have been frequently a matter of adjudication by the courts, since the laws governing municipal action differ in the different states and are frequently changed. Benefits are frequently paid to the widow of the employee of the city in case of death, and a pension is granted to minors. After a certain period of service, the employee may be retired on a pension, or a pension may be paid for disability acquired in the service of the city. Teachers' pensions are on much the same plan, although laws attempting to secure a compulsory contribution from the employee have been declared unconstitutional in several states, such as Ohio and Minnesota. The next step will probably be to require compulsory contribution. The arguments for and objections to such plans of insurance will suggest themselves, and since all these plans are yet in their developmental stages, no detailed account of them is here attempted.

Savings Bank Insurance. — Several states have also enacted legislation which aids their citizens with insurance in other ways than that of compensation insurance and pensions. In 1907 Massachusetts passed a law which permitted savings banks to establish departments to sell life and old age insurance. The cost of administration is sought to be kept low by its association with the banking activities and by the absence of solicitors. The past experience of providing insurance without solicitors has not proved successful, but it is hoped that the insurance under this plan will be solicited by organizations, such as labor unions, benefit associations, and employers who seek to have their members or workmen insured. The plan has not been in operation long enough to decide its success or failure.

Wisconsin also has passed a law under which a state department of life insurance under the supervision of the commissioner of insurance is created to sell life insurance. State insurance is in the United States only in the preliminary stages of discussion.

Government Insurance in Europe. — It is in the European and Australian countries that we find the best example of state activity in reference to insurance for the industrial classes. We shall select Germany, England, and the Australian countries as typical of the most advanced action in this direction.

Germany provides for compulsory accident, sickness, and old age insurance. The insurance of workmen against accidents dates from the imperial law of 1884, which with its later amendments requires compulsory accident insurance to be paid to practically all workmen, managers, and administration officials whose salary does not exceed $750 per annum. The enforcement and administration of the law is very largely in the control of the employers with state supervision. Mutual associations of employers in the same or closely allied trades or industries are formed. These associations determine the amount to be paid by each employer. This payment is based on the pay roll and the risk of the particular factory or plant.

The compensation to the injured workman includes the following: (a) medical attendance, including bandages, crutches, spectacles, etc.; (b) a weekly payment, based on the wage received, the extent and duration of the disability; (c) in the case of death a burial benefit and a pension to the dependents, if there are any. The workingmen's sickness insurance societies pay a sick benefit for a period of at least thirteen weeks, and of this sick benefit the employer contributes one third. The employers are thereby relieved from the payment for this period of time. The cash benefit for partial disablement is two thirds of the decrease in the earning power and for total disability two thirds of the wage. Free hospital treatment until cured and a reduced benefit to dependents may be taken in lieu of the cash benefits, but in case of total disability the cash benefit may be increased to the total wage.

In case of accidental death, a burial benefit is paid, and a pension to dependents; for the widow as long as she continues a widow and for the children until age 14. These pensions vary from 20 to 60 per cent of the average wage. If disablement of the workman continues beyond thirteen weeks, the amount to be paid is determined by these mutual associations of employers, but provisions are made by which the workman can appeal to a board of arbitration composed of two representatives of the employers, two of the workmen, and one appointed by the state. This board hears claims from injured workmen or from claimants for benefits on account of the death of the workman.

Compulsory sickness insurance is provided for practically all workmen except agricultural laborers, domestic servants, and those whose annual salary exceeds $200. This law was enacted in 1884 and its administration intrusted to the many societies which already existed for the purpose of providing sickness insurance. Many of these voluntary societies yet exist as independent organizations, but there is a tendency for them to decrease in the competition with the compulsory organizations. In the voluntary societies the members pay such premiums as they choose with the limitation that the payment must not exceed 2 per cent of the daily wage. In the voluntary societies, the employees make one third of the contributions and the employers two thirds. The benefits secured are as follows: (a) a minimum benefit in case of disability on account of accident or sickness for at least twenty-six weeks and at least one half of the daily wage; (b) medical aid; (c) in some cases hospital treatment and one half of the sick benefits paid to the family; (d) a funeral benefit of twenty times the average daily wage; (e) a benefit for women for six weeks after confinement. Additional benefits may under certain conditions be paid and the time extended to fifty-two weeks during which benefits may be received.

The German laws providing for insurance against invalidity and old age were passed in 1891 and 1899. All persons over 16 years of age receiving wages, clerks, and teachers who do not receive a salary in excess of $500 must be insured. The invalidity pension is paid regardless of age, and the old age pension begins at 70 regardless of whether invalidity has occurred. Invalidity is not paid in case of occupational accidents nor if the person is able to earn more than one third of his average wage. Old age pensions are limited to those who have contributed to the fund for at least twelve hundred weeks and invalidity pensions to those who have contributed at least two hundred weeks. The government pays all the expenses of administration and adds $12.50 yearly to each old age pension. The remainder of the cost is borne equally by the employer and the employee. The amount of the pension as well as the employee's contribution is determined by his average annual wage. If the recipient is receiving a pension from the state or a disability pension, the old age or invalidity pension is not paid, if either one with his personal income is in excess of seven and one half times the invalidity pension.

Although Germany has no insurance against unemployment, it will be recognized that she has by legal enactments devised a very complete system of workingman's insurance. The industrial progress of Germany during the last decade would seem to show that such a system of insurance for the industrial classes has placed no bar upon her development or power to compete with her opponents in securing trade, notwithstanding that she has paid out under these three plans of insurance over one billion dollars.

In England we have seen that no special protection was given to the workman before 1880 except what he could secure from the courts under the common law, governing the relation of master and servant. However, in 1897 a new law was enacted which permitted the servant to secure damages upon proof that he was injured in the employ of the master unless gross fault was proved on the part of the employee. In 1900 the principles of the previous acts were extended to the agricultural industry and in 1906 certain amendments were made which made possible the collection of damages for either an accident or an incapacity due to disease, inevitably connected with the trade. Employers are liable for payments to employees, including clerks and salaried employees receiving less than $1217.50 yearly. In case of death the maximum payment is $1460 and the minimum $730. In case there are no dependents, the employer must pay the medical and funeral expenses connected with the death of his employee. The amount paid in case of disability is determined by the duration of the disability and the weekly wage, the maximum benefit being $4.87 per week. If the disability is permanent, the compensation is made weekly throughout life. England has for many years encouraged the purchase of annuities, but the purchasers have always been comparatively few.

In 1908 England enacted an old age pension law. The person must have attained the age of 70, must have been a resident of the country twenty years preceding his application, and must prove that his yearly income is not in excess of $157.50; also that he has been industrious and that he has not within the past ten years been convicted of a criminal offense. The amount of the pension is graded from $1.25 per week down, according to the income of the recipient. The expenditure which resulted from this act was far in exceess of what was calculated, the first year's expenditures amounting to about $40,000,000. The fund is received from general taxation, no contribution to the fund being required from the pensioner.

A plan for sickness and unemployment insurance has been enacted which provides the following protection:

Nearly 15,000,000 men and women are included in the scope of the sick insurance fund. Every worker between the ages of eighteen and sixty-five whose earnings are less than $800 a year will be required to insure against sickness by the payment of eight cents a week, to which the employer will add six cents and the state four cents. By this means free medical attendance will be provided, maternity benefits granted, and in case of permanent disability, a life pension paid. Only the house building, engineering, and ship building trades, involving 2,500,000 workers, are to share in the unemployment insurance. The insurance of $1.75 a week to the man out of work through no fault of his own means only bare subsistence and can hardly prove an incentive to idleness, against which other precautions are taken; but other trades in time may be expected to demand equal treatment.

It must be understood that all these plans of insurance in the European countries do not supplant the work of private companies and mutual societies, each of which continues in operation. The activity of the government simply supplements private and collective activities. The friendly societies of England have especially given much protection for many years to the working classes in England.

Government Insurance in Australia. — In the Australian countries more advanced experiments are being made. In New Zealand the old age pensions are paid *in toto* from state funds. The same is true in New South Wales and Victoria. In each state it is considered the duty of the state to support the worker who has contributed to the productivity of the nation in his earlier years. The applicant for the pension must have reached the age of sixty-five and resided in the country twenty-five years previous to his application for the pension. He must have lived a temperate and industrious life. He must not have had a prison record of over four months during the last twelve years preceding the application, and must not have been in prison over one year at any time. He must have an honorable family record. The amount of the pension cannot exceed $130, and he is not entitled to any pension if his annual income exceeds $260. The pension is adjusted from $130 down, according to the income received from other sources. The requirements differ somewhat in the different countries of Australia, but the principle is the same in the above-mentioned countries.

New Zealand has a state department for accident and

liability insurance to afford employers their insurance. The laws governing the liability of employers are practically the same as in England. The amount which can be collected by the employee is dependent on the wages which he receives, as in England. The private companies have been quite able to meet the competition of the state in selling this form of indemnity.

Thus we see that insurance for the industrial classes has made great progress in its development since 1880 and its development in some countries will certainly be paralleled in other nations. Changes are annually being made in the different nations, and the student should familiarize himself with this topic by acquainting himself with the arguments for and against the plans, and the new proposals which are being made.

REFERENCES

Frankel, Lee K., and Dawson, Miles M.   Workingmen's Insurance in Europe.

Henderson, Charles R.   Industrial Insurance in the United States.

Seager, Henry R.   Social Insurance.

Schloss, D. F.   Insurance against Unemployment.

Lewis, Frank W.   State Insurance.

Willoughby, W. F.   Workingmen's Insurance.

Zacher, G.   Die Arbeiter-Versicherung im Auslande.

Benefit Features of American Trade-unions.   United States Department of Labor Bulletins, No. 22, May, 1899.

Report of the New York Liability Commission, 1910.

CHAPTER XII

RELATION OF THE STATE TO INSURANCE

The Bases of State Regulation of Insurance. — We have seen from the previous description of the character of insurance and the methods of its sale that it is a business which must concern itself with large numbers of individuals. It demands an agreement between sellers and buyers of a valuable thing — indemnity — in which the terms of the sale are frequently misunderstood. It demands the association of individuals in order to secure a thing which no one could secure for himself. It is a coöperation among many in which a general interest is present, but in which also an individual or a group of individuals may seek to benefit at the expense of the many. The contracts which are made, particularly in life insurance, continue for long periods of time and the settlements for which they provide cannot be enforced in most cases by the original party to the contract, but must rest either upon the good faith of the other party or upon the compulsion of a third party — the state.

Since the obligations of an insurance company are chiefly in the future, errors due to ignorance or dishonesty do not immediately disclose themselves. The policyholder cannot usually withdraw without loss to himself. The business of insurance, both on account

328

of the difficulty in comprehending the principles underlying it and also on account of the complexity of its
actual transaction, is such that the average policyholder
cannot determine for himself the soundness of the company. Even if he should discover evils in its operation,
he usually neither knows how to correct them nor
how to protect himself. The business of insurance is
almost wholly conducted with the funds of the policyholder, who receives for his payments a simple promise
to pay a sum at some future time.

There would therefore seem to be good reasons for the
activity of the state in order that the principles of just-
ness and equity may be preserved. The state should
not only protect the weak against the unjust activity of
the strong, but it should also prohibit large numbers
of its citizens from doing an injury to themselves. In
this last mentioned capacity, it should, for example,
prohibit a group of individuals from organizing themselves into an assessment company to do a thing which
past experience has shown to be impossible. The state
is particularly interested in compelling contracts to be
carried out, and since the insurance contract involves
rights and benefits extending beyond the lifetime of
one party to the contract, it finds an important sphere
of action in the insurance business. It is also inevitable
when a business has to do with so many persons, as does
insurance, that some of these persons will at times attempt to practice fraud on the group, and this practice the state must seek to prohibit. Although insurance is a business in which many are necessarily interested, its very character precludes the many from hav-

ing any direct part in the actual conduct of the business, and it is therefore incumbent upon the state to do what it can to protect the many against the possible carelessness, ignorance, or dishonesty of some officials of some companies.

It is coming to be more clearly recognized that the state amidst the present-day complexity of commercial activities and the intricacies of modern business organization cannot depend upon publicity and competition to secure protection to its citizens. If publicity simply means informing the public what an organization is doing, the state defaults its duty to its citizens by this negative approval of the thing done and leaves in many cases but an incomplete means of redress, and in other cases none.

Popular Fallacies Regarding Insurance. — Much of the confusion in thought and opinion, as to what the relation of the government to the business of insurance should be, arises very largely from a general ignorance or a mistaken understanding of what insurance is. The popular notions and sophisms of insurance are to be found in the case of scarcely any other business.

The first fallacy is, that insurance is a completely competitive business and therefore the public can benefit in the price by encouraging and compelling independent action on the part of all companies in selling their commodity. This fallacy will be treated more fully in a later part of the discussion, but at this point attention may be called to the fact that both in life and fire insurance a large part of the work of the company is to distribute a cost already entailed on the public by the mortality and burning rates. It is true that in all businesses there are overhead costs, and therefore there is a field for the play of competitive forces among the producers of the service; but a large part of the total cost in insurance is fixed by forces over which the producer has no control. In distributing this cost there may occur unjust apportionments of it and the overhead costs may be too large. Nevertheless, no amount of competition can directly affect for any one company the fixed charges which rest as a whole upon all companies.

The second fallacy is a popular notion that insurance is a business, suited for profit-taking, that is, profit in the technical economic sense. It is true that both life and fire insurance as conducted have often been and still are in some cases of this character. It is also true that denying to it these characteristics might seem to lead, as a logical conclusion, to a state monopoly of insurance. This is not, however, a necessary conclusion. Nor do life and fire insurance stand on a par as regards this profit-taking characteristic, for the reason that fire insurance has within it elements of risk, and also has demands for the enterpriser's ability which warrant under our present economic system, profit taking. It is believed, however, that the essential and fundamental characteristics of life insurance are such that only pure wages, rent, and interest are justified.

The third fallacy — In the third place it is generally believed that insurance is a peculiarly profitable business for those engaged in it; that is to say, that the stockholders or owners of the companies receive unusually high interest on the capital invested. This is supposed to be especially true in the case of fire insurance companies. Apparent proof of this fact is given by the quotations of the market value of fire insurance stock, some of which is many fold above par, and further by the large dividends of 20 to 30 per cent which some companies declare. These facts do not themselves warrant the conclusion that fire insurance stands out among other businesses as peculiarly profitable. The mere fact that no particular obstacles are in the way of any group of individuals organizing a life or fire insurance company, and the additional fact that there is always free capital seeking the highest possible return, irrespective of the nature of the investment, ought to be sufficient to prove the error in the conclusion. However, it must also be pointed out that the explanation of the returns in insurance, especially in fire insurance, as made by the companies, does not always express the exact financial condition of the business. It is often pointed out by fire insurance companies that the underwriting profit during the last fifty years has often been less than 1 per cent, and in some years has been nothing. This statement is correct, but it is not enlightening as to the financial experience of the fire insurance companies. The underwriting profit is only the remainder of the year's premiums after the loss payments and expenses have been deducted. Policies are written for periods of from one to five years which under the method of calculating the reserve previously described makes it impossible to take any one year's experience in fire insurance as a test of the profitableness of the business. The ratio of losses to $100 of premium has during the past fifty years averaged 57.85 per cent, and the ratio of expenses to premium receipt has been during the same period 36.42 per cent. Such a calculation of profit on the basis of mere underwriting profit leaves out of consideration the item of interest earning. But not all of the interest earned can be counted in determining the actual profitableness of fire insurance companies. The funds on which such a company has to earn interest during the year are the capital, the surplus, and the reserve. If the company has, for example, $1,000,000 of capital and $14,000,000 in surplus, and declares a dividend of 30 per cent on the $1,000,000 stock, this 30 per cent dividend resolves itself into a 2 per cent dividend on the total capital set aside for conducting the business, to say nothing of the risk involved from the fact that the stockholders are liable for an assessment on the stock in the event of a conflagration, if they wish to preserve all or a part of the accumulated surplus. However, this would not be an absolutely accurate method of calculating the actual profitableness of the business. The amount of capital which a company has invested in the business has, from the standpoint of calculating the earning, little significance. Its chief function is in determining the ownership of the company and only at times of crises in the affairs of the concern does it rise to importance in the financial aspects of the business. In an economic sense the real value of the company is not its capital value but what the business is worth or what it will sell for as a going concern. This going value or proprietary interest is determined by the capital, the surplus, and by a percentage usually about 30 per cent of the reinsurance reserve.

This assumes that a fire insurance company, if in a normal condition, can reinsure its business for about 70 per cent of the reserve. It will be recognized, then, that mere underwriting profit, that is, the difference between what is paid in to the company and what is paid out by the company, is not a full explanation of the company's net earnings. If the above described methods of calculating the actual profitableness of the business are applied to the fire insurance companies, it will be found that no excessive returns have as a whole been received. If the six largest, the six smallest, six medium sized companies, six new and six foreign companies are taken for application of the method, the following results are shown: The six largest United States companies have earned during the past twenty years 10.1 per cent, ranging from a profit in one year by one company of 31.4 per cent to a loss in one year by another company of 49.4 per cent. The rate of dividends for these companies, computed on this accurate method, has averaged for the twenty years 5.4 per cent, that is, they have distributed of this average earning of 10.1 per cent a little over one half in dividends and have kept the remainder in the business, allotting it to the surplus, which means that it may all be taken by a conflagration. Applying the same method of calculation to the other groups, results in an earning of 6.6 per cent for the six medium-sized companies during the past twenty years, and of this 3.3 per cent was used for dividends. The six smallest companies earned 4.5 per cent and distributed dividends of 3.4 per cent during the period. Of the six new companies three earned nothing during the period; of the six foreign companies, three lost money during the period. On the whole the investigation seems to show that it is likely to be only the old well-established companies which are profitable and also that there is a close connection between size, age, and success. In the second place it would seem to be clearly shown that the most successful companies have been earning about 10 per cent, of which 5 per cent has been placed back in the business. Ten per cent is considered a very good return in most business, but it must be recognized that 5 per cent is returned to the business and a risk of losing all of it is therefore incurred. Some return might be justified on this risk. These calculations were applied only to the larger companies. In many of the smaller companies the investors could doubtless have secured a better return by investing their capital in bonds, mortgages, or stocks other than insurance stocks. Nothing is here said in reference to expense. Whether the expense is or is not unnecessarily high is an entirely different question. All that is here attempted is to show that the common assumption that fire insurance is an extremely profitable business has no basis in actual facts. This, however, is not to state that a profit is not made, even an underwriting profit from certain states and on certain classes of risks. It is because of the fact that each state has control over rates, and these two previous facts that a large part of the discussion and dispute arise in reference to the rates and the profit of companies. A particular state or locality finds that the fire insurance companies have received a certain amount of premiums from the state or section and have paid in losses only a fraction of this premium fund. It is but natural to conclude that the companies are making a large amount of money, and to have no great desire to help pay for the losses in another state or locality by permitting the companies to charge the same rates.

In the fourth place it is a popular notion that life insurance has in it the primary elements of investment. This popular notion has been largely a result of some of the policies sold and the zeal of life insurance agents in selling insurance as well as in the excessive competition of companies for business. Insurance properly understood and sold can never compete with other investments. Life insurance is not an investing institution. It can never return to the buyer a profit. As a protection, as a mutual risk-assuming device, it has been greatly retarded in its true development by having had attached to it many of the appendages of an investment.

Lastly, the fallacy still persists with many that the insurance companies pay for the losses. The truth is, that the companies only act as collecting agencies for the policyholders and have no source of income and should have none except the premiums of the policyholders and the moderate rate of interest which these premiums earn when invested in long-time non-speculative securities. Nevertheless, many holders of life policies expect a company to return to them from some mysterious source sums far in excess of the premiums paid and their earnings. In the case of fire insurance policies, many object to becoming a coinsurer with the company of their property and in many states the legislatures have prohibited coinsurance and have enacted valued policy laws, both of which laws are essentially based on an assumption, that a particular policyholder may collect money from a company as distinct from the policyholders. Courts and juries are often ready to give decisions in favor of a claimant against an insurance company notwithstanding that a burden is thereby imposed upon other policyholders and not upon the company. Accident policies are made collectible by law in some states in case of suicide notwithstanding that the contract was never intended to include suicide among the list of happenings which would make the policy payable. The payment of premiums is forgotten in the payment of the loss. It is this failure to balance the many against the few, the public against the individual, the long view against the short view, which leads to so many popular fallacies.

The True Character of the Insurance Premium. — It must never be forgotten that the insurance business is peculiar in this one particular; the property of insurance companies is not made up of tangible or even intangible things distinct from the policyholders. The property is the premiums of the policyholders, exchanged for a piece of paper, expressing a contract. Even the securities held by the company are either actually or potentially the property of the policyholders. The officials and agents are in a true sense the hired employees of the policyholders. And this is true regardless of the mutual or stock character of the company. Insurance is even more than a public business like a railway. A railway company owns private property which is used in the service of the public, but an insurance company is service. It has no property other than the service it renders to the owners — the policyholders. Insurance of all kinds is essentially mutual, whatever modified forms this mutuality may take. It is but the voluntary contribution of the many to help bear the misfortunes of the few. Self-interest plays only a small part in that the bearer of the misfortune is unknown at the time the agreement is made. If a third party is introduced in addition to the individual members and the group — the first and second parties — it is only for the purpose of convenience, in that detailed and necessary work in operating the system is assigned to an employee, who becomes a middleman. This middleman simply collects the premiums and guarantees the payment of the losses, thus relieving the members of the group of any risk of assessments or premiums. Thus arises what is called stock insurance, the company selling a quasi commodity — indemnity; but even so, the business continues essentially mutual. No amount of surplus and assets would make possible a continuation of business or even the payment of the indemnity, if there were not this group of the insured, mutually bound together by the desire to protect each other against future misfortune.

Impelled by this motive of coöperation to protect each other, the life and fire insurance business has developed until it affects either directly or indirectly a large percentage of the people of the United States.

The stock fire insurance companies, alone, have risks in the United States of over sixty billions of dollars. There is an actual annual average loss of over $200,000,000. Not only is this actual loss distributed, but the distribution of the potential indemnity brings a state of security to the insured. It lies at the very foundation of the credit system.

In life insurance over twenty billion dollars of insurance is guaranteed by the ordinary and industrial companics, excluding assessment and other companies, just as mutual companies were excluded in the case of fire insurance. It is thus impossible to measure either the volume or importance of insurance.

Is Insurance a Public or a Private Business? — Two questions in relation to this business which has so wonderfully developed and which so intimately affects so many people are: *first*, Is it a public or private business, and *second*, Is it a competitive business? The answer given to these two questions largely determines the relation of the government to insurance. The first question, whether insurance is a private or public business, is assuming large importance at present, due to the discussion centering about rates. If insurance is a public business, then it follows that the government not only has a very extensive control over the prices charged for the indemnity and protection but also more substantial grounds exist for arguing that it should be made a state business, if not a state monopoly. Whatever may be the individual opinion as to the public or private nature of insurance, as a matter of fact the question as a purely legal one has been decided by the Supreme Court of the

United States in the case of the German Alliance Insurance Company *v.* Kansas, decided in 1914. (24 U. S. Sup. Ct. Rep. 612.) It was here held by a majority of the court that insurance was a public business. Business, said the court, may rise from a private to a public concern.

The decision pointed out that the risks in insurance are scattered over a large territory, and that therefore insurance rates are raised to a public issue. Contracts of insurance, therefore, have greater public consequence than contracts between individuals to do or not to do a particular thing whose effect stops with the individuals.

"To the contention that the business is private," said the court, "we have opposed the conception of public interest. We have shown that the business of insurance has very definite characteristics, with a reach of influence and consequences beyond and different from that of the ordinary business of the commercial world, to pursue which a greater liberty may be asserted. The transactions of a private character are independent and individual, terminating in their effect with the instances. The contracts of insurance may be said to be inter-independent. They cannot be regarded singly, or isolatedly, and the effect of the regulation is to create a fund of insurance and credit, the companies becoming the depositories of the money of the insured, possessing greater power thereby and charged with greater responsibility."

It was pointed out that the power to regulate interstate commerce existed long before the enactment of the interstate commerce law. That power, it said, however, was exerted " only when the size, number, and influence of these agencies had so increased and developed as to seem to make it imperative."

Is Insurance a Competitive Business?— As to the second important question; namely, Is insurance a competitive business, there would not seem to be reason for such extreme difference of opinion as exists, if the real character of insurance is understood. There are two aspects to this question. Confusion and misunderstanding result because these two aspects of the question have not been clearly kept in mind. The first aspect of the question is whether as a matter of fact monopoly exists. The second aspect of the question is, Is the character of the business such that it should be considered a monopoly; that is, Does its conduct invite and secure a play of the competitive forces in price making as in the ordinary competitive businesses? The first question is easily answered by stating that in 1914 there were about 253 different life insurance companies in business in the United States, and at the same date there were about 605 fire insurance companies. New companies are continually being organized. There are, therefore, different units selling this service and monopoly could only exist by proving that in each case of these 253 and 605 insurance companies, there was agreement as to the prices which were to be charged. This would need to be proven to exist among companies of such opposite interests as stock and mutual companies. The most superficial student of monopoly knows that it would be impossible to maintain an agreement regarding prices among such a large number of individual units. It is often argued that a monopoly must exist by some secretly maintained agreement on account of the fact that comparatively few large life and fire insurance companies have recently been established. The greater number of such efforts have failed. Statistics show that no company of the first rank has gained a footing in fire insurance during the past thirty years, and further that since 1841 of fire and marine insurance companies, 2249 have either failed or gone out of business in the United States. Likewise, statistics show that 274 life companies have either failed or gone out of business since 1850. But this is to be explained by the character of the business. This brings us to the second aspect of the question: viz. Is insurance by its character suited to the principles of competition? This is largely determined by the extent of control which each of the producers has over the cost of his product, and by the control that the consumer has over his demand for the product. As regards the producer — the insurance company — it is recognized that the life insurance company has no control over the mortality rate nor does the fire insurance company have any considerable control over the burning rate. These factors, the mortality and burning rate, are by far the most important ones in determining the price for the producer. There is only left for determination, operating costs, and some of these, such as taxes, are also fixed for the producer. Again, certain minor fixed charges exist. There remain only about one third of the total costs, — which may be denominated variable costs, — over which the individual producers — the companies

— have control. On the side of the consumer, the buyer of insurance, there is little control over the price and little choice of product. He can have but slight effect on the mortality and burning rate, and thus bargain in his purchase. He has no choice of product for there is no substitute for insurance protection. As the court well remarked in the Kansas case previously noted:

" We may venture to observe that the price of insurance is not fixed over the counters of the companies by what Adam Smith called the higgling of the market, but forms in the councils of the underwriters, promulgated in schedules of practically controlling constancy which the applicant for insurance is powerless to oppose and which therefore has led to the assertion that the business of insurance is of monopolistic character and that ' it is illusory to speak of a liberty of contract.'

" It is in the alternative presented of accepting the rate of the companies, or refraining from insurance, business impelling if not compelling it, that we may discover the inducement of the Kansas statute."

Evil Effects of Excessive Competition. — The results of competition have been disastrous enough in both life and fire insurance as proved by their effects. We need not theorize about this matter. In life insurance it has meant among other things the organization of companies on unscientific plans which in their operation have brought loss to many. It has meant unnecessary expense in an effort to secure business, and a perversion of insurance to investment, the issuing of semi-deceptive policies, the payment of unduly high salaries, commissions, and other accompaniments of unrestrained competition. In fire insurance the past and still too prevalent rate wars furnish ample evidence of the evil effects of competition.

" The universal effect of such periods of rate wars in fire insurance wherever and whenever they have occurred has been a cutting of rates to a point that was below the actual cost of the indemnity. If the rate war had been general, this would have meant the ultimate failure of the company, and rate wars of even local character lead, if long continued, to the dissolution of the smaller and weaker companies. The effect on all companies is weakening. The policyholder, to be sure, gets for a time his insurance very cheaply; too cheaply, for the weakening of the companies is not in the long run and on the whole an economic good, for there is just so much less protection behind the insured in case of a conflagration. The mutual character of insurance is so strong that nothing which tends to produce inferior protection can be for the public good. It has not done the policyholder any good to get cheap insurance if, when the time comes, the protection is found to be worthless.

" But this is not all. In a state of open competition the rates adjust themselves not to the hazards but largely to the strength of the insured, so that the man of influence, whose patronage is desired, will get his insurance too cheaply, as against the small man who is not in a position to drive a sharp bargain. That is, competition results in discrimination."

Such in brief is the elementary character of insurance. It is now for us to discuss the legal status of insurance as it expresses itself not only in the law and in the court decisions but also in the regulation of the business.

Supreme Court Decisions on Insurance. — From a long line of decisions beginning with Paul *v.* Virginia, and including such important cases as Nathan *v.* Louisiana, Ducat *v.* Chicago, Liverpool Insurance Company *v.* Massachusetts, Philadelphia Fire Association *v.* New York, Hooper *v.* California, Noble *v.* Mitchell, New York Life Insurance Company *v.* Cravens, Nutting *v.* Massachusetts, Equitable Life Society Company *v.* Clements to the late cases of the New York Life Insurance Company *v.* Deer Lodge County, Montana, and the German-American Insurance Company *v.* Kansas, several points in the legal status of insurance have been incontrovertibly decided.

First, insurance is not commerce nor is the policy an instrumentality of commerce. It therefore is a subject for complete state control, subject only to such limitations as the Federal Constitution lays down for the control of any property.

Second, insurance has certain characteristics which make it a public business for purposes of rate control. A state can therefore regulate insurance rates to the same extent that it can regulate the rates of any business of a public character.

Third, the insurance contract is a personal contract, a mere indemnity for a consideration against the happening of some contingent event which may bring detriment to life or property. Its character is the same, no matter what the event insured against, whether fire or hurricane, acts of man, or acts of God, storms on land or sea, death or lesser accidents. Nor does the character of the contracts change by their numbers or the residence of the parties. It is of course true that the ordinary life insurance contract is not peculiarly one of indemnity. It is also true that the courts of some states have refused to apply the fire insurance contract as one of indemnity.

Efforts to Secure Federal Regulation of Insurance. — Numerous efforts have been made to bring insurance under the regulation of the Federal Government. Elizur Wright, the first insurance commissioner of Massachusetts, made such a recommendation in 1865, and in 1866 a bill was introduced in Congress for this purpose. Several other bills for the same purpose have been introduced from time to time until it was finally recognized that such a law would in view of the decisions of the Supreme Court be unconstitutional. It is scarcely probable, in view of this court's decision, that Congress could make insurance interstate commerce by calling it such, for the court remarked in the early case of McCullough v. Maryland (4 Wheaton 316) " Should Congress under the pretext of executing its powers, pass laws for the accomplishment of objects not entrusted to the government, it would become the painful duty of this tribunal, should a case requiring such a decision come before it, to say that such an act was not the law of the land." The only hope, therefore, especially since the later decision of the Deer Lodge case, rests in securing an amendment to the Constitution which will bring insurance under the regulation of the Federal Government. Such an amendment was proposed to Congress in 1914, but it has not yet received affirmative action. The advantages of federal regulation are among others:

Advantages of Federal Regulation of Insurance. — First, there would be one uniform code of regulation. Some uniformity in insurance control has been secured by the adoption by one state of another state's laws and through the conference of state insurance commissioners, but there is yet very great difference in the detail requirements.

Second, there would be one standard policy for each kind and class of insurance.

Third, one official examination.

Fourth, one uniform method of valuing policies.

Fifth, a marked decrease in the expense of regulating insurance.

Sixth, one uniform method of taxation, although the state would have a coördinate power of taxation, as in the case of railways.

The disadvantages, theoretical and practical, are, among others:

First, the danger of centralized political control. This, however, would not seem to be serious.

Second, the danger of control by the insurance officials through such a centralized bureau as compared with the opportunity at present of controlling them through the many state departments.

Third, the difficulty of securing the repeal or amendment of unwise legislation. If at present a company is dissatisfied with the laws of a particular state or the administrative regulations of the insurance commissioner, it can withdraw from doing business in that state.

Fourth, the very great difficulty in prescribing regulation, especially as regards rates which would be applicable to the widely differing conditions in the different sections of a country so large as the United States. This would be more difficult in the case of fire than life insurance rates.

Fifth, the opposition that exists in some quarters of further centralizing control of business in the Federal Government at the expense of the states.

Sixth, the practical objection which the people of the states and their representatives in Congress would have in giving up such a lucrative source of revenue for the states by the loss of a part or all the revenue from the taxation of insurance companies.

The Basis of State Regulation. — Since the state is responsible for the existence of corporations, and since the rights granted to insurance corporations lead to the creation of trust funds, it follows that the state must see to it that these sacred obligations are met by the creature which it has called into existence — the corporation. At the time of the adoption of the Constitution and for many years later, the general principle of little government interference in industry was followed. Few evils, so far as insurance was concerned, resulted, for, as we have seen, little of insurance was transacted previous to 1835.

Character of Early Regulation. — Whatever supervision there was of the insurance business was at first primarily for the purpose of obtaining a basis for raising revenue, and this, it may be added, is still an important reason for supervision. In the licensing of companies and the prevention of fraudulent companies from operating within a state, the interest of policyholders was probably of secondary importance. In time, however, as the business grew in size and complexity, there was a growing realization that the state must take a more active part in regulating a business which affected so large a number of people. In addition, there had been organized many companies of a fraudulent character between the years 1825 and 1850, or, if not fraudulent, organizations which operated upon the unscientific plan of assessmentism. The evils which resulted from the operation of these companies were probably the most direct cause for the demand to arise, that the business of insurance be more closely supervised by the state. Previous to 1855 the state had been satisfied to lay down in general laws the terms under which an insurance company could be organized and operated. No detailed reports were required to be filed and no reserves to be maintained.

Massachusetts was the first state to establish a state insurance department. This was done in 1855, and the action of Massachusetts was followed by New York in 1859, by Connecticut in 1865, by Ohio in 1867, and by Michigan in 1871. Every state in the Union now supervises the insurance business, although in some states the department is only a separate bureau under the direction of some other department of state. Where there is no separate department, the work is usually placed under the charge of the auditor, treasurer, or secretary of state.

The departments or bureaus are supported by fees and taxes collected from the insurance companies, but the amount of funds collected bears no definite relation to the cost of maintaining the department.

Although Massachusetts established her insurance department in 1855, no standards of solvency were required until 1861. No other state established such standards until after the Civil War.

How Insurance Is Regulated. — Insurance is, therefore, now regulated in the following manner:

(a) By the general laws governing all business so far as they apply in their general terms to insurance.

(b) By special laws, enacted to govern the organization, operation, and liquidation of insurance companies.

(c) By the establishment of the office of a commissioner or superintendent of insurance who is given in the laws of many states wide discretionary powers of an administrative character in addition to his special statutory powers of enforcing the insurance laws.

This Commissioner or Superintendent is in practically all cases an appointive official, that is, the office is a political one. The result is that the official frequently changes. During a period of fifteen years, ending with 1914, only two such officials continued in office. Frequently the appointed official has no special insurance knowledge which qualifies him for the office. Yet the results are not as serious as might at first be supposed. The department under his supervision has become in most states a large one with the subordinates in charge of its divisions well fitted by training and experience. These department heads often continue from commissioner to commissioner's term of office and if the appointed commissioner is a man of good judgment, he soon becomes able with the aid of these subordinates to render good service to the insured public, the legislature, and the companies. Doubtless better results would be secured by longer tenure in office, since the commissioner is often replaced just at the time when he has become well informed and able to render directly better service, yet the actual results under the appointive system are not as serious as is sometimes argued. It does not follow by any means that " an insurance man " would make the best insurance commissioner for a state. The particular duties of the insurance commissioner cover a wide range of subjects.

There are in most states special laws which govern the organization of insurance companies. The terms under which such companies can be organized differ according to the character of the organization, such, for example, as the special laws governing the organization of a fraternal society or the ordinary level premium life insurance company. Since the latter companies do the greatest amount of the business and also are the ones to which regulation is chiefly directed, our description of the regulation of the organization and operation of life insurance companies may be taken as applicable to this kind of a company.

A very general requirement for such corporations is that they must deposit with the treasurer of state securities to the value at least of $100,000. This is a requirement for both stock and mutual companies proposing to insure lives on the level premium plan.

Massachusetts made this requirement of the New England Mutual, which was organized in 1835, twenty years before her state insurance department was established.

In some states there is a provision requiring the retirement of the stock of the proposed mutual company with a maximum interest paid upon the funds which have been advanced by the incorporators of the company, as a necessary capital to pay the large initial expenses of starting the company in business.

The laws governing the organizations of companies differ, of course, in the various states, but the general purpose in all cases is to lay down such principles as will insure the ability of the companies to meet their obligations.

The value of a deposit as a guarantee fund after the company is a going concern is very questionable, since the company is setting aside a reserve and probably a surplus. If the assets of a company are carefully inspected and the transactions of the company supervised, this would seem to give all the required safety, so far as solvency is concerned.

If a company organized in one state desires to do business in another state, it must comply with the conditions laid down by the state which it enters. Insurance is not commerce, according to the decision of the Supreme Court and the various states may lay down in detail the conditions under which a company is permitted to do business. They must satisfy the authorities of the state that they are able to meet their obligations. A copy of the charter, granted by the parent state, as well as a certificate showing that it is authorized to do business, is filed; also a statement of its financial condition showing income, disbursements, and a certificate showing that it has deposited with the officials of the home state a deposit, usually a minimum one of $100,000. It also files the valuation of its policies made by the insurance department of the home state and a copy of all the policies which it proposes to write. Its agents appointed or to be appointed must secure a license from the proper authority. Other information bearing upon the character of the company and its method of operation is secured by the proper state authority, usually the state insurance commissioner. If all this information seems to satisfy the state laws, the company is admitted by a certificate from the commissioner of insurance to do business in the state. The admitted company is then subject in its operation to the laws of the state on insurance. Some states intrust very large powers to the commissioner of insurance, while others lay down in detail the requirements for transacting the insurance business and require the commissioner to execute these laws with little discretionary powers. In either case the courts of the state can restrain the officials from violating the principles of equity.

Examinations of Insurance Companies. — In most states the certificate of the commissioner of insurance regarding the condition of the company is accepted in other states, but an examination of a foreign company can be made at any time and such examinations, although not infrequent in the past, are becoming less

2 A

frequent. One of the most important committees of the National Association of Insurance Commissioners is the committee on examinations. This committee acts as a clearing house of information for the various state departments of insurance. It has already done away with some of the evils connected with the numerous and sometimes unnecessary examinations made by numerous states. The examinations made by this committee are accepted in many cases by the state departments, although, of course, any state has the right to conduct a separate examination. The examinations made by this committee and used by the various state departments do not refer to the annual examinations, but to those comprehensive examinations of a company's business which are made from time to time, especially when suspicion arises concerning the conduct of a company's affairs. Such examinations would naturally be of companies doing business in several states at the particular time.

Independent of these special examinations each state makes an examination of its own companies. In some states this examination is required every year; in other states every two or three years. This annual, biennial, or triennial examination by the state department ordinarily concerns itself with an examination of the transactions of the company during the preceding calendar year. The examiners take the last annual report and verify it. The items of income and disbursement are checked from the company's books. The assets are inspected; all mortgages are inspected as to title and their proportion to the value of the property; the cash in office and banks is checked; and care is exercised to discover any weakness or any statutory violations of the investments. The liabilities must also be carefully investigated.

State Comity in Regulation Insurance. — The principle of state comity applies in many particulars, but it has far from accomplished complete uniformity. The National Association of Insurance Commissioners has done much in establishing uniformity in certain directions, such, for example, as providing uniform blanks upon which a company reports its condition to the insurance department. In many other cases, especially taxation, no uniformity is found. It is also generally true that home companies are favored over those of other states in one way and another. A favorite method is by a lower rate of taxation or no taxation at all on premium receipts.

Standards of Solvency. — The state has laid down certain standards of solvency by requiring the use of one of the accepted mortality tables and the valuation of policies must be made according to that table with interest at a specified rate per cent. In determining the reserve liability of a life insurance company the state insurance department generally uses mean — or midyear — reserves on the assumption that policies issued uniformly throughout the year are all, on the average, issued July first of that year, and hence when the valuation of a company's policies is made, as of December thirty-first of any year, the policies are all at their midyear. The midyear or mean reserves are obtained by taking the half sum of the reserves at the beginning and end of each year on the assumption that a full annual premium is paid on every policy. Consequently, deferred premiums to complete a full policy year are allowed in the assets. In industrial insurance the mean reserves just referred to are reduced by one half a net annual premium for a given kind and age, and deferred premiums are not allowed in the assets. On account of the heavy lapses in industrial insurance some reduction is usually made on first year reserves — about one half — and on second year reserves about one quarter.

In valuing assets certain rules are laid down for valuing stocks and bonds. The market value on December thirty-first has generally been used, but in some cases the amortization plan has been adopted, by which the values do not fluctuate with the market, but increase or decrease uniformly to par value so as to yield the same effective rate of interest throughout the period. Home office buildings and real estate owned by the company are valued by the local appraisers who know the value of the property.

Regulation as to Kinds of Business. — A requirement of many states is that a company is not permitted to write both participating and non-participating policies or, if both kinds are written, it is required that they be kept separate in the bookkeeping of the company. The tendency is for stock companies to write non-participating policies and mutual companies to write participating policies. It was urged that the evidence in the insurance investigation beginning in 1905 showed that in actual practice the equity of each kind of policyholders was not observed.

Dividend Distributions. — Annual distribution of dividends is a very general requirement. Standard provisions are required in all policies. These have to do with cash surrender values, options in settlement, loans, lapses, payment of premiums, and claims and many other subjects which are of general interest to all possessors of an insurance policy.

Regulation as to Investments. — The subject of investments is one upon which there has been a great amount of legislation. Not only has the state prohibited certain kinds of investments, as, for example, the permanent possession of real estate, but it has further limited them by specifying in what kind of securities the assets can be invested. This kind of regulation was adopted in many states before the establishment of the insurance departments, since the importance of having these funds securely invested was early recognized. The first restrictions were chiefly applicable to the original deposit, but by 1875 a number of states had restricted the investments of the general assets. At present the restrictions as to the character of the securities differ considerably in the different states. In all states investments in government bonds are permitted, although a few states limit the investment in bonds of other than the home state. Some confine mortgage loans to the home state of the company. Most of the states very carefully restrict the investments in corporation securities. New York prohibits all companies doing business in the state from investing in corporation stocks. Ohio follows the same practice. In the latter state, state and government bonds cannot be purchased when their market value is less than 80 per cent of their par value.

We may summarize the regulations regarding investments as follows as: (*a*) The tendency to prohibit investments in real estate except for Home Office Buildings is marked, but more liberality is found in regard to loans on real estate; (*b*) more liberal provisions regarding the investment in public securities and stricter regulations of the investments in corporation securities is the general rule.

Some states have shown a decided disposition to require a large amount of the reserve funds on policies to be invested in the securities of the state. So far as the legislation had for its purpose the protection of the funds by making possible a better knowledge of their actual value, there was some justification for the policy in the early days, when correct estimation of the value of securities could not be easily made. So far as the legislation has for its purpose the keeping of money within the state, it was more than questionable, for if the securities purchased must have a market made for them, this fact was at least presumptive evidence that these securities might not be desirable ones for an insurance company.

The purpose of regulating the investments of insurance has been to limit the investments to such securities as will bear the inspection of the public and guarantee the security of the funds. There are many who think that the restrictions are too severe and that a wide range of investments should be permitted under the supervision of the insurance departments. But the element of risk is so frequently present in corporation securities and the public demand is so insistent, and rightly so, for security as the first test of an insurance investment, that notwithstanding the greater return to be often procured from corporation securities, there is no immediate prospect that the field of investments will be widely extended.

Certain regulations have been attempted in regard to the remuneration of officials and agents. Some states have established a maximum salary to be paid to the president and maximum commissions to agents, and especially the amount of renewal commissions to be paid, that is, the amount paid to the agent on premiums subsequent to the first.

Most of the states have laws prohibiting rebating, that is, the reduction by the agent to the purchaser of the first premium; in most cases the penalties imposed apply only to the agent giving the rebate. There is a tendency in some quarters to punish both the recipient and giver of a rebate. No company or its employees is permitted in most states to issue any estimate misrepresenting the terms of any policy issued by it or the benefits or advantages promised.

New York also established a limitation on the amount of new business which could be written in any one year. This limit is decreasing in its percentage with the increase in the amount of business on the books of the company. The New York law also limits the amount of the contingent reserve or surplus which can be held by a company.

Liquidation of Companies. — Some states have enacted laws which give to the commissioner of insurance the power of liquidating companies that have failed or have been ordered to close up their business, or when one company's business is being absorbed by another. This is done with the view of protecting the policyholders for reasons that are obvious at such times when there is a temptation for the officials of the company to benefit at the expense of policyholders.

In other states, laws have been passed which give the Commissioner the sole power of licensing agents and revoking licenses granted. This is done for the purpose of securing a high type of agent. This power becomes especially important when an agent is guilty of rebating.

The Commissioner in many states is given certain powers over unauthorized business and surplus insurance. In the first case he prevents and prosecutes companies from writing business in the state without a license, or prosecutes those seeking to secure insurance on their property from such " outside companies." In the second case he grants the privilege to agents or brokers or property holders to secure insurance from companies not regularly admitted in case they cannot secure sufficient insurance from " admitted companies."

Taxation of Insurance. — The subject of taxation is one to which the companies have most consistently and continuously objected. These objections are based upon two grounds: First, it is argued that insurance is not a proper source of revenue for the state, and second, that there is no uniformity in the tax in the different states. It is argued that insurance is not productive; that it does not lead directly to the creation of wealth, but on the contrary aids greatly in the more equal distribution of wealth; that it is a fund set aside from income to care for those dependent upon the producer and thus relieves the state from supporting some, who otherwise would either become subject to their charity or would, through lack of adequate preparation, be inefficient producers and citizens; that the insurance policy is not a form of income-bearing property; that the premiums are a form of self-imposed tax.

It is urged that the policyholder must in the end bear the tax in the form of a higher premium, and thus the tax acts to discourage insurance by increasing its cost; that whatever of funds are collected from policyholders are so invested that they either bear a tax by their investment in real estate loans or aid the treasury of the state, if they are invested in state or local government securities. At the farthest those who object to taxation of insurance receipts would permit only such a tax as would support the insurance department of the state, that is, an inspection tax or fee. The taxes are usually levied on the gross premium receipts derived from the policyholders in the state, but in addition there is found sometimes a state license tax, a charge for filing the annual statement, agent licenses, and city and county fees.

The home companies are frequently exempted from paying some of these taxes or are taxed at a lower rate than foreign companies. This practice does not often accomplish the purpose intended, that is, it does not give preference to home companies, because most of the states have a retaliatory law which is automatic in its operation. That is, X state tends to tax the insurance companies of Y state at the highest rate levied by Y state on the insurance companies of X state.

The state tax on gross premiums, although in a few cases it is on the net receipts, varies from 1 per cent to 3 per cent. The amount collected by the states in the form of licenses, fees, fines, and taxes — excluding taxes on real estate owned — from ordinary life and industrial companies in 1914 was about thirteen million dollars. This was about 2 per cent of the total premium receipts of these companies during that year. It has been urged that the tax should be added to the premiums charged in each state and therefore assessed upon those policyholders whose state exacts the tax. Whatever theoretical justification this plan has as a matter of equity, it is practically impossible, since among other difficulties it would involve different rate books, policies, and reports for the different states, and add enormously to the bookkeeping work of the company and doubtless would be a violation of the antidiscrimination statutes of some states.

The reasons for the existence of the tax are not difficult to understand. The legislator in a democracy is constantly seeking revenue from sources from which objections will not be made. The large accumulations of funds by the insurance companies can be used without great popular objection. Notwithstanding that these funds are chiefly liabilities for obligations already incurred, they afford a ready source of revenue. The real owners of these funds — the policyholders — do not even perceive the burdens, since they are very numerous and the amount borne by each is very small. The availability of the funds for taxation and the absence of any great popular objection to the tax would therefore seem to be the chief reason for the tax. It is easy to get and therefore is taken without much consideration of the equity of the taking.

Reasons Assigned for Taxing Insurance. — There are, however, those who argue that theoretical as well as practical grounds justify a tax on Insurance, especially in all those cases where the insurance organization is in the form of a stock corporation. Capital has been invested in these stocks by the owners with the expectation of deriving a dividend in the same manner that capital is invested in other shares of stock. The results actually secured both in the case of life and fire stock insurance companies have generally justified the expectation. It is true that many stock insurance companies have failed, just as many mutual companies have failed. But there are many examples of success.

The reply that even in this case there is double taxation is not sufficient, for as every elementary student of taxation knows there are many cases of double taxation justifiable both in theory and practice. Insurance taxation may be a tax on thrift and saving, but so is all taxation. The distinction should be made first between that saving or thrift which is incurred for productive purposes and for the benefit of the individual saving and that incurred for the benefit of those other than the person saving. In the second place a distinction should be made between the number and character of those who benefit from the saving. If those of the insured group, that is, the policyholders, alone benefit from the saving of the individual members — the insured — and not second parties, such as the stockholders in a company, there would seem to be strong theoretical grounds to exempt these savings from any tax. The policyholders in a mutual company have banded themselves together to protect each other or their dependents against any existing risks. No one of the members expects to derive any special profit from the organization, and its benefits are open to any one who chooses to avail himself of it. If such organizations could be exempt from taxation as a distinct source of revenue for the state, these benefits would be granted its members at a lower cost. The state would be deprived of an easy source of revenue, but the ends of justice should always be of more importance to the state in its activities than matters of expediency.

So long as the stock company is a form of the insurance organization, it will be difficult to convince the legislator that insurance should be exempt from taxation. The tax is undoubtedly shifted to the policyholder in the form of a higher cost for his insurance.

The Annual Report. — The character of the annual report to a state may be indicated from the following items reported to the New York Department by a representative life insurance company.

1. Income and Disbursements; Assets and Liabilities in the form of a balance sheet beginning with the ledger assets of the previous year, and ending with

the gross assets as admitted by the Insurance Department.

2. An Exhibition of Policies, showing the number and amounts in force at the beginning and end of the year and the changes during the year. This is made for the State of New York on the basis of paid-for business only; for other states — as their laws require — either on a paid-for basis or an issued basis.

3. Business in the state of New York in brief — the copies going to other states containing an exhibit of the business in those states.

4. Gain and Loss Exhibit, showing actual expenses, interest and mortality in connection with legal allowances and office assumptions respectively; the profits from lapses and surrenders, gain and loss on investments, etc.

5. Premium Note account.

6. Schedule of cash and deposits of the Home Office with banks and trust companies in the United States and Canada; and cash with foreign banks, governments, and Branch Offices.

7. Special and General Deposit Schedules, showing in detail the securities deposited with the authorities of different states and countries in pursuance of legal requirements.

8. Real Estate Schedule, showing each parcel of property owned by the company, with particulars of cost, income, taxes, and improvements; also details of all purchases and sales made during the year.

9. Mortgage Schedule, with description, location, etc., of each piece of property mortgaged to the com-

pany; also an account of mortgage loans made, increased, reduced, discharged, or disposed of during the year; also showing the amount loaned in each state and foreign country.

10. Collateral Loan Exhibit, with similar information.

11. Bond Schedule, showing in detail the bonds owned with book, par, and market values; date of purchase and from whom acquired, interest received, etc.; also separate schedules of all bonds acquired or disposed of during the year, with the profit or loss on each lot sold.

12. Schedule of Bank Balances, showing the largest balance carried in each bank and trust company in each month of the year.

13. Schedule of Contested Policies, showing name and residence of insured, amount of Policy, reason for contesting; also all settlements of contested cases made during the year.

14. Schedule of Salaries, Compensation, and Emoluments of all persons or corporations, to whom $5000 or over was paid during the year.

15. Schedule showing all salaries paid for agency supervision.

16. Schedule showing all commissions paid on loans or on purchase or sale of property during the year.

17. Schedule of Legal Expenses, showing amounts, to whom paid, and for what service rendered.

18. Schedule of Expenditures, in connection with matters before legislative bodies, officers, or departments of government.

19. Dividend Schedule, showing dividends paid under

all forms of policies in various years and for various ages; including explanations of the methods by which dividends were calculated on all classes of policies.

20. Schedule showing in detail all money expended in connection with the election of directors.

21. In addition to this printed form Policy Valuation Schedules are furnished, showing in groups, by kind of Policy, amount of insurance, age of insured, and years in force, the data necessary for making a complete valnation of its Policy liabilities.

Some specific phases of the regulation of fire insurance need to be emphasized. Much of what has been previously discussed refers both to life and fire insurance. The method of organizing a fire insurance company, the requirements as to the investment of their funds, and the valuation of the reserve have also been described. The solvency of the large fire insurance companies is no longer a subject of particular concern to the people. Most of the legislation referring to this phase of the business has long been on the statute books, and its results in operation have been on the whole satisfactory.

Fire Insurance Rates the Chief Subject of Regulation. — The one problem in the regulation of fire insurance which has occasioned most interest is that of rates. It is but one aspect of the widely prevalent disposition on the part of legislative bodies to regulate prices in the interest of consumers. In fire insurance the rating problem is technical and therefore difficult of understanding for the legislator and the public. The efforts to regulate such rates are recent and no general agreement is found as to the best method to be used. The attempt to regulate rates arises from a desire both to protect the public from a supposed monopoly price and to secure equitable rates. The first desire has expressed itself in the numerous anti-combination laws which usually have attempted to prevent the fire insurance companies from making agreements to determine rates, and to observe them in practice and to agree upon the commission to be paid agents; that is, there has been a popular belief that fire insurance companies were frequently guilty of monopolistic action with its attendant public injury.

Antitrust Legislation and Insurance. — In the last quarter of a century there has been manifested a great public opposition to monopolies and suspicion is always alert on this subject. The fire insurance companies were observed to agree in their rates in many cases, but on risks, apparently the same to the superficial observer, the rates would be different. The public, which was not informed as to all the elements entering into a rate, very naturally concluded that the charges were both monopolistic and discriminatory. Associations of fire underwriters which often made rates were numerous. At first such monopolistic-appearing organizations of the fire insurance companies were attacked under the common law. The courts in general refused to hold such associations or similar ones among the companies to agree upon, fix, and maintain rates as illegal in themselves to the extent that the persons were guilty of an act justifying a criminal or civil action. At most these agreements to fix, regulate, and control the business of fire insurance were held to be unenforceable. If the restraint of trade which resulted was unreasonable in its effects upon the public interest, they could be dissolved. But few successful actions at law against such combinations under the common law principle of monopolies and combinations were had. When this common law principle had become expressed in the statutory antitrust laws of the various states, fire insurance organizations were attacked in the courts under these statutory laws. But when these laws were enacted, fire insurance organizations were not usually in the mind of the legislator as a monopoly to be thus regulated. It was common for these antitrust laws to refer in their terms to " merchandise and commodity " or similar business which did not include fire insurance. The courts very generally refused to interpret " trade," " merchandise," " commodity," and such words as including fire insurance. Since no relief adequate to the situation in the opinion of the public was to be had either from the common law or the antitrust laws, many states enacted specific anticompact or combination laws which applied specifically to fire insurance companies, although some states amended their antitrust laws to include specifically insurance companies. These laws have been upheld by the courts, since insurance has been held not only to be a public business but also not an interstate business within the meaning of the federal constitution.

Some of these laws are of a very stringent character, and only in a minority of the states is there a legal recognition of the fact that rates in fire insurance should be coöperatively made instead of being competitively made. The history of competitive rate-making in fire insurance is so full of examples of public injury that there is little intelligent opinion on the subject which would argue for its continuance. The chief interest of the public as well as of the insurance companies is in the stability and solvency of insurance. To secure these ends and at the same time receive fair rates two methods of rate-making are open.

How Rates May Be Made. — First, the state may fix and approve minimum rates, trusting to the forces of competition among the companies to prevent unduly high rates. The greater part of the evils connected with fire insurance rates have not resulted from high or maximum rates but from low rates; that is, all the attendant evils of rate-cutting and discrimination. Minimum rates, therefore, in a system of rate-fixing by the state are more important than attempting to establish specific rates for each risk and class of property.

Second, the State may allow the companies to combine for the purpose of making and maintaining rates, and supervise carefully these acts of the companies. Both of these methods are in practice in the United States, although but a few states have attempted to fix rates. This second method often takes the form of legalizing rating bureaus since these are the most economic agency for rate-making. These bureaus may be independent organizations or they may be composed of the representatives of the companies. The state through its department deals with the companies on the subject of rates through the bureau, and in some states these bureaus are becoming quite as much an agency to represent the interests of the public as the companies; that is, they act continuously as a force to compel individual companies to observe rates and are more closely related to the work of the insurance department of the state than to the offices of the companies.

In some states neither of the above methods are used; that is, the state simply requires the company to file rates with a state official; or the state official may be given power to supervise rates only in certain particulars, such as seeing that rates are not discriminatory. At the present writing there is no uniformity in the regulation of fire insurance rates in the different states, although the tendency seems to be toward state supervision of rates rather than state rate-making. Probably no other one thing would so much improve the fire insurance business as the adoption by all states of a state system of supervising rates which would compel all companies to coöperate in making and maintaining rates.

Discrimination and State Regulation. — Discrimination, which has too often been prevalent, would be largely removed, at least in the particular state, by such a system. It will require, however, a farsighted and broad viewpoint on the part of the regulating official if discrimination is to be avoided as between states. Due allowance should be made in the rates of each state for the conflagration hazard. Again, the mere fact that property of a similar character in one state enjoys a particular rate does not prove that the same rate is a fair one in another state because, as has been shown, there is a very wide difference in the burning rate in different states. This discrimination as regards states will probably be the most difficult problem in a system of state-supervised rates, since each state will think it is entitled to as low rates as any other state, just as the individual property owner or a village is disposed to think his or its rates should be as low as that of the neighboring property or village. Yet if the system of schedule rating is developed and the classified experience of companies is better collected and made public, there is hope of convincing both insured property owners and communities that the rates are fair. It has been too often the case in the past that neither the agent nor the company could give any satisfactory explanation to the property owner or the community for the difference in rates as compared with other property and communities.

Discrimination as to persons, as to property of the same kind, and as to communities and states has existed as an evil in fire insurance. The promise of its disappearance is in a system of combined experience, proper rating, enforced coöperation, and careful supervision by state officials.

No system of supervision will solve the problem of fire insurance rating in the sense that it is possible to determine what specific rates should be. Rates will continue to change with the varying conditions of building material, the construction and use of buildings, and the other fluctuating factors affecting the rates. But discrimination can be removed and equity as to classes of property secured. Finally, regulation of rates can do much to reduce the unnecessary fire loss by making those responsible for it bear the large cost, which results from their carelessness.

It is doubtless true that much of the legislation enacted to govern the business of fire insurance has been unwise, but the explanation of its origin and character is not difficult, nor are the insurance companies to be held blameless as a cause of it. There are many points of similarity between the railway legislation and the fire insurance legislation. The high-handed methods of some of the earlier railway administrators, the evils of the rate wars, the discriminations, and a multitude of lesser evils produced in the public mind an attitude of hostility to all railways which only in recent times has shown any indication of abatement. There was a tendency, as is common in social action, to go to extremes, and along with the constructive legislation, laws were enacted detrimental both to the public and the railways. Many of the reforms forced upon the railways are of permanent value, as, for example, the uniform system of reporting expense, and as in many other instances, such uniformity would hardly have been adopted voluntarily by the different companies.

In a like manner the public bill of indictment against the fire insurance companies is not without foundation. In fact many of the counts in this bill of indictment will stand the test of a careful investigation. The forms and results which the competition among fire insurance companies have assumed often have been beyond the comprehension of the public mind. The public has not only witnessed the violent cutting of rates at the time of rate wars, but it has also experienced a considerable variation of rates among the companies on the same risk in times of peace. It has observed that rates on apparently identical risks in the same locality, or in similar localities, have varied widely. This fluctuation in rates, now high, now low, now stable in the face of evident improved conditions, and unstable in the face of no changes, has caused the public to wonder if the fire insurance companies, collectively or individually, have any really scientific method of determining rates; whether, after all, rates are not a matter either of guess-work, or of charging what the traffic will bear; that is, the fire insurance companies were getting as much as they could, wherever they could.

Then, too, the apparently large expense of fire insurance companies has been a source of wonder to the public. Nor have the cases of over-insurance, careless inspection, and other attendant evils of excessive competition escaped public attention. When the companies have been called upon to explain and justify their acts, they have sometimes not been able to make an explanation satisfactory to the public, due partly to the fact that much of the explanation was technical, and partly to the fact that there was no satisfactory explanation to be made. The public itself is responsible for much of the difficulty. It has insisted upon competition in all respects and has paid the price for it. But when all allowance for the public's share in the situation is made, there remains a residuum of blame which must be borne by the companies. The chief source of this weakness is in the absence of standards in the fire insurance business. With the exception of a standard policy —

and it has many modifications — the fire insurance business has fewer standards than any business in the world. There is no standard for measuring hazards, no standard classifications, no standards of expense, no standards of accounting, and in fact no standards for doing a business, which, on account of its great complexity, is greatly in need of measuring units. The individual companies have been loath to join in coöperative movements to work out such standards, not primarily as they often assert because of fear of the law, but rather because the whole history of the business in the United States has placed a discount on such coöperation. It is very doubtful if this full coöperation, which alone will make possible a standardization of the business, will ever result except from public compulsion. The splendid work of the National Board of Fire Underwriters made an excellent beginning when it aided in the devising of a Standard Policy and even greater results are now promised through the work of its Actuarial Bureau.

The only prospect that the marked tendency to enact more restrictive fire insurance laws will be checked is for the companies to work out in coöperation, standards for the business. They must be able to explain more satisfactorily to the public how they make their rates, how they spend their receipts, how they classify the risks, what their losses are on classes of property and in different political divisions. The business of fire insurance is a public one and its relations to public welfare are so vital, and to other businesses so important, that in time the public will insist that it be conducted not only in the most careful and businesslike manner, but also that the methods be continuously open for public inspection and understanding. The courts have many times upheld the power of extreme control over the business of fire insurance, and public, or state, fire insurance promises no benefits which cannot better be secured by public control of the business under private ownership. Whatever reforms are needed can be best accomplished by the fire insurance companies themselves.

A greater degree of coöperation with the ends in view of restricting undesirable competition and of devising standards for the business is the great need of the fire insurance business.

REFERENCES

Insurance and the State. W. F. Gephart.
The Business of Insurance, Vol. III, Chaps. 67, 69, 72.
Yale Readings in Insurance, Chaps. 23, 24.
The Insurance Year Book 1915. Life, Casualty and Miscellaneous, pp. 1–86.

SELECT BIBLIOGRAPHY ON LIFE INSURANCE

The Actuarial-Mortality Investigation. Arthur W. Hunter, New York, 1914.

Alexander, William. The Life Insurance Company.

Annals American Academy of Political Science, Vol. XXXVI.

Ashley, W. J. An Introduction to English Economic History and Theory.

Benefit Features of American Trade-unions. United States Department of Labor Bulletin, No. 22. May, 1899.

Bowley, A. L. Elements of Statistics.

Brown, Benjamin F. The Brown Book of Life Insurance Economics.

Brown, Mary W. The Development of Thrift.

Dawson, Miles M. The Business of Life Insurance.
The Elements of Life Insurance.
Practical Lessons in Actuarial Science, Vol. II.

De Leon, Edwin W., and Moon, Sidney N. The Law of Liability.

Dicksee, L. R., and Blain, H. E. Office Organization and Management.

Dryden, John F. Life Insurance and Other Subjects.

Educational Leaflets. The Mutual Life Insurance Company.

Educational Series. The North-Western Mutual Life Insurance Company.

Elliott, Charles B. The Law of Insurance.

Fackler, Edward B. Notes on Life Insurance.

Farr, William. Vital Statistics.

Francis, John. Annals, Anecdotes and Legends: A Chronicle of Life Insurance.

Frankel, Lee K., and Dawson, Miles M. Workingmen's Insurance in Europe.

Fricke, W. A. Insurance. A Text Book.

Graham, W. J.   Romance of Life Insurance.

Gross, Charles.   The Guild Merchant.

Harbaugh, C. R.   The Selection of Risks by the Life Insurance Solicitor.

Causes of Disability.

Henderson, C. R.   Industrial Insurance in the United States.

Hendrick, B. J.   The Story of Life Insurance.

Hudnut, James M.   Studies in Practical Life Insurance.

Huebner, Solomon.   Life Insurance.

How to buy Life Insurance "Q. P."

Institute of Actuaries' Text Book.

Insurance Guide and Handbook.   Fifth Edition.

Jack, A. Finland.   An Introduction to the History of Life Assurance.

Jevons, Stanley W.   Principles of Science.

Journal of the Institute of Actuaries.

Lewis, Frank W.   State Insurance.

Newsholme, A.   Vital Statistics.

Pearson, Karl.   Chances of Death, Vol. I.

Grammar of Science.

Principles and Practices of Life Insurance.   Seventh Edition. The Spectator Company.

Proceedings of the Actuarial Society of America.

Proceedings of the Association of Life Insurance Presidents.

Proceedings of the International Congress of Actuaries.

Proceedings of the National Convention of Insurance Commissioners, 1889–1915.

Publications of the American Economic Association.   Third Series. Vols. VIII, X.

Publications of the American Statistical Society.

Reports Annual of State Commissioners of Insurance.

Report on National Vitality.   Parts I, II of Vol. III.   Senate Document, No. 676, Sixtieth Congress, Second Session.

Report of the New York Joint Committee of the Senate and Assembly on Life Insurance, 1906:

Report of the New York Liability Commission, 1910.

Report of the Ohio Liability Commission, 1910.

Report of the Royal Commission on Insurance. Part I. The Commonwealth of Australia, 1908.

Report of the Royal Commission of Canada on Life Insurance, 1907.

Richards, George. A Treatise on the Law of Insurance.

Roche, J. F. A Method of Handling Impaired Life Risks.

Schloss, D. F. Insurance against Unemployment.

Seager, Henry R. Social Insurance.

Stillman, Charles F. The Life Insurance Examiner.

Transactions of the Insurance and Actuarial Society of Glasgow.

Venn, John. Logic of Chance.

Walford, Cornelius. Cyclopedia of Insurance.

Wambaugh, Eugene. A Selection of Cases on Insurance.

Willard, Charles E. The A B C of Life Insurance.

Willett, Allen H. The Economic Theory of Risk. Columbia University Studies in Economics, History, and Public Law, Vol. XIV.

Willoughby, W. F. Workingmen's Insurance.

Wolfe, S. R. Inheritance Tax Calculations.

The Examination of Insurance Companies.

Yale Readings in Insurance, Vol. I.

Year Book, The Life Insurance, 1914. The Spectator Company.

Young, T. E. Insurance.

Young, T. E., and Masters, Richard. Insurance Office Organization, Management, and Accounts.

Zacher, G. Die Arbeiter-Versicherung im Auslande.

Zartman, Lester. The Investments of Life Insurance Companies.

INDEX

THE following pages contain advertisements of
books by the same author or on kindred subjects.

Principles of Insurance

Volume II — Fire

By W. F. GEPHART

Professor of Economics in Washington University

The volume on Fire Insurance, based on Professor Gephart's extended teaching experience and his practical experience in the business, has been written for the purpose of supplying a textbook on this subject as well as a guide for insurance men. It contains a clear and concise discussion of the underlying principles and of the practical considerations which arise in the conduct of the business. Professor Gephart has given chief consideration to the problems (far more complex and unsettled than those in Life Insurance) which center around the subject of rates and regulation by the state; but he has not neglected such other topics as the development of the business, the policy contract, the settlement of losses, and the finances of fire insurance. He has included also a discussion of fire waste and fire prevention in their economic aspects and in their relation to the price of fire insurance. Additional references to various phases of the subject are given at the close of each chapter.

THE MACMILLAN COMPANY

Publishers   64–66 Fifth Avenue   New York

Insurance and the State

By W. F. GEPHART

Professor of Economics in Washington University

228 pages, 12mo, $1.25

In this volume the author considers the fundamental principles of life, fire, and social insurance with a view to determining what should be the relation of the state to each of these kinds of insurance business. Confusion and conflict are the chief characteristics of the laws governing insurance in the United States. This exists not only between the states, but also between the states and the federal government. The question of public insurance is becoming increasingly important and some states have already ventured in this new field of activity with questionable results. Some states have regulated rates; others have made them for the companies. Some states tax insurance companies heavily, others lightly. Most states prohibit coöperation among companies through a fear of conspiracy for price or rate determination. All these and other related questions are discussed in this volume, not dogmatically, but by setting forth concisely the fundamental principles and practices of these different kinds of insurance. The answer to these mooted questions is left to the reader, or stated only by implication.

THE MACMILLAN COMPANY

Publishers   64-66 Fifth Avenue   New York

Social Insurance
A PROGRAM FOR SOCIAL REFORM

By HENRY R. SEAGER
Professor of Political Economy in Columbia University

Cloth, 12mo, 175 pp., $1.00

———————

Social workers, political leaders, editors, and teachers will rejoice that an economist of the first rank like Dr. Seager examines the growing evils of industrial accidents, illness, premature death, unemployment, and old age in this country, and shows us how their burdens may be carried collectively through the principle of insurance. European experience on this subject is already extensive. Dr. Seager studies it critically and applies it to a timely discussion of American facts and conditions in a most sane, courageous, and helpful little book.

———————

THE MACMILLAN COMPANY
Publishers   64-66 Fifth Avenue   New York

Readings in Money and Banking

By CHESTER A. PHILLIPS

Assistant Professor of Economics in Dartmouth College

Cloth, 8vo, 845 pp., $2.10

Designed for use chiefly in connection with a text or series of lectures, or both, on the theory and history of money and banking. The materials have been selected from a wide range of sources and in many instances have been specially adapted by the editor for classroom use. A few of the chapters are: A Symposium on the Relation Between Money and Prices, The Gold Exchange Standard, Foreign Exchange, Banking Operations and Accounts, State Banks and Trust Companies since the Civil War, Savings Banks, Clearing Houses, Agricultural Credit in the United States, Crises, The Federal Reserve System, The European War in Relation to Money, Banking and Finance. The readings have not been selected with regard to any particular text now on the market, but will be found equally useful and usable with all of the texts. Emphasis is placed upon the modern phases of the subject.

THE MACMILLAN COMPANY

Publishers   64-66 Fifth Avenue   New York